NOV 28

DATE DUE

GAYLORD   PRINTED IN U.S.A.

Wilderness Economics and Policy

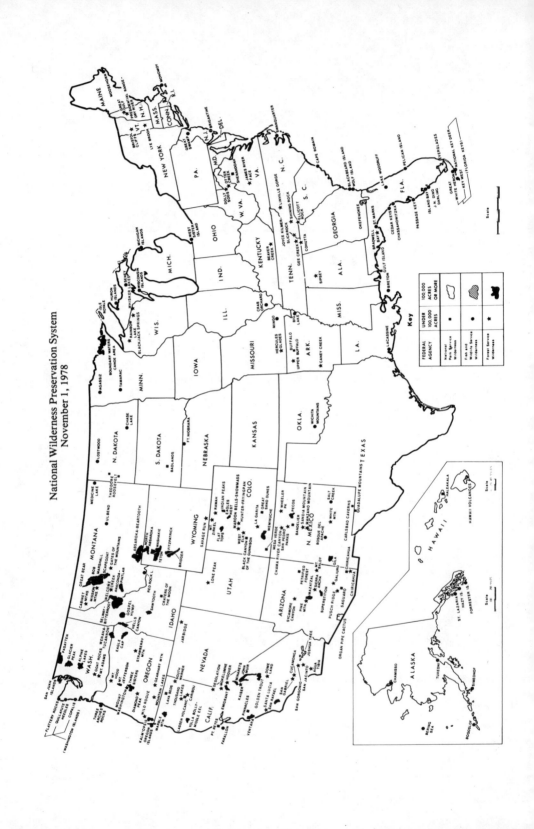

National Wilderness Preservation System
November 1, 1978

Wilderness Economics and Policy

Lloyd C. Irland

Lexington Books
D. C. Heath and Company
Lexington, Massachusetts
Toronto

Library of Congress Cataloging in Publication Data

Irland, Lloyd C
  Wilderness economics and policy.

  Includes bibliographical references and index.
  1. Wilderness areas—Economic aspects—United States. 2. Environmental
policy—United States. I. Title.
QH76.I74   333.9'5   78-24791
ISBN 0-669-02821-5

Published simultaneously in Canada.

Printed in the United States of America.

International Standard Book Number: 0-669-02821-5

Library of Congress Catalog Card Number: 78-24791

To My Parents

Contents

Contents

List of Figures

List of Tables
and Cases

Preface

In the debates of recent years, economic reasoning frequently has been abused and ignored in public discussions about wilderness. This book provides a brief overview of the economics and policy of wilderness preservation in the United States. It is based on the belief that economic thinking can contribute to a clearer public understanding—and thus to better policy decisions—about wilderness. In these pages I avoid recounting mathematical argument and methods of performing calculations, subjects that have been better treated by others. For the reader's convenience, I include extensive references to more technical works and to detailed case studies.

A talk delivered at the Thirteenth Biennial Sierra Club Wilderness Conference was the seedling from which this book has grown. It has passed through sapling stages used by students in my classes at Yale University, whose class discussions gave the ideas here a certain pruning and wind-firmness. I am indebted to the editors of *Environmental Law,* a review published by the Lewis and Clark School of Law—Northwestern Law School—for permission to reprint portions of this work, which appeared in 1976. This book is a snapshot of a tree that continues to grow, as the ideas summarized here are further applied by professionals and refined by scholars.

Readers are entitled to know on what experience the arguments of this book are based. Work as a U.S. Forest Service economist in the South and West, as a practicing preservationist, and as an analyst of the economic and environmental impact of recreation in Vermont and Washington provided much practical material and opportunities to explore the nation's backcountry. Reflections about the nation's timber supply convinced me that there is room in our nation's economy for a large wilderness resource. Teaching the economics of wilderness helped me search for themes and for ways of introducing economics to students. Finally, service with the Maine Forest Service has enabled me to observe, and occasionally participate in, major preservation debates in Maine.

In the growth of this book, encouragement, nourishment, and a challenging climate have been provided by many people, of whom I can only mention a few. Al Fox, of U.S. Forest Service Region 6, Dick Behan of Northern Arizona University, Roderick Nash of University of California at Santa Barbara, Michael McCloskey of the Sierra Club, Albert C. Worrell, my major professor and colleague at Yale, and William R. Burch, Jr. of Yale, encouraged me to proceed when early drafts needed more work. My work with students, some of whom are now fighting preservation battles of their own, encouraged me to believe it was worth doing. Lauren Brown and Jane Frost encouraged me to believe it could be done.

Competent typing by Helen Beaulieu helped it happen. The staff of Lexington Books has helped immensely. But, for all remaining knots, crooks, cracks, and twisted grain, I remain responsible.

Introduction

Wilderness is the raw material out of which man has hammered the artifact called civilization.
                                                                        —Aldo Leopold*

Wilderness, in a matter of decades, has blossomed from a refuge for a minority of hikers and naturalists to a noisy battleground of political conflict. On that battleground struggle representatives of the federal bureaucracy, of resource-based industries, and of citizen environmental organizations. Spokesmen for all these groups self-righteously assert that the public interest requires decisions favorable to their own constituency. All sides have mastered the ancient arts of lobbying and logrolling in Congress and in the statehouses; all have employed television and the press in attempts to sway public opinion. And some have resorted to the courts when other steps failed.

As a result, the controversies over the damming of the Grand Canyon, over the Redwood National Park, and over the North Cascades took place with considerable publicity. Not all the information generated was especially enlightening or objective. Hence, there remains considerable confusion about the economics of wilderness preservation in the United States.

On October 1, 1978, the National Wilderness Preservation System consisted of 16.5 million acres of land, shown by agency as follows:[1]

	Acres
Forest Service	14,762,561
Park Service	1,100,942
Wildlife Refuges	648,545
Total	16,512,048

The total remaining area of unroaded land in the fifty states has been variously estimated between 72 million and 210 million acres.[2] Considering the resource values, the sheer physical extent of these lands, and their historical, cultural, and recreational importance, wilderness land preservation certainly qualifies as a major public policy issue.

What are the roots of the concern for wilderness preservation? How did wilderness become a political issue? What are the provisions of the

---

*Aldo Leopold, *Sand County Almanac* (New York: Oxford, 1966), p. 241.

Wilderness Act and the recently passed Eastern Wilderness Areas Act? Have these laws been effective? What are the economic costs of reserving wilderness areas from commercial uses? What policy issues remain unsettled? To contribute to a more complete understanding of current wilderness policy, this book provides an overview of these issues.

The scope is restricted to the United States, although preservation issues occur worldwide. It is also restricted to issues normally described as wilderness—the preservation of substantial tracts of essentially wild land. Important preservation issues including coastal wetlands, endangered wildlife species, urban open space, and even the oceans and outer space, are not treated. Readers will, I expect, observe that many of the concepts applied here to wilderness can be applied to these other concerns.

The purpose of this book is to introduce concepts of economics useful in interpreting the justifications for preservation of wilderness areas, in analyzing the opportunity costs of wilderness preservation, and in studying management policies. In addition, I discuss existing wilderness policies and describe unsettled policy issues.

The major theme is the *mandate for preservation*. This mandate has its basis in the diversity of direct human wants supplied by untouched wildlands and in the significant scientific, educational, cultural, and ethical values they serve. The mandate has been implemented in the U.S. through an imperfect structure of legislation. Carrying out the mandate for preservation raises important economic questions, and specific land allocation choices may affect the economies of nearby communities. Economics provides tools that can be helpful in addressing these concerns but that cannot replace sensitive human judgment. Finally, the nation's wilderness patrimony must be managed, strange as that may seem, and management will in the future raise controversies as loud and emotional as those now seen over allocation decisions.

Notes

1. U.S. Department of Agriculture, U.S. Forest Service, *An Assessment of the Forest and Range Land Situation in the U.S.* (Washington, D.C.: 1979) Review Draft, p. 138.

2. George H. Stankey, "Myths of Wilderness Decisionmaking," *J. Soil and Water Conservation* 26 (September/October 1971): 183; John W. Duffield, "Wilderness—An Economic and Political Analysis" (Ph.D. diss. Yale University, 1974), p. 25.

Wilderness Economics
and Policy

1

Wilderness: The Mandate for Preservation

Introduction

In the midst of angry debates over the fate of the French Pete roadless area or the West Branch of the Penobscot, it is easy to lose sight of fundamental issues. The basic policy issues at stake in preservation policies and in decisions about individual areas are readily assembled from the reflections of those who have dealt with these problems.[1] They are a helpful aid to evaluating preservation decisions. They cannot, obviously, answer every issue by themselves—general principles never can.

Preservation of wildlands serves a wide range of public policy objectives. Objectives of a utilitarian character include both scientific and economic values. Broader objectives are nonutilitarian: man's relationship to the natural world, his ability to foresee future needs, and his ability to restrain short-term activities that threaten long-term values. Some of the most perplexing and costly preservation choices arise in the management of endangered species. This chapter outlines these considerations, which provide a mandate for preservation. Later chapters review the complexities of making intelligent judgments about the trade-offs always encountered in meeting this mandate.

This chapter divides the mandate for preservation into its scientific, economic, cultural, and ethical facets for convenience only, since many concepts employed do not fit this classification perfectly.

Utilitarian Justifications for Preservation

American attitudes toward wilderness spring from a rich variety of sources. By the seventies, fairly clear utilitarian concepts had emerged that form a conceptual foundation justifying the conservation of untouched wild areas (table 1-1). The most important utilitarian justifications are scientific and economic.

Scientific uses of wilderness include provision of baseline data on the working of undisturbed ecosystems, preservation of genetic information contained in rare ecosystems and species, and research stations that can operate without interference from other land uses.[2]

The scientific and economic concerns interweave with a range of ethical, religious, and scientific value statements about nature. But there are

Table 1-1
**The Mandate for Wilderness Preservation: Utilitarian and
Nonutilitarian Values**

Utilitarian Values

Scientific
    Preserving a sample of key ecosystems to ensure biotic diversity
    Conserving gene pools and potentially useful but presently unknown organisms
    Natural areas for research and ecosystem monitoring

Economic
    Providing backcountry recreation
    Conserving wildlife and fish
    Protecting watersheds and water quality
    Conserving scenic resources for tourism
    Avoiding diseconomies of development
    Promoting a balanced land use pattern

Nonutilitarian Values

Cultural
    Conserving a cultural heritage
    Preserving aesthetic values
    Providing educational opportunities

Ethical
    Providing for "rights of rocks"
    Providing scope for individual freedom
    Social value of exercising restraint

numerous practical reasons why preservation of wild areas can be economically justified.

Wildlands provide valuable recreation opportunities, for which some consumers are willing to pay substantial prices to enjoy. Some pay high rates for pack-trips through high alpine valleys. Others endure long journeys by auto or bus to reach mountain wildernesses for back-packing outings. The U.S. Forest Service estimates that National Forest wilderness use increased by 10 percent per year from 1946 to 1974. Total recreational use of all wilderness, including roadless areas, was estimated at about 12 million visitor-days in 1974.[3] For many areas, recreation uses may be only part—and occasionally a small part—of the basis for preservation.

Wild areas provide essential year-round or seasonal habitat for wildlife—including endangered and rare species such as the grizzly bear and the timber wolf. Mountain watersheds protected from road construction and grazing can protect the quality of water supplies, thus conserving fishery resources as well as aiding the provision of low-cost municipal water.[4] Scenic resources are a basic attraction drawing tourists to some regions. In such areas the visual integrity of the landscape is the community's basic economic asset—the ultimate source of most employment and income.

Finally, economic values include the diseconomies and disamenities that can be caused by development. Second-home developments are commonly scattered through valleys, requiring excessively costly provision of public services. Where drainage is poor and septic tanks fail, central sewer systems and waste treatment plants often have to be installed at burdensome expense. Pollution, erosion, and aesthetic blight caused by resource use or by construction can injure downstream water users, reduce fish and wildlife populations, and reduce visual amenities for large numbers of area visitors.[5]

Thus, land preservation may be dictated by the inability to exploit an area's resources without causing unacceptable loss of natural values and without inflicting high costs on other citizens and resource users. In such cases, the diseconomies of development reinforce the positive values placed on preservation for cultural, scientific, and economic reasons.

Wilderness plays a key role in our society's halting attempts to achieve a balanced pattern of land use. Rural land-use trends, especially in mountainous areas, are producing an unsound and unbalanced pattern of land use. Forest and range land is being rapidly converted to recreational lots and other uses. Land-sales projects registered with the Office of Interstate Land Sales Registration by 1973 included more than 1.8 million acres of land.[6] The availability of this land to the public for recreation has been reduced, and these acres may never produce commercial crops of wood or forage again.

Along the Appalachian range from Georgia to Vermont, recreational lot sales were, until the 1973-1974 real estate slump, a booming industry. An example is Rappahannock County, Virginia, near Shenandoah National Park, where real estate trading topped all other economic activities in dollar volume in 1973.[7] Parcel fragmentation and absentee ownership result. In some areas, a few second homes are appearing on these lots. Such developments, and the commercial establishments catering to nonresident vacationers, frequently spell the beginning of serious environmental, land-use, and public service problems.

To emphasize the role of wilderness in a balanced land-use pattern, consider the following:

1. A study of the ninety-six most urbanized counties in the twelve northeastern states found that from 1950 to 1960, 12,000 acres per year of land were urbanized.[8] One fourth of this was forest land.

2. In the Northeast's megalopolis, the Regional Plan Association projects that by 2019, an additional 8,530 square miles of land will be urbanized to provide for forty million additional inhabitants.[9] If the ratio of one-fourth forest still applies, this is more than 2,000 square miles of forest, or about 1.3 million acres.

3. From 1969 to the year 2000, a decline of 25 million acres in the nation's commercial forest land base is predicted by the U.S. Department

of Agriculture.[10] This decline is mostly due to land clearing for development.

4. Land consumed in coal mining, oil shale conversion, and related energy activities is expected to reach 10 million acres by the year 2000.[11]

The additions to wilderness in the lower 48 states being debated today do not seem large in relation to these figures. As a society we should be willing to provide for allocations of land to wilderness, just as we are prepared to accept the dedication of large acreages to development.

In serving the mandate for preservation based on these utilitarian values, tough decisions about trade-offs must be made. Some guidance in making such decisions is offered by the concept of a safe minimum standard. This approach was offered by S.V. Ciriacy-Wantrup, an agricultural economist.[12] The concept argues that society should plan to preserve a minimum standard of safety in decisions about resource supply, land use, or pollution control. The minimum standard should be set with due regard to the expected needs of future generations. In the case of wilderness preservation, a safe minimum standard approach argues for a bias toward preservation in land-use decision-making.

Plastic Trees and the Rights of Rocks: Nonutilitarian Justifications for Preservation

A firm basis for preserving a given area can often be based on practical considerations including wildlife, amenity values, scientific needs, and the diseconomies of development. But many persons find a purely utilitarian justification incomplete. Historic, cultural, and ethical arguments may also be brought to bear.

As American history was profoundly shaped by its wilderness, so have Americans remade the wilderness they encountered. The recent importance of wildlands in our history, then, gives wilderness a significant value as a cultural resource. As Leopold wrote, "If the forty-niners are worth commemorating on the walls of state capitols, is not the scene of their mighty hegira worth commemorating in several national prairie reservations?"[13]

Aesthetic appreciation of unique natural areas has a long history in this country, evolving from early fear and suspicion: "How frontiersmen described the wilderness they found reflected the intensity of their antipathy. The same descriptive phrases appeared again and again. Wilderness was 'howling,' 'dismal,' 'terrible.'"[14] Attainment of an economic and geographic distance from wilderness by most citizens has no doubt facilitated the emergence of a more favorable aesthetic view of wildlands.

As aesthetic appreciation of nature has grown, wilderness has come to be appreciated as an educational resource—witness, for example, the use of wilderness excursions by such groups as Outward Bound. One forest economist has suggested that wilderness be used as one pole of a planned program of introducing urban youth to nature step-by-step: "to provide at least some access to nature for practically all children, especially those who now grow up immersed in a man-made environment."[15]

Religious and ethical concepts demand due consideration in forming a mandate for preservation. Scholars have debated the significance of Christian religious doctrines in the development of modern exploitive attitudes toward nature—a debate that can only briefly detain us here. Thinkers have also pondered whether purely utilitarian values can ever form a satisfactory basis for protection of nature. Finally, ethical concepts such as the right of natural environments to protection from damage, the land ethic, and the ethical value of restraint have been offered in support of nature protection.

Many authors have argued that Western societies have drawn their basic attitudes toward nature from Judeo-Christian biblical traditions. These traditions, they say, justify human plunder of nature, or at least, indifference to environmental values.[16] They argue that the Old Testament mandate to multiply and subdue the earth has been taken literally, as the basis for a materialistic, manipulative attitude toward nature that places no restraints on human use of the earth. Christian thought, in this view, is hostile to an ethical relationship to nature.

There is no question that the Judeo-Christian traditions desanctify nature, thus diverging from other religious traditions that find gods immanent in trees, rocks, and mountains: ". . . Christianity encouraged special attitudes to Nature: that it exists primarily as a resource rather than as something to be contemplated with enjoyment, that man has the right to use it as he will, that it is not sacred, and that man's relationships with it are not governed by moral principles."[17] John Passmore, however, argues that the basic source of the Western attitude toward nature is not the book of Genesis, but the Greek scientific tradition. The Greeks, he argues, saw nature as a nonsacred collection of objects, connected by a physics emphasizing the atomic basis of matter and immutable natural laws, such as the laws of celestial motion. The Greek universe, as symbolized by Ptolemy's universe of epicycles, was a smoothly functioning machine. The Christian theology of the Middle Ages was heavily influenced by Greek scientific attitudes, and this accounts for the close identification of Christian thought with the Western attitude toward nature.

To the extent that the people who led the transformation of Europe and North America into industrialized market economies professed Christianity, there is a case for the environmental indictment of the Judeo-Christian traditions. To the extent that a specific Christian tradition—the Puritan

Ethic—led men to accumulate capital, to develop industrial technology, and to conquer much of the world in search of raw materials, there is an indirect influence as well. Perhaps the most important force in Western thought barring an ethical attitude toward nature is the development of the concept of private property and the dominance of the market in economic and social life. As Karl Polanyi points out, the critical social change in Europe that ended the Middle Ages was the transformation of labor and land into commodities, whose services were valued, not for their own sake or for their role in human life, but by an impersonal market.[18] The dominance of the market improved efficiency through specialization, far-flung foreign trade, and the drastic reorganization of society. The transformation of land into a commodity by parcelling it into legal units of private property encouraged absentee and foreign ownership and led the way for its exploitation to serve distant markets.

In a modern market economy, the social significance of land is no longer as the natural basis of community life: it simply is a source of crops and raw materials. The value of land is only instrumental—the discounted net return derived from using it to produce commodities. Intrinsic values are not prized. Naturally, conversion of land into a commodity favored the interests of the rising urban bourgeois class, who used it to break the political power of the landed aristocracy and to create a market in labor services by severing individuals and families from their medieval legal relationship to the land. The conversion of land into a commodity may have been justified by appeal to Christian theological concepts. It was undoubtedly promoted by the breakup of Medieval society under pressure of broad religious, economic, and political changes. But the process was clearly not demanded by any Old Testament injunctions. And it is the conversion of nature into a commodity that has produced the major environmental abuses of the twentieth century.

Passmore has identified a number of splinter traditions within the Judeo-Christian tradition toward nature.[19] These include the biblical concept of the shepherd's obligation to protect his flock and the occasional emergence of the idea that the Earth is not only for man. An example is God's mandate to Noah, who assembled in the Ark all species of creatures, not just those directly useful to man. Additional splinter traditions are the concepts of monastic life, which also occur in many other religions. Most monastic rules call for communal labor in farming, based on an organic relation to the land. Private property in land is not recognized within such communities. Finally, during the late Middle Ages, St. Francis adopted an attitude of reverence toward life that has retained an important place as a minority tradition.

All this is simply to argue that the Genesis view of nature takes a permissive stance toward man's use of the earth. But it is not the basis of a monolithic philosophy, nor is it the sole source of modern Western attitudes toward nature. The intellectual influence of Greek science and the conversion of land into a commodity at the close of the Middle Ages were of much greater importance. The development of a dynamic industrialized society, based on private property, capital accumulation, and the dominance of the market, may have also been promoted by a particular set of Christian ideas—the Puritan Ethic. But scholars do not agree on that point. In addition, as Passmore argues, the Western tradition of specialization in science has hindered the development of holistic thinking about environmental problems.[20]

In any case, Judeo-Christian ideas are not the only source of ethical notions about nature in Western thought. Passmore notes that a significant minority tradition has always been present in the concept of stewardship and cooperation with nature. A small group of thinkers adopted a conservative interpretation of the Genesis creation story—since God had created the earth, he intended that man disturb his creation as little as possible. As a result of these traditions, ". . . the West has never been wholly committed to the view that man has no responsibility whatever for the maintenance and preservation of the world around him . . ."[21]

In the end, Passmore finds that Western Judeo-Christian traditions contain the rudiments on which an ethic of nature protection can be built. It includes the concepts of stewardship and the tradition of reverence for life. It can also rely on general disapproval, in a property-oriented society, of vandalism. This disapproval, Passmore says, should place the burden of proof that it is necessary to develop a wilderness area firmly on the group proposing development, rather than, as is now the case, on the group proposing preservation: "the moral onus is on the one who destroys."[22]

Recently, discussion of a broader philosophy of man's relation to nature was touched off by Martin Krieger's well-known article in *Science*. Krieger argued that wilderness cannot be defined by reference to timeless, abstract criteria. He concluded that perceptions of nature can be created by human artifice and that it is the perceptions which are important for policy.[23]

Krieger argues that the satisfactions obtained from rare natural environments are producible. If so, this reduces the urgency of preservation of wild lands and would permit replacing lost wilderness values with artificial or restored environments.

Lawrence Tribe, responding to Krieger, argued that homocentric values could not provide an adequate philosophical basis for nature preservation. Tribe asserts that the potential replaceability of satisfactions derived from natural environments begs the question: ". . . we cannot simply assume that we must stand mute when confronting the ultimate question of whether we want our children, and their children's children, to live in, and *enjoy*, a plastic world.''[24] (Emphasis in original)

The answer to the dilemma posed by plastic trees is to base environmental policy on '' . . . a sense of reverence for whatever stands beyond human manipulation and its willed consequences, as well as a stance of criticism toward all that is given and a commitment to the conscious improvement of the world.''[25] What is needed, says Tribe, is environmental policy based not on homocentric values but on a sense of obligation to nature, a land ethic.

Mark Sagoff, in commenting on Tribe's proposals, argued for a different nonutilitarian rationale for nature preservation. Sagoff would base the obligation to preserve nature on society's sense of responsibility to its cultural heritage:

> The obligation to preserve nature, then, is an obligation to our cultural tradition, to the values which we have cherished and in terms of which nature and this nation are still to be described . . . The right of our citizens to their history, to the signs and symbols of their culture, and therefore to some means of protecting and using their surroundings in a way consistent with their values is as important as the right to an equally apportioned franchise . . .[26]

In a market-oriented society, a very different attitude toward preservation arises if natural areas are considered to have legal rights as do people and corporations. This approach has been advocated by Christopher Stone, in his widely acclaimed essay, *Should Trees Have Standing?*[27] According to Stone, history has been characterized by the process of granting legal rights to an expanding range of persons: from paterfamilias to wives and children; from property owners to racial minorities and former slaves.[28]

Stone proposes that the well-developed doctrines of guardianship be applied to natural objects. Certain statutorily defined classes of natural objects (rivers, marshes, forests) could be protected through permitting a conservation group to apply for a legal guardianship. The guardian would oversee the object's interests and could sue to prevent invasion of those interests. The rights would have three dimensions. First would be the object's right to sue in its own name (*Mineral King* v. *Morton*, in Justice Douglas' words). Second would be the right to have its own costs or damages, not merely the damages to visitors, considered. This would mean that losses to the fish, and not only to fishermen, would be considered. Third, the object would be a beneficiary in its own right. Damages assessed against invaders of its rights would be applied to attempting to correct the damages, not paid to a human group intervening on the object's behalf.

Adoption of Stone's proposals would have obvious and significant effects on public policy not only toward wilderness but also toward the entire natural environment. Tribe notes, however, that this immediate effect may not be nearly as significant in the long run as would be the effect on the evolution of social values:

> . . . most of the crucial environmental choices confronting industrialized nations in the last third of the 20th century will be choices that significantly shape and do not merely implement those nations' values with respect to nature and wilderness. . . . Choices of this type will also greatly alter the experiences available to the affected persons, the concomitant development of their preferences, attitudes, and cost-benefit conceptions over time, and hence their character as a society.[29]

Perhaps most widely quoted on man's responsibility for nature is Aldo Leopold, who formulated his notion of a land ethic from his experiences as a forester and wildlife manager. Leopold wrote that land policy should be based fundamentally on attempts to improve "land health":

> Individual thinkers since the days of Ezekiel and Isaiah have asserted that despoilation of land is not only inexpedient but wrong. Society, however, has not yet affirmed their belief. The land ethic simply enlarges the boundaries of the community to include soils, waters, plants, and animals, or collectively: the land.[30]

Roderick Nash has offered an additional ethical concept that he considers part of a mandate for preservation. This is the moral value of restraint. He argues that a decision to forgo the benefits of building a hydro dam to preserve a river requires the exercise of restraint, a willingness to place other values higher than economic growth:

> Here wilderness is primarily a symbol. When we establish and preserve a wilderness area we say, in effect, thus far and no farther to development. We establish a *limit* and in doing so we accept the concept of self-imposed limitations. . . . We challenge the wisdom and the moral legitimacy of man's conquest and transformation of the entire earth.[31]

He argues that the concept of restraint applies to the individual wilderness user as well, in that the hiker leaves behind all mechanical aids to transportation in favor of a personal contact with the wilds.

Ethics and Preservation: The Case of Endangered Species

The conservation of endangered species has evolved with a growing consciousness of the importance of ecological diversity. Earliest concerns were with large and spectacular species of birds and mammals, threatened by market demand for their fur or feathers. More recently, attention has been drawn to disappearing species among the plants, insects, fishes, and other creatures. An organization devoted to the preservation of rare butterflies has even emerged—the Xerces Society. Human activities modifying the ecosystem have increased the rate of extinctions beyond the previous norm (see case 1-1). Worldwide, there are about one thousand threatened animal species and perhaps twenty thousand threatened plant species.[32]

Practical reasons for conserving endangered species of plants and animals are numerous. The genetic diversity of natural ecosystems has been described as "a repository of some of society's most valuable raw materials."[33] Valuable services ranging from antibiotics to biological pest control agents have been discovered in previously little-noticed species—scientific laboratories the world over survey remote regions for such useful substances and organisms. Frequently, the most effective means of conserving species is through habitat preservation. It is unnecessary to list more than a few examples of species whose survival has been assured or enhanced by preservation of habitat, often together with other measures such as control of harvesting: whooping cranes, the California condor, desert pupfish.

Policies for state and federal protection of endangered species have increased in numbers and effectiveness, culminating in the Endangered Species Act of 1973. This act finally extended full federal protection to endangered species as defined by the Fish and Wildlife Service's Office of Endangered Species. The act spurred a series of state and federal studies designed to inventory and list all species considered endangered, rare, or threatened.[34] Federal agencies were directed to take steps to consider impacts on endangered species in their decision-making processes (see table 1-2).

A related issue concerns the geographic scope within which an organism or ecosystem is considered to be rare or endangered. The grizzly bear, for example, is not endangered worldwide, but it is becoming scarce in the forty-eight contiguous states of the United States. The same is true of the timber wolf. More locally, many species of plants are rare in Connecticut but widespread elsewhere. How should Connecticut citizens view threats to species that are perhaps on the edge of their ranges in Connecticut but abundant elsewhere? This question can only be answered after a much more thorough inventory of species and ecosystems has been done. An excellent model is the beginning effort completed for Connecticut by Joseph T. Dowham and Robert J. Craig. They note that species at the margin of their distribution are "important reservoirs of biological diversity. With increasing distance from a species' geographic center of distribution . . .

Table 1-2
Box Score of Species Listings as of September 30, 1978

	Number of Endangered Species			Number of Threatened Species		
	United States	*Foreign*	*Total*	*United States*	*Foreign*	*Total*
Mammals	33	227	260	3	18	21
Birds	67	144	211	3		3
Reptiles	11	47	58	10		10
Amphibians	5	9	14	2		2
Fishes	29	10	39	12		12
Snails	2	1	3	5		5
Clams	23	2	25			
Crustaceans	1		1			
Insects	6		6	2		2
Plants	20		20	2		2
Total	197	440	637	39	18	57

Species currently proposed (approximate)	
Animals	158
Plants	1,850
Critical habitats proposed	73
Critical habitats listed	33
Recovery teams appointed	64
Recovery plans approved	18
Cooperative agreements signed with states	22

Source: *Endangered Species Technical Bulletin* 3 (October 1978).

populations tend to become geographically isolated, restricted in habitat, and less dense . . ." As a result, these fringe populations:

> . . . are also of great significance to man in providing an important source of genetic variation used in developing new strains of economic plants and animals. Characteristics such as wilt resistance and frost hardiness in crop and garden plants are mostly derived from peripheral populations adapted to extreme environmental conditions at their range limits.[35]

Fundamentally, however, the management of endangered species must be based on a clear understanding that ethical, not practical, considerations must govern society's decisions.[36] Ethically, the matter may be simply stated. It is simply that human societies have no right to deny survival to any living species. It is true that extinctions have occurred throughout geologic time; human societies need not seek to prevent natural extinctions. It is the increase in extinction rate—wholly because of human action—that is morally intolerable. Further, as many naturalists have noted, the extinctions of many species have been caused by ignorant actors in pursuit of tiny and fleeting gains.

This view goes beyond Passmore, who inquires into the basis for asserting the ethical necessity of protecting endangered species. He states that moral arguments are not available to show that destroying endangered species is intrinsically wrong. Passmore concludes, however, that the value of ecological diversity and the reverence for life do provide partial justification for species preservation. As an additional justification, he cites general social disapproval of vandalism.

The most noted clash of recent years between resource development and an endangered species is the Tellico Dam case. The TVA had virtually completed the Dam on a branch of the Little Tennessee River. The presence of the only known population of the snail darter (figure 1-1) led to a court fight and a major legislative battle resulting in adjustments to the 1973 Endangered Species Act. The controversy also produced a fine piece of applied benefit-cost analysis, as the staffs of TVA and the U.S. Fish and Wildlife Service sought to explore the issue. In the process, they discovered a rich diversity of alternatives.[37]

The Mandate

A mandate for preservation exists. It is based on a wide range of social benefits from the preservation of untouched wild land. These values include scientific, economic, cultural, and ethical values. The benefits accrue not

Figure 1-1. The Snail Darter. (U.S. Fish and Wildlife Service photo by Dr. David Etnier, University of Tennessee.)

only to those who hike or hunt in preserved areas, but to many nearby resource users as well as to distant, and unaware, citizens. The fact that only a minority of the population is currently aware of these values makes them no less real.

Case 1-1. Endangered Western Trouts

Management policies for wildlands and back-country fisheries in the Western states have severely reduced populations of rare western trouts.[a] Species of particular interest include the Colorado River cutthroat, the greenback, the Lahontan cutthroat, the Paiute trout, the Gila trout, and the Arizona native trout. These fish have been reduced to threatened and endangered status by massive stocking of hatchery rainbow and cutthroat trout. Overgrazing, logging, road-building, and other practices have destabilized streambanks and degraded stream habitat for these species.

Wilderness preservation plays an obvious role in preservation of populations of these rare fish. Preservation can eliminate some, but not all, of the management practices that reduce suitable habitat. Beyond mere designation of an area for wilderness, however, a number of active management measures should be taken:

1. Survey of waters to collect specimens from suspected pure populations and to locate potential sites for re-introduction.

2. Taxonomic study of collections to identify pure populations.

3. Protection and possible improvement of habitat.

4. Introduction into barren or chemically treated waters isolated by some barrier against contamination by non-native trouts.

5. Establishment of special regulation fisheries where applicable.[b]

[a] R. J. Behnke, and Mark Zarn, *Biology and Management of Threatened and Endangered Western Trouts,* U.S. Department of Agriculture, Forest Service, Rocky Mountain Forest and Range Experiment Station, General Technical Report RM-28, August 1976.

[b] Behnke and Zarn, p. 8.

Notes

1. For a full exposition, see Roderick Nash, *Wilderness and the American Mind* (New Haven, Conn.: Yale University Press, 1967; Michael Frome, *Battle for the Wilderness* (New York: Frederick A. Praeger, 1974); Aldo Leopold, *A Sand County Almanac* (New York: Oxford University Press, 1949; Michael McCloskey, "The Wilderness Act of 1964: Its Background and Meaning," *Oregon Law Review* 45 (June 1966): 288-314. Also, Roderick Nash, "Wilderness: To Be or Not to Be," in William R. Burch, Jr., ed., *Nature and Human Nature,* Yale School of Forestry and En-

vironmental Studies, New Haven, Conn., Bulletin no. 90, 1976; and Joseph L. Sax, "Freedom: Voices from the Wilderness," *Environmental Law* 7 (Spring 1977): 565-574.

2. Jon Ghiselin, "Wilderness and the Survival of Endangered Species," *Living Wilderness,* Winter 1973-1974, pp. 23-27; J. F. Franklin, R.E. Jenkins, and R. Romancier, "Research Natural Areas: Contributors to Environmental Quality Programs," *Journal Environmental Quality* 1 (1972): 133-139; H.T. Odum and E.P. Odum, "Natural Areas as Necessary Components of Man's Total Environment," *Transactions, 37th North American Wildlife and Natural Resources Conference* (1972), p. 178; The Nature Conservancy, *The Preservation of Natural Diversity: A Survey and Recommendations* (Washington, D.C.: 1975); New England Natural Resources Center, *Protecting New England's Natural Heritage* (Boston: 1973).

3. U.S. Forest Service, *The Nation's Renewable Resources—An Assessment, 1975,* Forest Resource Report no. 21, Washington, D.C., June 1977, p. 77.

4. For a recent example, see U.S. Congress, Senate, Committee on Energy and Natural Resources, *Management of Bull Run Reserve, Oregon,* Publication no. 95-98, July 26, 1977.

5. For examples, see W.E. Shands and P. Woodson, *The Subdivision of Virginia's Mountains* (Washington, D.C.: Central Atlantic Environment Center, 1974); Brian Payne, Richard Gannon, and Lloyd C. Irland, *The Second-Home Recreation Market in the Northeast* (Washington, D.C.: U.S. Department of Agriculture, Bureau of Outdoor Recreation, 1975).

6. Richard L. Ragatz, *Recreational Properties,* Report to U.S. Council on Environmental Quality, U.S. Department of Housing and Urban Development, and the Appalachian Regional Commission (Eugene, Oreg.: R.L. Ragatz Associates, 1974), p. 83.

7. Gene Wunderlich, *Land along the Blue Ridge: Ownership and Use of Land in Rappahannock County, Va.,* U.S. Department of Agriculture, Economic Research Service, Agriculture Economic Report no. 299, 1975.

8. H.W. Dill and R.C. Otte, *Urbanization of Land in the Northeastern U.S.,* U.S. Department of Agriculture, Economic Research Service, Publication EAS-485, 1971.

9. Boris S. Pushkarev, "The Atlantic Urban Seaboard: Development Issues and Strategies," *Regional Plan News* no. 90 (September 1969): 1-26.

10. U.S. Department of Agriculture, Economic Research Service, *Our Land and Water Resources,* Miscellaneous Publication 1290, 1974.

11. Robert Fri, "Energy Imperatives and the Environment," in Charles J. Hitch, ed., *Resources for an Uncertain Future* (Baltimore: Johns Hopkins University Press, 1977), p. 50.

12. S.V. Ciriacy-Wantrup, *Resource Conservation: Economics and Policies,* 3d ed. (Berkeley, Calif.: University of California, 1968).

13. Aldo Leopold, *A Sand County Almanac* (New York: Oxford, 1966), p. 243.

14. Nash, *Wilderness,* p. 26. Reprinted with permission.

15. E.M. Gould, "Wilderness: What Are the Opportunities?" *Journal of Forestry* 73 (January 1975): 8 (reprinted with permission); also N.R. Scott, "Toward a Psychology of Wilderness Experience," *Natural Resources Journal* 14 (April 1974): 231; Betty B. Rossman and E. Joseph Ulehla, "Psychological Rewards Associated with Wilderness Use," *Environment and Behavior* 9 (March 1971): 41-66.

16. See especially, Lynn White, Jr. "The Historical Roots of Our Ecologic Crises," *Science* (10 March 1967) pp. 1203-1207; and Douglas H. Strong and Elizabeth S. Rosenfield, "Ethics or Expediency: An Environmental Question," *Environmental Affairs* 5 (Spring 1976): 255-270.

17. Reprinted by permission from John Passmore, *Man's Responsibility to Nature* (New York: Charles Scribner's Sons, 1974), copyright © 1974 John Passmore.

18. Karl Polanyi, *The Great Transformation* (Boston: Beacon, 1957), chaps. 6, 15. Also J.F.A. Taylor, *The Masks of Society* (New York: Appleton-Century-Crofts, 1966), chap. 3.

19. Passmore, *Man's Responsibility to Nature,* chap. 1.

20. Ibid., p. 48.

21. Ibid., p. 40. Reprinted with permission.

22. Ibid., p. 124. Reprinted with permission.

23. M.H. Krieger, "What's Wrong with Plastic Trees?" *Science* 79 (2 February 1973): 453, reprinted by permission, copyright 1973 by the American Association for the Advancement of Science.

24. Lawrence Tribe, "Ways Not to Think about Plastic Trees: New Foundations for Environmental Law," *Yale Law Journal* 83 (June 1974): 1327. Reprinted with permission of the Yale Law Journal Company, Fred B. Rothman & Company, and the author.

25. Tribe, "Ways Not to Think about Plastic Trees," p. 1340. Reprinted with permission.

26. Mark Sagoff, "On Preserving the Natural Environment," *Yale Law Journal* 84 (December 1975): 265, 267. Reprinted by permission of the Yale Law Journal Company, Fred B. Rothman & Company, and the author. For further discussion, see Lawrence Tribe, "From Environmental Foundations to Constitutional Structures: Learning from Nature's Future," *Yale Law Journal* 84 (January 1975): 545; also, Joseph L. Sax, "Freedom, Voices from the Wilderness," *Environmental Law* 7 (Spring 1977): 565-574.

27. Christopher Stone, *Should Trees Have Standing? Toward Legal Rights for Natural Objects* (Los Altos, Calif.: William Kaufmann, Inc., 1974).

28. A basic objection is raised by Passmore, who argues that nonhuman creatures do not possess "rights," *Man's Responsibility to Nature,* p. 116.

29. Tribe, "Ways Not to Think about Plastic Trees." Reprinted by permission of the Yale Law Journal Company and Fred B. Rothman & Company.

30. Leopold, *Sand County,* pp. 203-204. On the evolution of Leopold's thought, see Susan Flader, *Thinking Like a Mountain* (Columbua, Mo.: University of Missouri Press, 1975). Leopold's land ethic has repeatedly been urged as a basis for U.S. land policy. See, most recently, G. Barney, *The Unfinished Agenda* (New York: Crowell, 1977).

31. Nash, "Wilderness," p. 38. Reprinted with permission.

32. Norman Myers, "An Expanded Approach to the Problem of Disappearing Species," *Science* 193 (16 July 1976): 190-202. See also his book, *The Sinking Ark* (New York: Pergamon Press, 1979). Also, U.S. Council on Environmental Quality, *Environmental Quality,* Seventh Annual Report (Washington, D.C.: Government Printing Office, 1976, pp. 408-415; Erik Eckholm, *Disappearing Species: The Social Challenge,* World Watch Paper no. 22, Washington, D.C., July 1978; U.S. Department of the Interior, Fish and Wildlife Service, *"Endangered and Threatened Wildlife and Plants, Federal Register"* 41 (27 October 1976): 4718. Some human activities, farming, for example, may maintain habitat and thus assist rare species: Joseph T. Dowhan and Robert J. Craig, *Rare and Endangered Species of Connecticut and Their Habitats,* State Geological and Natural History Survey of Connecticut, Department of Investigations, no. 6., 1976. Don A. Wood, *A Bibliography on the World's Rare, Endangered, and Recently Extinct Wildlife and Plants,* Environmental Series no. 3, Oklahoma State University, Environmental Institute, 1977, offers 114 citations in the field.

33. Myers, "An Expanded Approach," p. 198. Reprinted by permission, copyright 1976 by the American Association for the Advancement of Science.

34. D.M. Henderson, et al. *Endangered and Threatened Plants of Idaho,* University of Idaho, Forest, Wildlife and Range Experiment Station, Bulletin no. 21, 1977, is one example. See also note 32.

35. Dowhan and Craig, *Rare and Endangered Species,* p. 10.

36. This is not to ignore arguments offered by economists. See, for examples, R.M. Bishop, "Endangered Species and Uncertainty: The Economics of a Safe Minimum Standard," *American Journal of Agricultural Economics* 60 (February 1978): 10-12; F.T. Bachmura, "Economics of Vanishing Species," *Natural Resources Journal* 11 (October 1971): 674-692; R.C. Amacher, R.D. Tollison, and T.D. Willett, "The Economics of Fatal Mistakes," *Public Policy* 20 (Spring 1974): 411-441;

C.W. Clark, "Profit Maximization and the Extinction of Animal Species," *Journal of Political Economy* 81 (July 1973): 950-961; Jon R. Miller, "A Simple Economic Model of Endangered Species Preservation in the U.S.," *Journal of Environmental Economics and Management* 5 (1978): 292-300; J.R. Miller and F.C. Menz, "Some Economic Considerations for Wildlife Preservation," *Southern Economic Journal* 45 (January 1979): 718.

37. Tennessee Valley Authority and U.S. Department of Interior, *Draft, Alternatives for Completing the Tellico Project* (Knoxville, Tenn., 10 August 1978). For another useful case study, see W.E. Phillips, *The Conservation of the California Tule Elk* (Edmonton, Alberta: University of Alberta Press, 1976). Also, J. Verner, *California Condors: Status of the Recovery Effort,* U.S. Department of Agriculture, Forest Service, Pacific Southwest Forest and Range Experiment Station, General Technical Report, PSW-28, 1978.

2 From Hot Springs to the Gates of the Arctic: Development of U.S. Preservation Policy

In the 1840s, the U.S. Congress designated the Hot Springs area in Arkansas as a national preserve, to preserve it for possible future tourism. In the late 1970s, the Congress was considering proposals to create millions of acres of wilderness in Alaska, including the Gates of the Arctic (figure 2-1) and the Wrangell-St. Elias National Parks, each of which would preserve more than 8 million acres of snowcapped, glacier-shrouded peaks and valleys. During the intervening years, public interest in preservation shifted, and the focal point of leadership shifted as well, from senior elected officials like Theodore Roosevelt, to agency officials like Stephen Mather of the National Park Service and Bob Marshall of the Forest Service, then

Figure 2-1. Gates of the Arctic, Alaska. (National Park Service Photo.)

to activist citizens' groups such as the Save the Redwoods League, the Sierra Club, and the Wilderness Society.

The history of wilderness preservation in the United States has been capably reviewed elsewhere.[1] For now, a brief review of major themes will suffice. Three broad periods may be identified. From colonial days to about 1900, steps were taken in an ad hoc fashion to preserve specific notable natural features, such as Hot Springs and Yosemite. From the turn of the century to the mid-fifties, conscious wildland preservation policies were developed. This period was characterized by administrative action at the federal level, encouraged by the small conservation movement of the day. Since the mid-fifties, political conflicts over wildland resource use emerged on a broad scale. A new period of legislative struggle and administrative innovation ensued. At the urging of active citizens' groups, Congress found itself dealing with a series of multi-million-acre preservation decisions. Simultaneously, there emerged a broad interest in saving natural areas to preserve small unique ecosystems for scientific reasons. Sparked by nongovernmental groups, this natural area movement has involved federal agencies as well and has built a sizeable citizen constituency for preservation.

Ad Hoc Preservation

In colonial times, various actions of the Crown and of colonial governments have been cited to show the existence of preservation or resource conservation policies. The Broad Arrow Act, which reserved large white pine trees for the Crown, was an example. But wildland preservation in this period was hardly an economic or political issue.

In the confederation and early federal periods, federal policy debates centered on the most expedient methods of promoting the settlement of the Old Northwest, and later, the Louisiana Purchase, the Oregon Territory, and the regions conquered from Mexico. In the 1820s, concern over supplies of ship-building timber led Congress to establish several reserves of live oak and pine timber in the southeastern states. These reserves were never fully protected or managed, and they simply reflected official concern for military supplies, rather than a resource management or conservation policy.[2]

In 1864, the first major federal step in wildland preservation was taken. In that year, the nucleus of the future Yosemite National Park was donated to the State of California for use as a public park. The Park was later ceded back to the federal government, and it is now the centerpiece of a cluster of federal reservations protecting that unique area.

Eight years later, in 1872, President Grant proclaimed the Yellowstone National Park, in a region of natural wonders explored several years earlier by several parties of explorers.[3] Whereas Yellowstone Park represented a victory for nature advocates, it was in no sense an expression of a policy favorable to wildland preservation. Proponents prevailed on the basis of their argument that the Park would preserve a valuable tourist resource and that the developable resources of the area were unimportant. As Roderick Nash put it, "it is clear that no *intentional* preservation of wild country occurred."[4]

In 1885, the New York legislature created the Adirondack Park, which was later protected by constitutional amendment in the 1890s. The moving force for this action was the pressure of New York commercial interests, who saw the Park as the only means of preserving the water supply for the Erie Canal and for New York's growing cities. These interests were allied with tourism groups, conservation groups, and local landowners interested in preserviang the area's scenery. The Adirondack Park has grown to encompass several million acres of state-owned land and millions more of private land within the "blue line" defining the region. It has spawned a smaller satellite, in the Catskill Range to the southeast, which protects reservoirs supplying New York City's water.

The period from European settlement to about 1900, then, was one of occasional, ad hoc efforts to preserve a few areas of outstanding importance. Reasons for these actions were specific and pragmatic—tourism or water supply. They expressed no general public view as to the desirability of committing a fraction of the nation's land to preservation.

Emergence of Preservation Policies: 1900 to 1950

In the conservation era of the early 1900s, several major natural resource policies fell into place and were fitted with administrative machinery to give them effect. That these policies resulted from several decades of conscious debate recently has been shown by J.A. Miller.[5] They were not accidental or happenstance occurrences, as they have appeared to some conservation historians. The movement of the forest reserves from the Department of the Interior to the Department of Agriculture in 1905 marks a significant turning point. At that time, the forest reserves, created under authority of the 1891 General Land Law Revision Act, came under the control of the new U.S. Forest Service.[6] The young agency survived concerted attempts to bar further creation of reservations, to bar the agency from charging grazing fees, and, later, to donate the forest reserves, renamed national forests, to the states. The price of this survival was a commitment to the West's development-oriented philosophy of resource management. This philosophy, in any event, was congenial to Forest Service Chief Gifford Pinchot and his agency staffers.[7]

At this time were sown the seeds of the division that persists within the conservation field today—conservation as development of resources versus conservation as preservation of resources. This division was symbolized by the fact that Pinchot stood opposite conservationist John Muir over the issues of grazing on the national forests and authorization of the Hetch Hetchy reservoir in Yosemite National Park.[8]

Theodore Roosevelt's administration greatly expanded the national park system. In addition, Roosevelt established several important wildlife refuges, which were later pulled together into a national wildlife refuge system by act of Congress in 1929. In 1916, the Congress established the National Park Service, to provide professional management of the growing list of parks, monuments, and related areas.

Immediately after World War I, the Forest Service was faced with a host of management problems, ranging from locating boundaries and preventing trespass to developing recreation. Timber harvests were low, and the dominant resource use was grazing. The Forest Service also faced competition from the newly created National Park Service, which was eagerly seeking new fields for expansion. References to recreation values began to appear in the public statements and documents of the Forest Service. A young Forest Service landscape architect, Arthur H. Carhart, surveyed the recreation potential of the Quetico-Superior country of northern Minnesota and studied the Trappers Lake country in the White River National Forest in Colorado.[9] He attempted to persuade his superiors that certain national forest wildlands could be of the best use to society in their natural state. He was instrumental in obtaining administrative classification of these areas as wild areas. Another Forest Service employee, Aldo Leopold, worked for wilderness in Arizona and New Mexico. He persuaded his regional office to establish the Gila Wilderness in southern New Mexico in 1924. Leopold, a capable writer, expressed his case to his fellow foresters in an eloquent 1921 article, and to the general public years later in his famous *Sand County Almanac*. Leopold emphasized the need to preserve large wild areas to provide for the recreational needs of hikers and sportsmen, which he expected to increase in the future.

At that time, Leopold based his view of the need for wilderness on the need to provide backcountry recreational experiences, which he correctly predicted would be in increasing demand. As Leopold saw it, a wilderness area should be: ". . . a continuous stretch of country preserved in its natural state, open to lawful hunting and fishing, big enough to absorb a two weeks' pack trip, and kept devoid of roads, artificial trails, cottages, or other works of man."[10]

In the late 1920s, Chief W.B. Greeley of the Forest Service ordered a survey of potential wilderness lands, with a view to standardizing by regulation the procedures that had grown up, willy-nilly, in the regional offices. In 1929, the resulting L-regulations were promulgated. These regulations permitted the Chief to establish a series of primitive areas, which would be maintained in primitive condition "for purposes of public education, inspiration, and recreation."[11] By 1933, sixty-three primitive areas had been established on the national forests.[12]

In the 1930s there emerged another forceful personality who was to significantly affect wilderness policy. This was Robert Marshall, independently wealthy, a plant-pathologist-turned-recreation-administrator for the Forest Service. His benefactions provided the financial foundation for the Wilderness Society, which remains an active force for the cause of wilderness.[13]

Written under Marshall's influence, the U-regulations were issued in 1939, shortly after his death. These three regulations remained policy until passage of the 1964 Wilderness Act. Regulation U-1 authorized the establishment of wilderness areas 100,000 acres or more in size to be created by order of the Secretary of Agriculture. Such areas could also be modified, on due notice, by the Secretary. Regulation U-2 provided that areas between 5,000 and 100,000 acres in size could be designated as "wild areas" by the Chief of the Forest Service. Regulation U-3 provided for establishment of roadless areas, primarily for recreation.

The prevailing pattern was one of conserving wilderness values by administrative action. No proposal for national forest wilderness raised sufficient interest to command Congressional attention, for market demand for National Forest resources remained low. In several instances, large areas were transferred to the Park Service from Forest Service administration. In 1940, timber harvests were still small, and mineral developments were few. In the national parks and wildlife refuges, management attention was devoted to mission-oriented resource development—serving the growing tourist boom on the parks and managing game species of fish and wildlife on the refuges. Land acquisition for these purposes progressed steadily, reflecting steady congressional support for parks and wildlife.

The period of conscious preservation saw a professional corps of managers and scientists assembled in the Forest Service, Park Service, and Fish and Wildlife Service. National attention was drawn not to proposals for new wilderness areas—these were handled quietly by administrators—but to proposed invasions of the national parks by dams or railroads.

In this period, however, political debts were incurred by the resource agencies as the price for larger land bases, budgets, and staffs. The I.O.U.s were held by the resource interests, including timber, water, grazing, wildlife groups, and the congressmen representing them. As demands on the national forests, parks, and wildlife refuges grew, these groups expected first priority in service and in resource decisions. And more and more, agency psychology came to terms with the interests of development-oriented groups. This trend precipitated the third major period in wilderness preservation policy—the era of conflict, dating from the mid-fifties.

Era of Conflict

After World War II, the resurgent home-building industry caused an unprecedented boom in the lumber and plywood industries. An all-time record in home-building set in 1950 was not exceeded until 1972. The price of national forest timber rose, and the volume harvested grew rapidly— from 3.5 billion board-feet in 1950 to about 12 billion board-feet in the early sixties. Rising timber harvests slowly altered the appearance of the national forest landscape in previously remote areas. Bulldozers pushed roads into untouched valleys. Ragged bare patches appeared, as old growth stands were clear-cut. In some cases, boundaries of existing wilderness areas were redrawn around valleys containing valuable timber. National parks were scenes of roadbuilding, campsite development, and traffic congestion. Conservationists became convinced that administrative discretion was not a reliable protection for the wilderness in the national forests and parks. They responded by promoting new protective legislation, and by adopting new tactics.

New Legislation

The first wilderness bill was introduced in Congress in 1956 by Senator Hubert Humphrey. The bill called for a wilderness commission, which would study additions to a wilderness system, and for immediate protection of existing wilderness and primitive areas. The Wilderness Act was passed, considerably altered, in 1964. Its legislative history is ably recounted elsewhere;[14] its substantive provisions are discussed in the next chapter.

The period around 1960 saw a broadening of the National Park Service mission with the establishment of national seashores and national recreation areas. As the Park Service struggled with its Mission 66 program to expand the recreational capacity of the parks, it confronted an increasingly critical environmental movement. By the late sixties, the major preservation groups were convinced that the Park Service was mismanaging the park system by catering to an auto-oriented, superficial clientele of two-hour visitors and Winnebago campers.[15] This critique was a basic theme of a major report issued by the Conservation Foundation in 1972.[16]

Simultaneously, concern for endangered species of creatures slowly broadened from its original concern with large hoofed mammals, rare birds, and furbearers. A series of endangered-species acts culminated in the 1973 Endangered Species Act, which gave substance to an emerging federal policy of protecting threatened species.[17]

The effort to save the Grand Canyon from dam building drew attention to the fact that the nation's stock of free-flowing rivers was declining rapidly.[18] A move for a systematic response to the issue grew out of a Department of the Interior study of several streams in the Ozarks, which blossomed into the National Wild and Scenic River study. The study became the basis for the Wild and Scenic Rivers Act of 1968.

The era of conflict was marked by major confrontations over resource use between the organized conservation and development-oriented groups. These conflicts lifted preservation decision-making out of agency hands and placed the basic policy issues squarely before the Congress. The issue of preservation became a significant new theme in old debates where it had rarely been heard—major debates over the trans-Alaska pipeline and over clearcutting on the national forests were based on fundamentally preservationist arguments. By the late seventies, the Congress, the states, and federal agencies faced the largest preservation decisions in history—the preservation of Alaskan wilderness, completion of national forest roadless area reviews, and survey of Bureau of Land Management lands for wilderness potential.

New Tactics

The era of conflict is not over. The period is notable for its dramatic legislative progress, but perhaps of greater long-term significance are important changes in tactics. The major innovations are the development of highly organized citizens' groups to serve as pressure groups in preservation causes and the use of litigation.

The organized citizens' conservation movement is not new. Groups such as the Audubon Society, the American Forestry Association, and the various sportsmen's clubs have been important in the history of conservation policy. What is new, however, is the rapid growth of groups with an explicitly preservationist program, which appeal to a broad group of persons interested in the outdoors and in conservation. The Sierra Club, perhaps best known, is well advanced in national, regional, and local organization. Its local groups are supported by newsletters and by a superstructure of regional offices and conservation committees. The Club operates a legal defense fund and a nonprofit foundation to promote research. It reaches a wide audience through its monthly magazine and a series of books.

What distinguishes today's Sierra Club from the earlier conservation movement is first its professionalization. The group has become organized much along the pattern of existing trade associations and pressure groups. It enlists the aid of many persons who devote so much time to Club business as to be virtually paraprofessionals in the group's work. Second, the Club and its sister citizens' groups are distinguished by their extraordinarily wide range of interests—based on the realization that the entire world biosphere must be protected if the group is to achieve its objectives. This breadth of interests has drawn the preservation groups into fields such as nuclear power, population growth, and marine resource problems. The Sierra Club, with its extensive organization, can operate at the program level in the U.S. Congress and in state legislatures, while its local chapters operate at the project level—promoting specific parks and wilderness areas, and opposing dams, freeways, or other projects.

The maturing of the conservation-oriented citizens' group as a major institution in modern society is attested by the considerable attention the movement has drawn from sociologists.[19] The conservation groups' demand for influence has generated a move among the resource-managing agencies to design explicit procedures for incorporating public views into the administrative process.[20]

The citizens' groups have made shrewd use of litigation to gain leverage in the decision-making process. Through litigation, they and the major public interest law firms have virtually created the emerging field of environmental law.[21]

Privately Sponsored Preservation

The American conservation movement includes a long tradition of privately sponsored land preservation for public purposes. Best known, perhaps, are the major benefactions of the Rockefeller family, who provided the core lands for national parks in the Great Smokies and the Grand Tetons, and for Acadia in Maine. The redwood purchasing program of the Save the Redwoods League is prominent in California. Groups such as Ducks Unlimited and the Audubon Society have long owned preserves to foster their own particular interests.[22]

Since the early fifties, a highly professional group, the Nature Conservancy, has come to the fore by using the tools of the modern real estate trade to foster conservation objectives. The Conservancy has assisted in the preservation of more than one million acres of land in less than thirty years. It frequently acts as a broker and short-term landholder, until properties can be transferred to public agencies. In such cases, the Conservancy retains rights through reverter clauses to assure that the new owner does not abuse its preservation responsibilities. Recently, the

Conservancy has begun to retain specific parcels in its own hands, establishing local preserve management committees to oversee them.

Conserving Endangered Ecosystems—The Natural Area Movement

The natural areas movement originated with a group of scientists, members of the Ecological Society of America, who met in the 1920s and determined that a sample of America's remaining ecosystems should be preserved for the future. This concern broadened from strictly scientific values to a more general interest in the importance of biotic diversity, landscape integrity, and environmental education. Today, the natural area movement presents a bewildering institutional diversity—from groups such as the Nature Conservancy and Ducks Unlimited, who buy land and broker land deals for public agencies, to obscure federal committees charged with inventorying research natural areas.

A major review by The Nature Conservancy offered four rationales for preservation of natural diversity.[23] First, natural areas provide "libraries of information," which can be resorted to for more detailed ecological understanding at any time. This is especially so for rare ecosystems, since they add significantly to the total range of conditions available for study. Second, they can serve as ecological monitoring stations, helping scientists detect broad environmental changes such as effects of temperature change or of pollution. It is well established, for example, that in stressed stream ecosystems, biotic diversity declines. The trends in diversity in streams can serve as an integrating index of biological purity and ecosystem health. Third, undisturbed natural areas can serve as ecological baselines against which to compare the effects of man's manipulations. A large area of undisturbed grassland ecosystem would serve as a valuable comparison to farmed or grazed lands nearby. The natural system would demonstrate, for example, the effects of climatic trends, so that such effects could be taken into account in appraising productivity of the managed grasslands.

Finally, designated natural areas can help guide land-use planning by identifying landscape features—whether topographic, geologic, or ecological—that deserve preservation. As the Conservancy report observed:

> It seems just short of miraculous that the preservation of diversity has not become a basic raison d'être for land use planning. Instead, the land use planning movement has concentrated upon matters of carrying capacity and development constraint. Most likely a good deal more could be accomplished by gearing the effort toward protecting what is valuable.[24]

All the justifications presented apply to the need to devote tracts of sample ecosystems strictly to scientific research. Uses would include the study of undisturbed natural ecosystems, monitoring of planned management strategies, and analysis of long-term successional trends. A prime example is the Hubbard Brook Ecosystem Study, conducted in a small experimental forest in the White Mountains of New Hampshire. This multiyear study has yielded important insights into ecosystem energy flows and material flows in the northern mixed forest.[25] To be effective, research natural areas often have to be protected from all other land uses, even hiking and camping.

In 1974, federal agencies managed a total of 369 research natural areas, encompassing almost 1.7 million acres of wildland. The major agencies involved were the Fish and Wildlife Service, the Forest Service, the National Park Service, the Energy Research and Development Administration, and the Bureau of Land Management. These are supplemented by a number of systems at the state level.[26] Another nationwide program is the Natural Landmarks Program, which maintains a registry of important natural features.[27] On the state level, the Nature Conservancy's Natural Heritage program has promoted similar efforts: by 1977, ten states had completed detailed inventories of natural areas.

Existing international programs for promoting preservation of important natural features are varied. The worldwide activities of the International Union for the Conservation of Nature are well known. The United States cooperates with UNESCO in its Man and the Biosphere (MAB) program. The program aims to provide a global, comprehensive framework for preservation of large examples of major biotic provinces, for conservation, research, and education. To date, twenty-eight reserves have been selected in the United States. Several experimental forests, which have been manipulated for research, are included. These are included under the concept of linked reserves, "since rarely will a single tract be able to adequately fulfill all functions—preservation, research, and education . . ."[28]

Notes

1. Roderick Nash, *Wilderness and the American Mind* (New Haven, Conn.: Yale University Press, 1967); H.K. Steen, *The Forest Service* (Seattle, Wash.: University of Washington Press, 1976).

2. See standard histories of the public lands, such as: P.W. Gates, *History of Public Land Law Development* (Washington, D.C.: U.S. Government Printing Office, 1968); E. Richardson, *Dams, Parks, and Politics—Resource Development and Preservation in the Truman-Eisenhower Era* (Lexington, Ky.: University Press of Kentucky, 1973); also,

M. Clawson and R.B. Held, *The Federal Lands* (Baltimore: Johns Hopkins, 1957).

3. E. Clary, *The Place Where Hell Bubbled Up* (Washington, D.C.: U.S. Government Printing Office, 1972).

4. Nash, *Wilderness,* p. 112 (emphasis in original). Reprinted with permission.

5. Joseph A. Miller, "Congress and the Origins of Conservation, 1865-1900" (Ph. D. diss., University of Minnesota, 1973).

6. 16 U.S.C. 471.

7. S.P. Hays, *Conservation and the Gospel of Efficiency* (New York: Atheneum, 1974), chaps. 3, 7.

8. See Nash, *Wilderness,* chap. 10 for the Hetch Hetchy story.

9. Ibid., p. 185.

10. Aldo Leopold, "The Need for Wilderness," *Journal of Forestry* 19 (November 1921): 718-721.

11. Quoted in Wildland Research Center, *Wilderness and Recreation,* Outdoor Recreation Resources Review Commission, Report 3 (Washington, D.C.: U.S. Government Printing Office, 1963), p. 20.

12. Wildland Research Center, *Wilderness,* p. 19.

13. Marshall's own wilderness philosophy was forcefully expressed in his "The Problem of the Wilderness," *Scientific Monthly* 30 (February 1930): 141-143.

14. Nash, *Wilderness,* pp. 220-225; Michael McCloskey, "The Wilderness Act of 1964 . . ." *Oregon Law Review* 48 (June 1966): 297-301; Michael McCloskey, "Is the Wilderness Act Working?" in E.R. Gillette, ed., *Action for Wilderness* (San Francisco: Sierra Club Books, 1972), p. 22.

15. An eloquent expression of this view is Edward Abbey, *Desert Solitaire* (New York: Simon and Schuster, 1968), p. 39ff.

16. Conservation Foundation, *National Parks for the Future* (Washington, D.C., 1972).

17. C.W. Fawcett, "Vanishing Wildlife and Federal Protection Efforts," *Ecology Law Quarterly* 1 (Summer 1971): 520.

18. T.Watkins, et al., *The Grand Colorado* (New York: Crown, 1969) and Nash, *Wilderness,* p. 227ff. tell the story of the Grand Canyon controversy. D. Mann, *The Politics of Water in Arizona* (Tucson, Ariz.: University of Arizona Press, 1963) provides valuable background. Also, F. Hannay, "in Memoriam: Rainbow Bridge . . ." *Ecology Law Quarterly* 4 (Spring 1974): 385.

19. See, for example, J. Harry, R. Gale and J.C. Hendee, "Conservation: An Upper-Middle Class Social Movement" *Journal of Leisure Research* 1 (Summer 1969): 246; W.B. Devall, "Conservation: An Upper Middle Class Social Movement: A Replication," *Journal of Leisure Research* 2 (Spring 1970): 123; National Committee on Voluntary Action,

Environmental Volunteers in America (Washington, D.C., 1973). In W.R. Burch, Jr., N.H. Cheek, Jr., and L. Taylor, eds., *Social Behavior, Natural Resources, and the Environment* (New York: Harper and Row, 1974) are found valuable essays by Morrison, McEvoy, and Gale.

20. J.C. Hendee et al., "Using Public Input . . .," *Journal of Soil and Water Conservation* 29 (March-April 1974): 60; and L.C. Irland, "Citizen Participation—A Tool for Conflict Management on Public Lands," *Public Administration Review* 35 (May-June 1975): 263; M.E. Gellhorn, "Public Participation in the Administrative Process" *Yale Law Journal* 81 (January 1972): 359; W.B. Devall, "The Forest Service and Its Clients . . .," *Environment Affairs* 2 (1972-1973), p. 732.

21. J. Sax, *Defending the Environment—Handbook for Citizen Action* (New York: Vintage, 1970), especially chaps. 4-6; G.P. Thompson, "The Role of the Courts," in E. Dolgin and T.G.P. Guilbert, eds., *Federal Environmental Law* (Washington, D.C.: Environmental Law Institute, 1974), p. 226.

22. A survey by the Nature Conservancy received nineteen responses out of thirty groups thought to be engaged in private preservation efforts. The Nature Conservancy, *The Preservation of Natural Diversity* (Washington, D.C., 1975), appendix 4.

23. Ibid., part 1.

24. Ibid., p. 33.

25. G.E. Likens et al. *Biogeochemistry of a Forested Ecosystem* (New York: Springer Verlag, 1977).

26. The Nature Conservancy, *Preserving Natural Diversity,* appendixes 3, 4.

27. Anne LaBastille, "The Natural Landmarks Program of the U.S.," *Environmental Conservation* 3 (Spring 1976): 31-32.

28. Jerry Franklin, "The Biosphere Reserve Program in the U.S.," *Science* 195 (21 January 1977): 262-267, reprinted by permission. For an up-to-date inventory covering federal lands, see Federal Committee on Ecological Reserves, *Directory of Research Natural Areas on Federal Lands* (Washington, D.C.: U.S. Government Printing Office, 1977). For examples of regional and state-level inventories, see Clifford C. Garmain, William E. Jans, and Robert H. Read, *Wisconsin Scientific Areas 1977: Preserving Natural Diversity,* Department of Natural Resources, Technical Bulletin no. 102, (Madison, Wisconsin, 1977); and Center for Natural Areas, *A Preliminary Listing of Noteworthy Natural Features in Maine,* Critical Areas Planning Program, Maine State Planning Office, Augusta, Maine, June 1976; Gary S. Waggoner, *Eastern Deciduous Forest,* vol. 1, *Southeast Evergreen and Oak-pine Region,* National Park Service Natural History Theme Studies (Washington, D.C.: U.S. Government Printing Office, 1975).

3 Implementing the Mandate: Legislation for Preservation, 1964 to 1974

The era of conflict in conservation policy produced four major pieces of legislation establishing preservation policy, three of which applied primarily to the federal lands. These three laws—the 1964 Wilderness Act, the 1968 Wild and Scenic Rivers Act, and the 1974 Eastern Wilderness Areas Act—set forth policy goals and established similar programs of instant designations followed by study programs with time deadlines. The fourth law was the Endangered Species Act, which applied to all lands in the United States. These laws emerged from intense partisan debate. Preservation advocates never succeeded in achieving as much "instant" preservation as they desired. All three acts embody a judgment that the process for designating areas for preservation should be a deliberate one, conducted by the agency already administering the land, with potential commercial values that may be affected fully considered.

The Wilderness Act of 1964

The Wilderness Act was a landmark of conservation policy. It provided for an immediate classification of less than 10 million acres—an acreage that appears insignificant when compared to the areas at stake in Alaska or on the Bureau of Land Management lands. But it established a study process that became the model for subsequent laws, and it placed wilderness preservation on an equal footing with other objectives of federal land-use planning.

The Debate

The wilderness system existing in the fifties had largely taken shape by 1939, through administrative measures promoted by a minority of dedicated individuals. That system was regarded by the Forest Service as a tentative series of reservations, whose boundaries were subject to adjustment as demands for timber or other resources grew. The system was created with little public debate, nationally or regionally. As early as 1951, Howard Zahniser, a leader of the Wilderness Society, proposed that wilderness on the national forests be protected by congressional action. In 1956, bills sponsored by the

Wilderness Society were introduced by Senator Hubert H. Humphrey and Congressman John Saylor.[1] The bills called for designation of a series of units on the national forests, parks, and wildlife refuges as well as on Indian reservations. A Wilderness Council was to be established, which would oversee this process and recommend additional areas and management policies to the President.

These proposals precipitated a seven-year marathon wilderness debate in the Congress, involving nine separate hearings and generating more than 6,000 pages of hearing prints.[2] Mining and timber industries opposed the various wilderness bills because they restricted commercial uses of public land. Particularly strong opponents were the mining interests, who, as we shall see, succeeded in extracting concessions to their viewpoint. The resource-managing agencies at first considered the bill a challenge to their professional competence and autonomy, and argued that congressional wilderness decision-making was unnecessary.

The act that emerged from this struggle in 1964 bore little resemblance to the proposals offered in 1955 and 1956.[3] The compromises made during that period have been complained of since.[4] A brief review of the act's provisions seems useful here.[5]

Provisions—What the Act Did

The Wilderness Act established a process for determining the ultimate size of the National Wilderness Preservation System (NWPS). This was far from the conservationists' original goal, which was a bill that would establish the system immediately. The Congress, however, chose to establish a procedural route through which proposed areas would become part of the wilderness system. To accomplish this, the Congress provided for a process of reservation and review—a pattern extensively used later. The process has three major components—provisions establishing an "instant" system, a study procedure for establishing additional areas, and management guidelines.

First came the initial establishment of the system. In 1964, the existing wilderness areas on the national forests became the charter members of the NWPS. This initial system totalled about 9.1 million acres. This included the Boundary Waters Canoe Area in Minnesota, which was later to become the center of further controversy, finally resolved in 1978.

Beyond the existing wilderness areas, the areas next in order of contention were the primitive areas, totalling about 5.5 million acres at that time. Congress directed the Forest Service to present proposals on these areas through the President within ten years. The proposals were to be aired at public hearings—a significant departure from past procedure and one that recognized the wide public interest in the issue. State and county governments were to be specifically invited to comment. The primitive areas were to be protected from development pending completion of the studies. Each report was to be accompanied by a U.S. Geological Survey field survey of the area's mineral potential. The act required that this study process encompass lands adjacent to primitive areas which are predominantly of wilderness value.[6] This provision sparked litigation which is discussed below.

Areas on existing national parks and wildlife refuges were not controversial for their extractable resource values, since they were already largely reserved from such uses. But conservationists argued for wilderness areas there as well. They believed that the Park Service and the Fish and Wildlife Service, with their commitments to mass recreation, and to wildlife management, were unreliable stewards of wilderness. The act adopted this view. It required the Secretary of the Interior to report within ten years on the suitability for wilderness of all roadless units on the national parks and wildlife refuges larger than 5,000 acres, and also on all islands in the refuge system.

Conservationists complained that the lengthy study-hearing-legislation route placed an unreasonable burden on wilderness advocates:

> There is a curious double standard here: on the one hand, if we conservationists want more wilderness preserved we have to go through endless reviews and hearings, exposed at every step of the way to fullscale attack by industry. On the other hand, if de facto wilderness is to be logged there are no hearings or reviews whatsoever, no chance for public scrutiny except in the most pro forma sense.[7]

The most important compromise involved mining. The mining industry opposed the act on the grounds that minerals must be developed wherever they are found. The act provides that mineral exploration may continue on national forest wilderness areas until December 31, 1983.[8] In addition, subject to regulation by the Secretary of Agriculture, actual mining development may be permitted on valid claims after that date.

Nonprovisions: What the Act Did Not Do

The Wilderness Act is often presented as a ringing declaration by Congress of its determination to conserve wilderness values. Instead, the act is actually a result of political compromises between positions taken by the opposing interests. Despite its ringing statement of policy, it is in fact a grudging concession to conservation by the interest groups who then dominated public land policy. It was wrung from those groups by a handful of determined congressmen and by the growing political skill and power of the organized conservation movement.

For this reason, it is useful to examine what the act did not provide. Briefly, the act did not provide for a ban on mining, nor for an agency with funding to manage wilderness and act as an advocate for new areas. It did not mandate a review of roadless areas on the national forests outside of existing primitive areas, and it overlooked the vast lands controlled by the BLM. In short, its review process omitted far more de facto wilderness than it included. Finally, it did not include in the instant system any more areas than the minimum, noncontroversial amount—the lands within existing national forest wilderness.

The failure of the act to ban mining was a blow to conservation interests, who began to perceive its seriousness in the sixties and early seventies as mining companies began to plan operations in Idaho's White Cloud Peaks and in Washington's Glacier Peak area.[9] Political pressure on this issue was so intense that the Forest Service did not issue its regulations on mining until the early seventies. The mining issue returned to haunt all parties to the debate when it became a critical issue in the debate over eastern wilderness.

The early conservationist proposals for wilderness legislation provided for a wilderness council or agency. At least in principle, a wilderness agency could have served to manage existing areas and to carry out the study program prescribed for new proposals. It could have been free from the mission-oriented biases of the existing agencies. Existing agencies and their corresponding committees in the Congress did not view such a prospect with pleasure. The Congress made clear its distaste for additional bureaucracy:

> No appropriation shall be made available for the administration of the National Wilderness Preservation System as a separate unit nor shall any appropriations be available for additional personnel stated as being required solely for the purpose of managing or administering areas solely because they are included within the National Wilderness Preservation system.[10]

Whatever the advantages and disadvantages of a wilderness council might have been, the Congress was unwilling to delegate decisions of such political significance to any existing or proposed agency, council, or commission.

The 1964 act dedicated for preservation and study only a fraction of the potential unroaded land in the national forest system, considering less than 15 million acres for instant or study status. Later study showed that about 67 million acres of unroaded land in units larger than 5,000 acres remained in the national forests. The Wilderness Act provided no mandatory review of potential units on 475 million acres of public domain land, which was not required until passage of the 1976 Federal Lands Policy and Management Act.

From the conservationist viewpoint, the most disappointing thing the act failed to do was simply to designate more acres as wilderness. The instant system incorporated only areas that had already been protected for decades and in which the resource-oriented industries had little interest. The Congress in 1964 was unable to go farther than this.

The act's compromises resulted in serious unresolved conflicts, which have led interested parties to the courts to promote their interests. [11]

The Wild and Scenic Rivers Act of 1968

Rising public sentiment for wilderness preservation was accompanied by an increased interest in the preservation of free-flowing streams. Concern for riverine wilderness has been a major theme of the conservation movement, which has fought major battles—Hetch Hetchy, Echo Park, and the Grand Canyon—over preserving wild waterways. The movement for a Wild Rivers preservation program arose out of a 1964 study proposing an Ozark wilderness waterway. [12] In 1965, an Interior Department study inventoried remaining wild waterways and proposed a program for their preservation. Following several years of debate, the Wild and Scenic Rivers Act was enacted in 1968. [13]

This act followed the precedent of the Wilderness Act by establishing an instant system of preserved areas and defining a program of study with a schedule for completion of reviews on a series of study rivers. Eight rivers were protected in the instant system, including 392 miles of river. A deadline of 1978 was set for completion of reports and recommendations on an additional twenty-seven study rivers with a total length of 4,650 miles.

The act provides for management of rivers by agencies currently managing adjacent lands. To date, most of the river reaches included in the system flow through or near federal lands. In several cases, however, significant land acquisition or land-use controls would be required to protect river corridors. The act limits federal control of land in river corridors to a total of 320 acres per stream mile, roughly a quarter-mile strip on each side of the stream. It encourages the use of easements to control development on private lands.

The act creates three classifications of stream reaches. More than one classification may occur on a given protected river. The most strictly protected is the wild river category. In such streams or in wild reaches of protected streams the mining laws are not in effect, and dams may be constructed only by permission of Congress. In scenic and recreational reaches less stringent limitations prevail. Standards for inclusion of such reaches are much broader than for wild river reaches. On some streams proposed for protection, recreational reaches consist of streams flowing through open, lightly developed rural areas and even near suburban developments. The National Wild and Scenic River System consisted of 1,655 miles of federally protected waterways by 1977 (table 3-1). By that year, 51 study streams had been designated. The largest unit was Montana's 219-mile Flathead, of which 98 miles were in the Wild category.

Following the lead of the federal act, and in some cases stimulated by that act, many states have established their own wild river systems. At the end of 1972, twenty-two states had passed wild river preservation legislation.[14] In most states the number of stream miles preserved under such legislation has been small.

Eastern Wilderness

After the passage of the Wilderness Act of 1964, a period of ferment began in which the land-managing agencies worked out wilderness study procedures, began to prepare reports to Congress, and inventoried potential wilderness areas. The act stimulated a massive effort by conservation groups to identify, study, and propose additional areas. By the late sixties the Sierra Club and the Wilderness Society had made considerable membership gains in the eastern states and had created regional chapters and groups in those areas. By the time the Forest Service began its roadless area review in the early seventies, conservation groups were ready.

The 1964 Wilderness Act established several eastern areas. It provided a specific management regime for the Boundary Waters Canoe Area in Minnesota. It also established the Shining Rock and Linville Gorge wilderness areas in North Carolina and the Great Gulf Wilderness in New Hampshire. These steps protected about 26,000 acres of wilderness plus

Table 3-1
The National Wild and Scenic Rivers System, 1977, 19 Rivers

Classification	River Miles
Wild	681.05
Scenic	452.7
Recreational	448.4
Total	1,655.15

Source: U.S. Council on Environmental Quality, *Eighth Annual Report,* (Washington, D.C.: U.S. Government Printing Office, 1978), p. 88.

almost 900,000 acres of canoe country. In 1969, the Alabama Conservancy proposed a Sipsey Wilderness of roughly 12,000 acres in the Bankhead National Forest. The Conservancy's efforts to present the Sipsey proposal to the Congress stimulated the later debate over eastern wilderness. The Sipsey was finally included in the NWPS under the 1974 Eastern Wilderness Areas Act. In its roadless area review, the Forest Service adhered to its "purity" policy and included only three areas in the East—one each in North Carolina, Florida, and Puerto Rico. Failure to include more eastern areas was one of the major criticisms lodged by conservation groups against the Roadless Area Review and Evaluation (RARE) list.

The first omnibus eastern wilderness bill was Senate 3699, introduced in June 1972 by Senator George Aiken of Vermont. This and companion bills died in the 92d Congress, but similar bills were immediately introduced in the 93d Congress. The Forest Service, maintaining its view that no eastern areas qualified under the 1964 act, countered the omnibus eastern wilderness bills with administration proposals, providing first for a separate eastern system, apart from the 1964 act, and later for a program of wilderness studies without any instant areas.[15] In the second session of the 93d Congress, positions moved slowly toward accomodation. After much debate, the act passed both houses in the final days of the 93d Congress and was signed by the President. The act followed earlier precedent by establishing a series of sixteen instant areas and providing for a study program with a 1980 deadline for an additional seventeen areas.[16]

Throughout the debate over eastern wilderness areas legislation, proponents referred to the scarcity of wilderness in the East. The discussion centered exclusively on the national forests with few references to other ownerships. Considering the Eastern states to include the states east of the Plains, the various bills proposed included at most about 600,000 acres of national forest land. In 1974, this acreage was in fact only a fraction of the dedicated eastern wilderness then in existence—a total of 2.3 million acres (table 3-2). The state-controlled areas of Baxter State Park and the Allagash Wilderness Waterway in Maine and the Adirondack and Catskill Parks in New York accounted for more than half of the total. The 900,000-acre Boundary Waters Canoe Area was at the time not strictly wilderness but was under limited management and served a wilderness recreation clientele. The small wildernesses on wildlife refuges added an additional 34,500 acres.

As of mid-1974, an additional area of 2.3 million acres in the East was under consideration for wilderness, including the 625,000 acres in the Eastern Wilderness Bill. The largest units were in the Great Smokey Mountains National Park and the Okefenokee National Wildlife Refuge. Adding the areas of existing and proposed wilderness, we find 4.3 million acres of wilderness remaining in the East. This is only 0.5 percent of the land area of the states involved. In its RARE-II review, the U.S. Forest

Table 3-2
Eastern Wilderness—Statistical Summary as of Summer 1974
(*acres*)

	New England	*Eastern States*[a]
Existing		
States	224,000	1,313,000
National forests	5,600	913,600
National parks		
National wildlife refuges	5,100	34,500
Total	234,700	2,261,100
Proposed		
States	unknown	unknown
National forests (S. 3433)		
Instant	41,900	252,400
Study	72,400	372,900
Total	114,300	625,300
National parks		1,240,000
National wildlife refuges	5,200	439,000
Total	125,100	2,304,300
Total existing and proposed	359,800	4,304,300
Total land area (millions of acres)	40.3 (0.9)[b]	750 (0.5)[b]

Sources: correspondence with *Fish and Wildlife Service, National Park Service*, Haight, 1974; U.S. Congress, Senate, *Wilderness Areas Act of 1974*, Calendar no. 771, Senate Report No. 93-803, May 2, 1974.

[a]States east of the Plains; includes Minnesota and tier of states on west bank of Mississippi River plus NF areas in East Texas

[b]Percentage of total land area that is total existing and proposed wilderness

Service identified in the East 325 roadless units totalling 2.4 million acres. This is roughly 10 percent of the National Forest land area in the eastern states.

Wilderness on the Public Domain

As noted earlier, the 1964 Wilderness Act did not address lands with wilderness potential on the public domain. The public domain lands administered by the BLM include remote stretches of Alaska, and vast western deserts and mountain ranges. Used mostly for grazing, with occasional mining and logging, these lands include a number of significant natural areas.[17] Under its classification authority, the Bureau had designated eleven primitive areas by 1976, totalling 234,000 acres. In addition, the BLM had created forty-four natural areas totalling 272,000 acres.[18] This administrative system did not mandate full review of all potentially significant lands, nor did it provide full interim protection for lands deserving study.[19]

In the early seventies, a BLM organic act was proposed, to provide a statutory management mandate for the national resource lands, to replace the lapsed classification-and-multiple-use authority, and to repeal a list of out-of-date statutes. The proposals were vigorously debated, with much of the discussion involving conflicts over grazing leases and mandatory wilderness review. As finally passed, the Organic Act did provide for mandatory wilderness review.[20]

The BLM is to review all roadless areas five thousand acres and larger, and all roadless islands, within fifteen years. The resulting recommendations are to be reported to the President for his transmittal to Congress. The act explicitly requires the procedures and criteria of the 1964 Wilderness Act. In 1978, the BLM circulated a draft plan for its study procedures and for interim protection of candidate areas.[21]

Endangered Species Acts

Although wildlife protection is one of the oldest concerns of the organized conservation movement, federal protection of endangered species is a recent development. This is due in part to the durable legal tradition that nonmigratory wildlife are under the jurisdiction of the states. In 1966, a weak Endangered Species Act was passed which provided for listing of species but allowed no actual federal regulation if states failed to act. The act's principal effect was on the programs of federal agencies. In 1973, the final step was taken: federal protection of endangered species became a reality.[22] The act provided improved control over United States-foreign trade in products of endangered species, and mandated the U.S. Fish and Wildlife Service to designate critical habitats for endangered species. In addition, acts dealing with marine mammals, wild horses, and burros were passed.

But the act did not eliminate all controversy. In 1978, significant amendments to the Endangered Species Act were enacted.[23] The amendments responded to the conflict created by the desire of the Tennessee Valley Authority to build the Tellico Dam, which would wipe out the only known habitat of a small fish, the snail darter. In 1978, the U.S. Supreme Court halted construction on the nearly completed dam. Dam proponents and others pressed for a statutory balancing procedure that would allow actions detrimental to endangered species when the benefits of such actions were of sufficient public importance. The amendments were required in any case to reestablish administrative authorities, which lapsed in late 1978.

The 1978 amendments created an exemption procedure under which a project can be constructed despite its impact on an endangered species. The procedure calls for cabinet-level review when an agency seeks to construct a project that may damage a population of an endangered species. A request for exemption must be considered by a three-member board of review. If the board recommends further consideration, it reports to an Endangered Species Committee, which consists of six cabinet-level officials and a state representative appointed by the President. The committee's recommendations are subject to further review by the Secretary of the Interior. If a project is exempted from the act's prohibition, mitigation measures are required, and performance is monitored by the Council on Environmental Quality.[24]

Other Preservation Policies

The objectives of wildland preservations are supported by a number of additional public laws and policies in addition to laws designating specific areas and defining study procedures.

Specific legislative protections, such as the Wilderness Act, the Wild and Scenic Rivers Act, and endangered species laws, can provide for preservation of specific areas, but only, in general, on public land. Even under existing legislative protections, further ambiguities of management policy remain. But a more serious difficulty is the limited reach of policies aimed at protecting specific parcels of land. Such policies are of little use in implementing a broad land ethic.

Environmental quality legislation such as the 1972 Federal Water Pollution Control Act Amendments and the 1970 Clean Air Amendments can play a role in assuring environmental preservation.[25] Enforcement of nondegradation policies for air and water quality can guide development away from wild areas or even bar disturbances such as mining or timber harvesting. Preservation of wetlands and marine estuaries have been aided by these policies.

The National Environmental Policy Act articulates an apparently clear policy toward environmental protection.[26] But it does not represent a nonutilitarian rationale for preservation. The act's language makes clear that the goal is to provide for environmentally sound development.

Three broad legal approaches toward preservation have received attention recently—granting rights to natural objects, the public trust doctrine, and the use of constitutional guarantees to promote preservationist policies through litigation or otherwise.

The public trust doctrine is based on the ancient Roman concept under which the sovereign held title to mineral resources. Joseph Sax has applied the doctrine to modern environmental quality problems in a path-breaking article. He argues for legislative recognition of a public trust in the nation's common pool resources of air and water.[27]

Considerable attention has been given in environmental litigation and in scholarly commentary to deriving environmental protection mandates from basic constitutional guarantees. This approach has as yet made little headway in the courts.[28] In a number of states, however, constitutional conventions have faced the issue in incorporating environmental bills of rights in revised constitutions.

Appraisal

By 1977, the three major land preservation acts had provided the means for designation of most of the 14.4 million acres in wilderness at that time. The review-study-legislation process involved considerable delay in decision-making. After passage of the 1964 act, for example, no new areas were designated until 1968. By 1974, congressional action had been completed on only thirty-seven units comprising about 2 million acres. The Congress received proposals for the last 181 units—mostly small islands and park service units—by 1974.[29]

The act's narrow terms, however, left untouched the large wilderness decisions—national forest roadless areas, Alaska, and the public domain. In the Alaska case, the land selection and congressional planning process was provided for by the Alaska Native Claims Settlement Act. For the public domain, the wilderness issue was resolved by an overall reform of the legal mandate for the BLM.

The formal procedures provided for in the three major acts were unable to resolve long-standing and deep conflicts over several important areas. These included major wilderness and river preservation controversies. The final prohibition of dams in the Grand Canyon was accomplished in the Colorado River Basin Project Act of 1968 and later strengthened in the Enlargement Act.[30] Dams proposed for the New River in North Carolina and for Hells Canyon in Idaho were dealt with in separate legislation. Complex land-use decisions in large wild areas were handled separately from the normal wilderness study process for Washington's scenic Alpine Lakes[31] and for Idaho's Sawtooth National Recreation Area.[32] These highly controversial areas were handled through proposals that did not move through the planned wilderness evaluation process. This approach enabled the Congress to respond to pressure for action on these areas, and to design special management regimes appropriate to the needs of each area.

The legislative study processes established in 1964 and 1968 did not foresee the quantum leap in public interest in preservation of the seventies. The result was that more active preservation groups were able to obtain favorable consideration for proposals not provided for in the original legislation. By this process, the list of study rivers for the wild and scenic

designation grew to fifty-one by 1977. Large areas of roadless land were
included in endangered American wilderness bills, which opponents accused
of circumventing the orderly wilderness study process.

The pressures for wilderness allocation of remaining national forest
roadless lands became so great by the late seventies that the Carter Administration undertook a new roadless area review (RARE-II) which was to settle
the de facto wilderness arguments once and for all (see chapter 8). At this
writing, the RARE-II proposals are being sent to Congress. This development was the natural outgrowth of the completion of the 1964 act's orderly and limited study process, which simply omitted vast areas from
consideration.

The three major land preservation acts, then, represented the product
of an era with a patient attitude toward preservation. They employed a
decision-making model based on rational evaluation of the costs of
wilderness decisions; the model allowed ample time for decision-making
and review. This pattern was followed, with variations, in the Alaska debate
and in the BLM review process. Their work was largely completed by the
late seventies, so that preservationist attention turned to the national forest
roadless areas, the BLM lands, and to broader concepts of natural area
preservation based on intensive inventory and protection of small units
through state programs. The three acts of 1964, 1968, and 1976 thus played
a key role in America's progress toward fulfilling the mandate for
preservation.

In protecting endangered species, progress has been somewhat slower,
impeded by a few spectacular conflicts between preservation and
development. By 1978, a tentative policy consensus had developed that a
heavy burden of proof must be sustained by any proposal to deliberately
endanger survival of a plant or animal species. Detailed inventories of
species are underway. The basis for further progress is in place.

Notes

1. U.S. Congress, Senate, Committee on Interior and Insular Affairs,
1956, *Hearings on S. 4013, National Wilderness Preservation Act,* June 19
and 20, 1957, p. 37.

2. R. Nash, *Wilderness and the American Mind* (New Haven, Conn.:
Yale University Press, 1967), p. 221.

3. 16 USC 551, see documentary appendix.

4. Michael McCloskey, "Is the Wilderness Act Working," in
E.R. Gillette, ed., *Action for Wilderness* (San Francisco: Sierra Club,

1972), pp. 22-23; D. V. Mercure, Jr. and W. M. Ross, "The Wilderness Act, a Product of Congressional Compromise," in R. Cooley and G. Wandesford-Smith, *Congress and the Environment* (Seattle, Wash.: University of Washington Press, 1970).

5. Interpretation of the act's provisions are in Michael McCloskey, "The Wilderness Act," *Oregon Law Review* 45 (June 1966): 288; J.M. McCabe, "A Wilderness Primer," *Montana Law Review* 32 (Winter 1971): p. 19. For a careful analysis of the designation process as actually applied in Congressional action, see J.W. Duffield, "Wilderness: A Political and Economic Analysis" (Ph.D. diss., Yale University, 1974), chaps. 2 and 8-11.

6. Sec. 3(c).

7. B. Evans, "Preserving Wilderness in the Northwest," in Gillette, *Action for Wilderness* (San Francisco: Sierra Club, 1972), p. 34.

8. Sec. 4(d), 2, and 3.

9. John H. Hammond, Jr., "The Wilderness Act and Mining—Some Proposals for Conservation," *Oregon Law Review* 47 (June 1968): 447.

10. Sec. 2(b).

11. Cases are ably reviewed in K. Haight, "The Wilderness Act: Ten Years After," *Environmental Affairs* 3 (1974): 275.

12. J.V. Tileston, "Status of the Wild and Scenic River System," in Gillette, *Action for Wilderness*, p. 134. See also documentary appendix.

13. The act is discussed in detail in A.D. Tarlock and T. Tippy, "The Wild and Scenic River System," in *Environment Law Review* (1971).

14. U.S. Department of the Interior, *Outdoor Recreation—A Legacy for America* (Washington, D.C.: U.S. Government Printing Office, 1973), p. 44.

15. For other versions of the Forest Service role in the eastern wilderness debate, see D. Barney, *The Last Stand* (New York: Grossman, 1974), pp. 95-105; and G.O. Robinson, *The Forest Service* (Baltimore: Johns Hopkins, 1975), chap. 6.

16. U.S. Congress, Senate, *Eastern Wilderness Areas Act of 1974,* S. Report 93-803, Cal. No. 771. Reviews the issues, describes the compromises reached, and provides detailed inventory data on the proposed areas.

17. T.S. Watson, Jr., "The Lands No One Knows," *Sierra Club Bulletin* 58 (September 1973): 5-9.

18. U.S. Department of the Interior, Bureau of Land Management, *Wilderness Review Procedures, Draft,* Washington, D.C., February 1978. Processed.

19. John D. Foster, "BLM Primitive Areas—Are They Counterfeit Wilderness?" *Natural Resources Journal* 16 (July 1976): 621.

20. PL 94-579, 90 Stat. 2743, Sec. 603. See documentary appendix.

21. U.S. Bureau of Land Management, *Wilderness Review Procedures.*

22. Endangered Species Act of 1966, 16 USC 668; Endangered Species Act of 1973, 87 *Stat* 884 (1973). For history, see W.D. Palmer, "Endangered Species Protection: A History of Congressional Action," *Environmental Affairs* 4 (1975): 255.

23. Endangered Species Act Amendments of 1978, P.L. 95-632. For description of the amendments, see U.S. Fish and Wildlife Service, *Endangered Species Technical Bulletin* 3 (October 1978).

24. The act mandated specific studies of Tellico (snail darter) and the Grayrocks Dam (whooping crane) within ninety days of its passage.

25. 42 USC 1857; 33 USC 1251.

26. National Environmental Policy Act of 1969, 42 USC 4341.

27. J. Sax, "The Public Trust Doctrine in Natural Resource Law," *Michigan Law Review* 68 (January 1970): 471.

28. See P. Soper, "The Constitutional Framework of Environmental Law," in E.L. Dolgin and T.G.P. Guilbert, *Federal Environmental Law* (Washington, D.C.: Environmental Law Institute, 1974), p. 21. Also, Soper addresses Constitutional protection for environmental values directly. For additional literature, see L. Tribe, "From Environmental Foundations," *Yale Law Journal* 85 (January 1975): 546 (his note 9); W.D. Kirchick, "The Continuing Search for a Constitutionally Protected Environment," *Environmental Affairs* 4 (1975): 515, provides a full and up-to-date review.

29. Haight, "The Wilderness Act," pp. 278-279. For a comprehensive summary and listing of all proposals and their status in 1974, see "The Tenth Year," *Living Wilderness,* Winter 1973-1974, p. 9ff.

30. P.L. 90-537, (1968), and P.L. 93-620 (1975).

31. P.L. 94-357; see also U.S. Congress, Senate, Committee on Interior and Insular Affairs, *Alpine Lakes Area Management Act of 1976.* 94th Congress, 29 Session on H R 7792, June 22, 1976.

32. 16 U.S.C. 460 (1972).

4

Basic Economics of Preservation

Introduction

Economic arguments are frequently abused by participants in debates over preservation policy. This is true on all sides of the issue, whether over an individual area or over broad preservation policies. In a nontechnical way, this chapter provides an overview of the economics of preservation. Further analysis of specific resources is given in succeeding chapters. This is not a cookbook—more technical descriptions of methods are given in the references. Economics has commonly been applied to instrumental values of wildlands—commodities. Economists have recently extended their analyses to the appraisal of intrinsic, nonutilitarian, values as well.

The "idols of the marketplace" have frequently hypnotized economists and others analyzing preservation. One group asserts that social decisions should be guided totally by calculations of social cost and benefit, reckoned in dollars. They believe that ultimately we will be able to measure all relevant values in dollar terms. They despair that their computer models and refined calculations are not taken more seriously by decision-makers. Politicians, who must steer an imperfect course amid impossible short-term conflicts, are ridiculed and distrusted by these analysts.

Another fraternity, citing instances of inept and incomplete quantification, rejects all attempts at systematic analysis in wilderness decision-making. This group believes that the essential spiritual and aesthetic benefits of wilderness should be given supreme consideration in decision-making, and that measurement can only mislead.

This chapter attempts to provide an approach to systematic analysis in preservation decision-making. It avoids the worship of numbers but recognizes that responsible decision-makers demand coherent and understandable analyses displaying the consequences of decisions. The concepts of economics provide useful organizing principles for such analyses. First, this chapter reviews the public nature of preservation—the reasons why unhindered private markets fail to provide adequately for preservation. It then reviews the insights offered by the new economics of conservation. Final sections offer a general framework for systematic analysis of preservation decisions.

45

Political Economy of Preservation

The appropriate management of the nation's wild lands and waters is inescapably a public issue for two basic reasons. First, much of the remaining wildland resource is now in public ownership. Second, the private economy based on private property and market exchange is unable to give the proper weight to preservation values in its decisions. This is because of the inevitable publicness and concern with the future of such decisions. Also, private markets may significantly undervalue the future importance of flexibility. These three concepts—publicness, concern with the future and flexibility are of powerful importance for wildland allocation decisions.[1]

Public Ownership

Wilderness is an unavoidably public issue, since most remaining wilderness is on public lands. Decision-making therefore relies on bureaucratic and legislative institutions. The nation's 760 million acres of federal land are administered by several federal agencies. The Bureau of Land Management (BLM) manages the remaining public domain lands, mostly in Alaska and the arid western states, plus offshore lands in federal control and certain revested lands in Oregon. The U.S. Forest Service controls 186 million acres of national forests and grasslands, which contain the bulk of currently designated wilderness. The National Park Service administers about 26 million acres of national parks, monuments, national recreation areas, and other smaller units such as historical parks.[2] Since the lands concerned are not available for resource development, they are de facto wilderness. The U.S. Fish and Wildlife Service (formerly Bureau of Sport Fisheries and Wildlife) administers the national wildlife refuges. A large number of wildernesses have been created on these lands, but many are small units consisting of barren islands with no alternative uses. The fact that most of the potential wilderness is federally owned, then, means that wilderness decisions are unavoidably made through pressure politics, letter-writing campaigns, congressional hearings, and logrolling. In addition, state and local governments own about 29 million acres of forest land, and additional areas of rangeland. In several states, wilderness reserves have been created on such land.

The areas now in dispute on BLM lands, in Alaska, and in national forest de facto wilderness will be dealt with by this imperfect machinery for government decision-making, rather than through an imperfect market.

Apart from the public ownership of much of the nation's wildland resource, the publicness of preservation results from the inability of private markets to meet the long-term social objectives of the mandate for preservation. This is because of the publicness, concern for the future, and flexibility of the preservation problem.

Publicness

The U.S. economy is a mixed one, based on private ownership of land and productive capital. It contains large sectors devoted to government production (Corps of Engineers hydro dams), to production solely for government agencies (defense and space industry), and to income redistribution (welfare agencies). Still, the dominant means of organizing production and employment is the private market. Private markets are excellent means of organizing many economic activities. This is especially true for goods and services that can be characterized by their "privateness":

1. Their consumption is divisible and exclusive among consumers, and potential consumers may be excluded for nonpayment.[3]
2. The activity is small in relation to the surrounding community, so that its decisions about employment levels, output levels, and pricing are not matters of life or death for the relevant community.
3. Its production is not accompanied by side effects—erosion, air pollution, or release of toxic wastes—that adversely affect other producers or consumers.
4. The product's consumption does not produce adverse side effects on nonusers.
5. The activity does not involve irreversible commitments of resources that cannot be replaced.

The values on which the mandate for preservation is based are scientific, cultural, and economic. Those that are strictly economic do not, for the most part, share the characteristics that would lend them to efficient production in private markets. When markets do not exist or do not seem to perform adequately in guiding production, economists speak of market failure. Market failure for preservation is essentially because of the publicness and concern for the future of the resource and its important services. The services of wilderness that are most compelling guides to public policy are not divisible in consumption. Exclusion for nonpayment is not possible. The intrinsic values of wilderness such as aesthetics and preservation of natural ecosystems generally fall in this category. Some authors refer to those values as "existence" values.

Whereas users may be excluded from enjoying some of the benefits of wilderness for nonpayment, wilderness benefits are enjoyed by many members of society, some of whom live at great distances from the area. Speaking of Utah's Aquarius Plateau, Stegner notes, people "can simply contemplate the *idea,* take pleasure in the fact that such a timeless and un-controlled part of earth is still there."[4] A private owner of the Aquarius Plateau would be providing services to distant persons who might never enter his gate to pay admission. He would therefore be inclined to preserve too little of the Plateau in its natural condition, other things being equal.

Interestingly, the one wilderness service that partakes most of private characteristics is recreation. As long as congestion is avoided, recreation is an almost perfectly private service. It is divisible in consumption, and it is at least technically possible (although in some areas it may not pay to do so) to exclude users for nonpayment.

Decisions about the allocation of the wilderness resource are public in another basic way. They affect the welfare of different communities and groups in society. Resource-dependent rural communities, consumers of resource products, recreationists, and concerned wilderness devotees all will be affected by decisions about a particular wild area. Even when occurring on private property and made by private firms, nothing can obscure the public nature of these decisions. The local impacts of coal development in the Great Plains provide an excellent example. Similarly, decisions about wilderness in southeast Alaska are essentially decisions about the future size of that area's timber industry and employment base.

In addition, the developments in or near wild areas frequently have adverse effects on third parties through pollution or otherwise.[5] These are termed "externalities" by economists, since their effects are external to the balance sheet and profit-and-loss statements of the individual firm. A large body of literature deals with the best ways to reduce pollution and other externalities. It is enough for present purposes that the rule-making, contract-enforcing, and regulatory role of government is essential in all the approaches that have been offered so far.

In sum, decisions to allocate wildlands to different uses are affected with the public interest and cannot be made properly by private decision-makers. This is because of: the indivisible and nonexclusive nature of the important services of wilderness; the effects wilderness decisions have on different groups; the side-effects of development; and the conflicts be-tween consumers of the same resource. Wilderness has many of the characteristrics of what economists call a common pool resource. Proper management demands a recognition of user interdependence and cannot be achieved without joint action.

A final ingredient of publicness may be briefly noted. Some classes of goods are produced under a general social value judgment that production or consumption of that good is socially desirable and should be compelled by society.[6] Examples include the required consumption of education by children and the fluoridation of water supplies. Some wilderness advocates use arguments that suggest that they view wilderness as a merit want—as a service that society should supply because of its intrinsic goodness. Wilderness as a merit want can be justified by appeal to the mandate for preservation.

Concern for the Future—The Social Discount Rate

Preservation decisions partake of an inevitable concern for the future that confounds analysis and makes public decisions difficult, especially in a society facing uncertain future availability of natural resources. The first problem is how to forecast how future citizens will value wild lands. If appreciation and use of wilderness grows in the future, individuals a century hence may well feel that too few wilderness acres were saved in the seventies. Individuals may have no current desire to visit a wilderness area, but they might be willing to pay a positive sum to preserve the right to do so in the future. The phenomenon is known as "option demand."[7] In some existing markets, options exist and are traded regularly, real estate and securities being prominent examples. For wilderness areas, there is no way to obtain information about the option value individuals place on their services. Estimates of benefits realized by current users will therefore underestimate the total social benefit from preservation. Positive option demand simply means that there is an economic value in preserving flexibility.

The second problem is that, even if we assume that future preferences for wilderness will resemble today's, we are comparing benefits and costs that will accrue to different generations. The problem of valuing time streams of future costs and benefits accruing to different generations has puzzled generations of economists. The problem of discounting the future gains and losses to make them comparable to present ones is so important that it must occupy a substantial discussion here.

Time Preference and Social Discount Rate

Time preference is the extent to which individuals (or society) apply a discount factor to future benefits or satisfactions when comparing them with the present. What is the relative value of a dollar's income to me today in comparison with a dollar's income in ten years? The concept may be illustrated with a simple example.[8] Consider a security that offers a payment of one dollar per year, free of tax, guaranteed against all risks, forever. How much would you pay for such a security, one offering a dollar a year in purchasing power with certainty forever? If you would pay $5, then your discount rate is 20 percent. The $5 sum is said to be the present net worth (PNW) of a future stream of $1 payments discounted at 20 percent. Many people seem to have discount rates lower than this, since they are willing to invest in savings certificates yielding from 5 to 8 percent before tax. But saving is a complex process, so such an inference is only a first approximation. Few would be willing to pay an infinite price for the above security. So few individuals have zero rates of individual time preference. And some individuals have such high discount rates that they consume income rapidly with no provision for saving.

Many economists would argue that since society should have a time horizon spanning generations, social time preference should be lower than individual time preference. Most commonly quoted on this view is the economist A.C. Pigou.[9] Pigou argued that social decisions should be based on a low discount rate, to reflect the role of government as guardian of the interests of the unborn. Other economists have searched for theoretical reasons why the social and individual rates of time preference should differ, but those discussions need not detain us.

Basically, four theories have been proposed for measuring the social discount rates:[10]

1. Opportunity cost of funds in the private sector refers to the returns that could be earned by private companies on the same capital, or to implicit returns on consumption by individuals.
2. Government borrowing cost refers to the interest rate paid on government bonds.
3. Arbitrary rates are based on assuming an appropriate rate, based on professional or political consensus.
4. Agnostic theories: some economists deny that there is a social discount rate. Others see unavoidable contradictions in using it for decision-making.

Capital, Savings, and Growth

The social rate of discount has been widely discussed in the literature on capital accumulation and economic growth. In outline, the issue is this: if output depends on the stock of capital, then our heirs will enjoy a higher standard of living, the larger is their capital stock. But to make that capital stock larger requires us to save (sacrifice consumption) today. The question is, then, what is the rate of saving (investment) that harmonizes the conflict between the interests of those alive today, versus the interests of future generations?

Economists have formulated a "Golden Rule of Saving" for an abstract answer to this question. The answer is, in a golden age, a generation should save to create capital for the future just that share of income that it would have preferred past generations to invest. Theorems also exist that show the optimal policy for reaching the golden age. "Growth-men" argue that society should increase its saving rate to hasten arrival of the golden age.

One of the most famous rules was given by Frank Ramsey who argued that society should apply a zero discount rate, arguing that, in society's overall investment policy, time discounting is inappropriate.[11]

These formulations do not yield specific answers, but they do point to the central issue: that social decisions about the aggregate level of saving represent ethical judgements about the trade-off between present and future welfare. We invest money to clean up our nation's water not only because we expect to benefit, but because we desire to bequeath clean waters to our heirs. It should also be noticed, however, that promoting economic growth through lower discount rates would hasten the consumption of exhaustible resources, not to mention the other environmental alterations involved. This ties the argument, then, to questions of project feasibility and intergenerational consumption of resources.

The Feasibility of Development Projects

The rate of discount used has a profound effect on the financial feasibility of dams and other government public works projects. This is because using low interest rates minimizes the effect of high capital costs and maximizes the value of distant project benefits. Despite bitter controversy, public works proponents have succeeded in having projects continue to be evaluated at low discount rates.[12]

Extraction Rate for Exhaustible Resources

Clearly, the optimal rate of exhaustible resource extraction for a private firm depends on the cost of its capital. Its view of the future is heavily determined by how heavy its interest charges are. At high interest rates, optimum depletion is more rapid than at low rates. From society's viewpoint however, the discount rate expresses the trade-off between present and future satisfactions. A high social discount rate implies little concern for the needs of the distant future. A low discount rate implies, on the other hand, that use of exhaustible resources should be stretched as far as possible into the future. If the social discount rate is lower than private capital market rates, then private enterprises will deplete resources at a rate that is too fast from society's standpoint.

In determining the intertemporal allocation of nonrenewable resources, then, the basic decision is an ethical one. Solow notes:

> . . . even well-functioning competitive markets may fail to allocate resources properly over time. . . . the future brings no endowment of its own to whatever markets may exist. The intergenerational distribution of income or welfare depends on the provision that each generation makes for its successors. The choice of a social discount rate is, in effect, a policy decision about that intergenerational distribution.[13]

A society provides a complex heritage to future generations. This legacy consists of four things:

1. A natural environment, complete with reserves of oil, gas, and other depletable minerals, and stocks of renewable resources
2. A stock of capital—roads, factories, schools
3. A stock of scientific and technical know-how
4. A heritage of culture and institutions

There are some who believe that the prospects for human survival are determined by the first item only. Such a view argues for extremely slow extraction of the earth's mineral wealth. There are good grounds for believing that the last three items are more important to long-run human survival. But the stock of capital and know-how can only be created with wealth that is partly derived from consuming nonrenewable resources.

The question of intergenerational equity in resource use is one of the most perplexing and difficult matters in resource policy. One answer is, "we owe it to posterity to leave as much coal in the ground as we can." This answer cannot tell us how much should be left. Further, it ignores the fact that at some point, a generation will be facing the last lump of coal. If we cannot leave that generation with a flexible social system, and a large stock of capital and technical knowledge, it will become extinct. Leaving coal is not enough. Another answer is: "As far back as we can remember, each generation has been richer than the last. We expect this to continue. Therefore, by restraining our use of resources today, we are arguing for a subsidy from the poor to the rich." This is a variant of the question, "what has posterity done for me lately?"

It should be clear that both answers are inadequate as foundations for policy. Yet it is not clear just what can take their place. One complicating factor is that many exhaustible resources are simply transformed in form when removed from the earth. They are not literally consumed, as is the case for energy. Many metals are used in buildings and equipment that provide services for years or decades into the future. Clearly, the concept of consumption in thinking about such materials is oversimplified.

What use, then, is the concept of social time preference in thinking about wilderness preservation? Most economists accept that society's time horizon must be longer than that of individuals, so that the social discount rate should be relatively low. This rate should be employed in evaluating projects or policies that affect society's welfare over long time periods. In any event, it is clear that private-market interest rates do not accurately reflect even individual—much less social—attitudes toward the distant future.

Adoption of a low social discount rate has been advocated by those who believe that society should promote economic growth by promoting capital investment. More rapid growth, however, means accelerated consumption of resources and of wild areas, other things being equal. Low social discount rates argue for stretching the consumption of exhaustible resources over time for larger periods than would be preferred by private resource owners; low social discount rates favor the construction of capital-intensive and environmentally damaging public works projects such as dams, levees, and long-distance water diversions. Acceptance of a low social discount rate thus has contradictory implications for the economics of wilderness preservation.

More generally, we see that the arguments over the social discount rate are part of an argument about valuing a natural heritage. The intrinsic values of a preserved wildland heritage can only be expected to grow in the future. These future intrinsic values must be compared with the present intrinsic and instrumental values of preservation and with the instrumental values that could be obtained by development. The best to hope for in such a comparison is the wise use of economic analysis to clarify issues. Tidy numerical answers are not available.

Flexibility

Wilderness allocations often involve decisions with irreversible consequences. Many private economic decisions are irreversible. If I decide to scrap my car, that decision becomes difficult to change after the hulk has gone through the shredder. But I can easily buy a new car. It is not irreversibility itself, then, but irreversibility combined with irreplaceability that is of public concern. A decision to build a dam in the Grand Canyon is irreversible, at least within future time periods of interest to citizens now living. Decisions about unique resources that promise to be irreversible demand public control. Economists have debated whether irreversibility itself creats analycially significant problems.[14]

A basic demand for an economic system is flexibility—to allow it to adapt to changing ecological and economic conditions. Preservation of wildlands is one form of policy that can avoid premature commitment of land to specific short-term uses. Few wilderness advocates, however, see wilderness allocations as being flexible or subject to future revision. They like to perceive them as permanent.

To help in achieving preservation purposes while preserving flexibility, a middle ground is needed. It will be desirable to manage sizable areas of backcountry in ways that avoid premature commitment to either permanent wilderness or to single-purpose development. Such an approach is essentially a commitment to retain options for the future. Option-retaining strategies are often followed by private decision-makers, whereas examples of government improvidence are legion. Still, the long-term public importance of flexibility gives it a major role in the public nature of preservation policy.

The New Economics of Conservation

New economics of conservation is a phrase that has come to be applied to the ideas and their applications first stated clearly by J.V. Krutilla in his path-breaking 1967 article.[15] The basic concept of the new economics of conservation is that economic growth has differential effects on the supply and demand for different environmental resources. Economic growth requires the use of larger and larger areas of land for residential structures, transportation, mineral extraction, and other uses. For example, from 1959 to 1969, urban and transportation developments consumed open land at a rate of 880,000 acres per year.[16] Additionally, natural watercourses are increasingly disturbed by improvements for hydropower generation or for navigation. Economic change may also release land from intensive uses to revert to a wild state. Across large areas of the Eastern United States, millions of acres have gone out of agricultural uses and reverted to forest. Further, millions of acres that were once heavily cut for timber have regrown. Many of the areas now in the eastern wilderness system are of this type—once heavily logged, now far from markets and in limited demand for wood production. Whereas economic change has offsetting effects on land uses and open spaces in different regions, it generally reduces the remaining area of untouched wilderness.[17]

As population grows and per capita income rises, opportunities for effective use of leisure rise. Improved transportation and the availability of leisure in larger time blocks (paid vacations) are the most important factors. In the United States, these trends have accompanied an increasing appreciation of outdoor activities. A growing subculture has emerged whose members seek strenuous outdoor experiences in remote uninhabited areas.

These backpackers and other wilderness users form the backbone of organizations that have been effectively promoting the cause of wilderness preservation. As economists say, the consumers' willingness to pay to actually use wilderness areas or to see them preserved has risen. The large dues-paying memberships of organizations devoted to wilderness preservation illustrate this.[18] At the same time, economic growth depends on ever-increasing improvement in technology and labor skills, together with rising inputs of natural resource products. So it would appear that there is an unresolvable conflict between the desire for wilderness preservation and the need for more raw materials, both of which are increased by the process of economic growth. But, say the new economists of conservation, growth itself provides its own way out of this dilemma. The force that comes to the rescue is technological change.

Man's supply of natural resource products depends on his ability to overcome nature's resistance to his efforts to extract useful services from the earth. Some areas—the Sahara Desert, for example—are extremely resistant to the extraction of useful services. Yet a human group possessing the required capital and know-how can obtain valuable groundwater or oil from the Sahara. The jungle islands of fabled South Seas were said, on the other hand, to be favorable to human efforts to extract useful services. Abundant food grew in forest and shallow tidal waters; water and building materials were readily at hand. Prosperity required only the effort of harvesting these resources, at little effort with relatively simple tools.

Economic growth provides societies with the tools needed to overcome nature's resistance and equip themselves more lavishly with capital and energy. Technological change allows the cumulative reduction in the human effort required to obtain food, energy, and materials. Technological advance does this in four ways:

1. Technological change provides alternate sources of the same services provided by a given resource product. For example, as the real cost of aluminum has fallen, it has replaced iron in beer cans and copper in much electrical wiring.[19] In forest products, technological advances have permitted the use of different species of trees for plywood, lumber, and paper-making.

2. New technology permits the processing of a given resource product with fewer inputs of capital and labor. It thus reduces the real costs of resource products.[20]

3. Improved technology makes possible the attainment of higher yields from existing raw material sources. The average efficiency of coal use in electric power generation has improved sevenfold since 1900. The average level of utilization of timber cut has risen from roughly 40 percent in the forties to nearly 100 percent today in some locations.

4. Many useful substances in nature occur in obscure locations. They

do not become economic resources until they are found. Thus, the technology available for exploration at a given time limits the ability to extract resources from the earth. In the case of oil, major offshore finds have been made possible by improved methods of geophysical prospecting and by technology capable of drilling wells in extremely deep water under difficult weather conditions. Since the development of offshore drilling and exploration capabilities after World War II, offshore reserves have been discovered that now yield about one-fifth of the world's oil production.

Discovery has in the past been the most important means of augmenting resource supplies, in contrast with more intensive utilization of known reserves. For example, known world reserves of major materials increased dramatically from 1950 to 1970:

	Percentage Increase
Iron	1,221
Manganese	27
Potash	2,360
Bauxite	279

In contrast, reserves of tin barely increased (10 percent), while tungsten reserves fell (30 percent).[21]

How does this relate to the conflict between wilderness needs and the demand for energy and raw materials? By cumulatively reducing the real costs of extracting the earth's raw materials, technological change reduces the economic opportunity cost of removing from use a given resource deposit. Every year, improved technology makes available new sources of the same services provided by a given material or makes possible the discovery of additional deposits of that material. Therefore, the economic loss from forgoing development of a wild natural area is really less than it appears, based on today's costs and prices.[22]

The new economics of conservation, then, asserts that rising population and income lead to increased consumer demand for preservation of natural areas. At the same time, technological progress effectively expands society's supply of raw materials, so that the nation can afford to reserve wild areas from extractive uses in spite of increasing demands for raw materials.

The recent revolution in raw material prices has caused many observers to overlook the declining resource prices of the previous century and conclude that the earth has arrived on a new plane of resource scarcity. Whereas this view may be correct, it appears to overemphasize the experiences of the past few years. There is no reason to believe that the increases in real prices of recent years will continue indefinitely. In fact, downward price pressures (partly because of the current recession), are appearing in the markets for many major resource products. It is likely that resource prices will remain at a new higher plateau, from which the forces of technical change will begin anew in the continuous search for lower cost material sources, for more efficient processing methods, and for more economical methods of product use.

One development is significant, however. It seems likely that energy prices will remain on a plateau several times higher than their level in the sixties. Since resource extraction is highly energy intensive, this fact will remove from the economic supply those marginal deposits whose development would require the most energy. The results will be tighter supplies and increased attempts to find substitutes for energy-intensive commodities such as copper and aluminum.

A Systematic Approach to Preservation Decisions

This section provides a brief overview of standard procedures employed by economists in analyzing a public decision. It is not meant to provide all needed formulas or technical methods but to suggest a framework for approaching the problem. References to more technical treatments are provided along the way.

The framework proposed here is summarized in table 4-1. It provides a structured presentation of information bearing on a particular preservation problem, but it does not crank out an answer that settles the matter. It will allow, if applied carefully, the analyst to produce information that will help clarify objectives, benefits and costs, and values affected by a proposed action. An analytical framework cannot show which option is best—it cannot make a decision. Only a publicly accountable individual or group charged with decision-making can do that.

The Right Questions

The most important part of an analysis is establishing a set of "right questions" to guide further study. In this case, the right questions are: what are the objectives and what are the options available for meeting those objectives? Any given preservation policy, or a proposal to preserve a given tract of wildland, will be aimed at specific objectives. It is likely, however, that groups interested in the proposal will have differing objectives. In such cases, analysts should identify conflicting objectives and estimate how different options affect those conflicting objectives. For example, in establishment of wilderness in Alaska, one group desires maximum protection of natural processes. Another group desires preservation of traditional subsistence activities such as hunting and fishing. Still another

Table 4-1

A Systematic Approach to Analyzing Preservation Decisions

I. The right questions
    A. Identify major objectives of preservation appropriate to the case in hand. Express any notable side-objectives. Is the purpose to conserve an endangered animal or plant? To preserve a unique recreational resource? To avoid downstream damage from logging or development?
    B. Identify options. Set forth the options available for achieving the objectives, including:
        1. alternative sizes and locations of land areas
        2. regulatory requirements for included and nearby areas
        3. acquiring more information, such as mineral surveys
II. Appraisal—describing outcomes
    A. Measure benefits in physical or biological terms, relative to stated objectives, for each option. Express benefits quantitatively, where possible, or indicate their nature in general terms as data allow.
    B. Express in physical or biological units the known direct and opportunity costs of each option.
    C. For all costs and benefits where appropriate, express in dollar values.
    D. For both A and B, express as time streams, if relevant, accounting for expected future changes. If uncertainty exists as to the value of key variables, employ best available estimates and express in terms of means and ranges where possible.
    E. Identify alternative sources of the benefits and opportunity costs reviewed in A and B.
III. Comparing options
    A. Express benefits and costs in terms of present worth (PW) at a range of discount rates.
    B. Compare $PW(B)$ with $PW(C)$ in terms of B/C or $B - C$. Display with qualitative descriptions of other major values at stake.
    C. Assess local and national economic impacts of each defined option, if needed. Review possible mitigation measures, if needed.
    D. Assess the impact of options on other values identified in the mandate for preservation or raised by affected parties to the decision. Present in brief narrative or tabular form.
IV. Analysis
    A. Using explicit criteria, rank the options identified and summarize impacts of the recommended alternative, if one is selected.
    B. Present a full summary of all above analyses in a form comprehensible to the interested parties and decisionmakers, identifying all value conflicts and controversies over data. Provide highly technical analyses as supporting appendixes. Summarize and evaluate major previous analyses of the same problem. Identify all known and suspected sources of bias in the data and assumptions employed in the analysis.
    C. Subject the analysis to review by all interested parties. Analyze responses and make any required adjustments.

---

group desires continued access to valuable minerals. In the Alaska case, then, an analyst is faced with rating proposals against these three somewhat conflicting objectives. As a practical matter, of course, most of the analysts involved work for only one of these groups, so their task is simplified.

    For any particular objective in a given problem, there is often a range of options for meeting that objective. The universal presence of side objectives will complicate matters. For example, suppose it is desired to protect Hells Canyon on the Snake River. It may also be desired to protect native elk winter range. Are other objectives appropriate as well? How long a stretch of protected mainstem will protect the canyon? How wide a corridor is required to meet this primary objective and the side objectives? What are alternative ways to meet or circumvent the needs for power that would be generated by dams in Hells Canyon? How important is Hells Canyon to the elk?

Describing Outcomes

It is a truism that benefits only have meaning in relation to previously stated objectives. If the objective of preserving Hells Canyon is to save a rare plant, then recreational benefits of a wild river are not at issue. In fact, recreational uses may be a cost, if they threaten survival of the plant. All benefits may not be quantifiable. In such cases they should be described as clearly as possible for each identified preservation option. In many cases, the benefits of preservation will need to be stated in terms of changes from the status quo as a result of preservation. For example, many wild areas experience no increases in recreation use after designation as wilderness. Where this appears likely, it is not proper to claim the existing level of recreation as a benefit of preservation, unless the objective of preservation is to prevent a development that would eradicate the activity entirely.

Where an area is adjacent to existing large wildernesses, it may be difficult to reasonably claim recreation benefits. Large concentrations of wilderness such as central Idaho, the North Cascades, and the Smoky Mountains possess such vast unexplored recreational wilderness already that recreation alone probably cannot justify major additional wildernesses unless alternative uses of the land involved are nonexistent. Preservation may be worth considering for other reasons, which should be clearly specified in setting objectives. This principle applies to all potential benefits of preservation or of development. In the case of recreation benefits of a large dam, they may be small if a nearby reservoir already has sizable undeveloped capacity.[23]

Opportunity costs are the benefits forgone as a result of a management decision—such as the forgone timber production opportunity included in a wilderness area. Straightforward biological and physical measures usually suffice to measure their extent for a given area. For minerals they may represent educated guesses only.[24]

In identifying opportunity costs, alternative sources of the lost services should be clearly identified, so that the likely adjustments that can be made are identified. If policy or management changes could mitigate the opportunity costs, such changes should be clearly identified and evaluated for cost and effectiveness. As an example, in some eastern national forests, planned timber harvests cannot be sold for lack of markets. When timber is removed from the market for a wilderness area, it can be replaced with sale offerings in other areas to maintain local wood supplies. The same principle is applied to wildlife, developed recreation, or any other service that may become an opportunity cost of a wilderness area or wild river.

Opportunity costs are forgone opportunities, but they usually do not represent actual transfers of cash. This is especially true in wilderness decision-making. The recreationists or the managing agency may not need to compensate anyone for the value of an unclaimed mineral deposit under a wilderness area.[25] Other costs, however, are more direct. The managing agency will construct trails, employ rangers to patrol the area and clean up the campsites, and incur fire protection and other management costs. These direct costs are often substantial in relation to specific categories of direct benefits and must be considered in analyzing wilderness proposals. There is entirely too little published information on this subject. A recent study by R.W. Guldin, cited earlier, has suggested how large these costs may be for small eastern wilderness areas (see table 4-2). Without detailed information on future management plans, it is difficult to determine to what extent these costs reflect startup costs due to wilderness designation, since the area shown was designated only in 1974.

Consideration of costs and benefits leads naturally to the subject of greatest controversy in wilderness decision-making: valuation. It is held by

Table 4-2
Costs of Providing Wilderness Recreation, Lye Brook Wilderness, Green Mountain National Forest, Vermont, Fiscal Year 1977
(*dollars*)

Item	Amount
Total costs	
Annual direct management cost	36,774
Capital costs, annual equivalent[a]	26,876
Net opportunity cost of timber	19,573
Total cost	83,223
Unit costs	
Cost per acre (12,424 A. in fiscal year 1977)	6.70
Average cost per user (2,980 in fiscal year 1977)	27.93
Average cost per visitor day (7,011 in fiscal year 1977)	11.87

Source: Richard W. Guldin, ''An Economic Model of the Costs of Wilderness Management Incurred by the United States Forest Service'' (Ph.D. diss., Yale University, 1979), p. 101.
[a]Capital outlays in fiscal year 1977 amortized at 6 3/8 percent to convert to annual equivalent cost.

some that a view cannot be valued, and that therefore the methods of economics cannot be applied to wilderness decisions. However that may be, decision-makers often request information on specific quantifiable impacts of proposed decisions. Some of the relevant impacts can be expressed directly in dollars, because they are marketable commodities such as timber. In other cases, reasonable proxies can be established. For a wide range of values, however, dollars are inappropriate measures.

Thorough description of outcomes can be of considerable aid to decision-makers. As an example, some of the effects of allocating all road-less areas on two national forests are shown in table 4-3. The study from which the information was taken also provided qualitative estimates of the impact on a range of environmental values.

Valuation: Apples, Oranges, and Dollars

For some costs and benefits it is appropriate to translate apples and oranges into dollars. Such arithmetic accomplishes several purposes. It expresses

Table 4-3
Four-decade Financial and Employment Effects of Withdrawing Roadless Areas and Reallocating Funds to Intensive Management: Two Sample National Forests.

Item	*Willamette National Forest*		*San Juan National Forest*	
	Base programmed harvest	*Change from base with 100 percent withdrawal of roadless areas*	*Base programmed harvest*	*Change from base with 100 percent withdrawal of roadless areas*
Acreage of regulated commercial forest land	1,171.0	− 195.0	681.0	− 243.0
Harvest in millions of cubic feet/year	115.4	− 12.5	17.3	− 4.6
Payments to counties (millions of dollars/year)	58.0	− 4.0	0.9	− 0.2
Present net worth: 10 decades at 5 percent (millions of dollars)		− 281.4		+ 7.6
First decade average annual total employment (person-years)	18,215.0	− 1979.0	868.0	− 233.0

Source: Roger D. Fight et al., *Roadless Area—Intensive Management Tradeoffs on Western National Forests*, U.S. Department of Agriculture, Forest Service, 1978, pp. 39, 45.

material flows in terms that are meaningful to some decision-makers, and it allows comparison among values at stake in different areas. For example, 1,000 board-feet of pine stumpage may be worth $5 in one place, but $50 in another. The differences in value resulting from local supply and demand, species, size, quality, and logging cost are clearly relevant to decisions. Translations into dollars also aid in aggregating the apples and oranges into useful totals, so that board-feet of timer, animal unit-months of grazing, and tons of ore can be added and compared.[26] It may also be appropriate to give dollar values to various forms of recreation experience, since recreation is essentially a private service. It may require arbitrary assumptions or tedious analysis to derive the prices, however.

Using dollars to obtain totals can be dangerous. At some point, the apples differ too much from the oranges for them to belong in the same grocery basket. For example, consider two baskets, each containing $5 worth of groceries. One contains twenty-five apples. The other contains 2 pounds of steak. To some of us, these are groceries, and the $5 tells us something. To a vegetarian, however, describing the baskets as groceries is misleading. So aggregation can conceal important differences. This is true whether the aggregation is performed by weight, by dollar prices, or by simply counting the articles. Since aggregation can be misleading, it is important to present the basic physical quantities for each item considered.

There are some situations where apples are so different from steak as to make aggregation impossible. This is true, for most people, of human life, scenery, or opportunities for solitude. Placing dollar values on such things and lumping them into aggregates will conceal more than it reveals, and hence it should be avoided. Every citizen, and every decision-maker, will place different values on these things and should not be asked to accept those provided by so-called objective analyst. It should be noted, however, that valuations of all of these things are implicit in everyday decisions. Society does not escape the need to compare apples and oranges. But such comparisons should be recognized for what they are and not concealed by technical procedures, no matter how reasonable such procedures may seem to some.

Some problems of appraisal must be briefly noted. Economists believe that prices of standardized goods, traded on competitive markets, provide good measures of the social values of commodities. Competitive markets are found wherever large numbers of well-informed buyers and sellers trade a standardized commodity. Lumber is a good example. Steel is not. Cigarettes are an intermediate case. Where prices are formed under competitive conditions, quotations will be easily obtainable, and they will be useful guides to values. But in most natural resource markets, sellers and buyers are few, imperfections often exist, or the resource itself is not traded at all. Whereas lumber is sold on competitive markets, sawtimber on the stump is sold on markets with few—or only one—sellers and frequently with few buyers. In some cases, markets for the resource do not exist. Metal ores in the ground are rarely traded, although markets may be said to exist in some areas for petroleum exploration rights and for ownership of proven deposits. Worse yet, resources may be sold at arbitrary prices—as is true of grazing rights on federal lands. Worse yet, the prices may be zero, as is true for backcountry recreation. When arbitrary prices such as these exist, analysts must seek comparable prices from private markets or must estimate the net value of the service.

At best, each service should be appraised at its resource-level value—its value in or on the ground. A stand of trees derives its net value from its value as lumber minus all costs of harvesting and processing it. Although the lumber may be worth $50,000 in New York City, most of that value is in inputs that add value to the trees themselves. If it costs $50,000 to cut, load, mill, and ship those trees, then their net value is zero. When resource-level prices are not obtainable, appropriate imputations must be made by deducting costs from values at higher levels of processing. In some markets—metal ores, for instance—the necessary information may be unobtainable.

What matters for decisions, however, is the expected future level of values for resources, not the current levels. For most purposes, analysts agree to use current prices, even though they know that prices will change in the future. Working out the impact of possible future price levels may be helpful, as, for example, when timber demand in a region is expected to rise due to growing local markets. When price relationships can be expected to change in a predictable fashion, as in the relation between scarcity value of wild streams in relation to the value of electricity, such trends should be accounted for. Values of marketable commodities are obtained by residual value appraisals, which may reach great complexity.[27] For services that are not marketed, a number of approaches may be suitable. The greatest attention has been devoted to recreation. The key problems are projecting use levels and benefits per user. Methods used to project benefits per user include the merit-weighted user-day, proxy-demand curves, direct interviews, and market information.

Recreation is enough of a private good to make the attempt at appraisal worthwhile, and it will be considered here to provide an example. Estimates of benefits hinge critically on methods used to project user-days on a given stream. Under current techniques, projections have high degrees of error, so that recreation benefit estimates are relatively unreliable. Causes of error include:

1. Inability to account for the influence of nearby alternative opportunities
2. Inability to predict future incomes, tastes, population growth, and trans-

portation improvements; these factors often have caused recreation use to be underestimated.

3. Difficulty of forecasting user response to crowding. Congestion on streams can affect user choices. As congestion increases, potential users will turn elsewhere, as the quality of the experience declines.

Current participation rates are often used as a basis for demand prediction, but J. Knetsch has warned against reliance on them for demand prediction.[28]

User benefits can be evaluated in a number of ways, some of which are highly technical. The appropriate measure of recreation benefit is consumer willingness to pay. This is true in all cases where exclusion for nonpayment can be applied, as it usually can in outdoor recreation. For services commonly provided free or at arbitrary low prices—the general rule in water-based recreation—determination of willingness to pay presents serious conceptual and empirical problems.[29]

Under current Water Resources Council guidelines, the merit-weighted user-day is used by federal agencies to assess recreation benefits. The method specifies a range of values per user-day that are applied to estimated attendance to derive total benefits: General recreation (swimming, picnicking) is valued at $0.75-$2.25; specialized recreation (low-intensity uses in remote areas, white water canoeing) is valued at $3-$9.[30]

Interestingly, several rigorous studies of recreation demand have found that willingness to pay for outdoor recreation experiences often falls close to these apparently arbitrary ranges.

Total willingness to pay can be derived by computing the area under a correctly specified proxy-demand curve for use of a given stream. Commonly, travel cost or time expenditures are used to establish a proxy for the price of a recreation-day. A huge literature debating theoretical and statistical problems of this approach has arisen.[31] These methods require extensive interview data, so they can be expensive and time-consuming. Their accuracy is still relatively low. In return, however, they can yield, when properly employed, information useful in predicting future use and benefit levels.

It is possible to interview recreation users and attempt to obtain direct responses about their willingness to pay to enjoy a given activity. In a major study of this kind, J. Horvath and coworkers asked a sample of recreationists in Southern states how much benefit they derived from, and what sums they would have to be paid to forgo, the enjoyment of a day's use of different types of recreation.[32] They arrived at the following average benefit levels:

	Per day
Fishing	$43.00
Hunting	47.00
Wildlife enjoyment	71.00

Studies of this kind face the difficult problem of eliciting information that truly reflects how a person would behave in an actual choice situation. It is not known whether any of the study respondents would actually pay $43.00 to enjoy a day of fishing.

Although outdoor recreation activities are often thought of as nonmarketable, there do in fact exist markets for some recreation services. There are well-developed markets in duck-hunting leases and deer leases in many areas of the country. It is possible to find out what an acre of deer habitat or a good duck blind leases for per year. It is possible to find out what recreationists are actually willing to pay to enjoy boating, camping, swimming, or fishing at existing private facilities. But there are few examples of private-market prices for the enjoyment of a wilderness river.

Users of wild rivers will often spend considerable sums in nearby towns. Guided float trips provide jobs and spending flows in rural areas. These economic impacts may be important and worth estimating, but they should not be confused with the economic value of the resource itself. Similarly, the user's total expenditure on the sport cannot be used for a valid measure of the value to users of a given river.

Comparing Options

The first step in comparing options is to assemble those values appraised in dollars and obtain present values (PNW). The calculations are aided by tables and computer programs that are readily available. These values must be computed using specific values for the discount rates.

Discounting Costs and Benefits

Parties at interest will rarely agree on the discount rate to use in evaluating a development proposal—developers will want a low rate, whereas conservationists will want a high one. For preservation proposals, however, preservationists will usually attach a zero rate to the benefits of the natural ecosystem. Since perceptions of appropriate discounting procedure vary so widely, an analysis should present present values based on a range of discount rates, including a zero rate for future services of the natural environment.

Comparing Costs and Benefits

The simplest comparison would be, for all items expressed in dollars, net benefits, or: $PW(B) - PW(C)$ at each discount rate, where B = benefits and C = costs. Where apples and oranges problems are significant, a table displaying the dollar items and the other measured values should be provided. Another familiar presentation is the benefit-cost ratio: $PW(B)/PW(C)$. When apples and oranges are involved, the B/C ratio will be less useful as an overall summary measure.[33]

When a range of options is examined, a suitable display comparing the options by $B - C$ and other values, will be required.

Analysis

Once the objectives and options have been constructed, then evaluated in terms of costs and benefits, it is necessary to analyze the information obtained in a meaningful way. Based on the objectives identified and on other explicit criteria, the options should be ranked according to their desirability. Where objectives conflict or are unclear, or where differences exist over the discount rate to be employed or over the values to be assigned to key variables, a number of rankings may be required. It may require considerable ingenuity to express these differences clearly without presenting a confusing mass of tables of comparisons. Better, however, to be explicit about conflicts and uncertainties than to attempt, by introducing spurious assumptions, to boil them all down to one or a few numbers.

The results of these exercises should be presented in written form to be used by interested observers and the appointed decision-makers, whether they are a district ranger and staff or the U.S. Congress. The analysis does not cease with completion of a report. Interested parties may question assumptions, or contribute new data. The initial recommendation may be overturned by a higher decision-maker, requiring additional analysis and study. The ultimate decision-maker may decide that some important issue has not been sufficiently studied and may send the matter back for further consideration.

When objectives are multiple, as is often the case, they usually conflict. The different options will then stand in different order of desirability when ranked by reference to the different objectives. Decision-makers are accustomed to such situations and will welcome analyses that present them explicitly and show precisely how the different objectives conflict and how the different options available allow them to deal with the conflicts presented.

In many proposals to create wild rivers or wilderness areas, the issue will be whether the likely social benefits of a proposed development such as a dam, road, or mine will justify the long-term damage to a wild area. It then becomes necessary to study in detail the true economic costs and benefits of the development proposals. It may be found that the net benefits to society do not in fact exist, and the proposed projects should not be undertaken even if one values wilderness at zero. This may be due to heavy public subsidies in the form of flat grants or low-interest financing, or due to failure to charge users for the value of appropriable resources (mining claims) or for use of common pool resources (water pollution). It may be due to faulty decision-making by federal development agencies in failing to adequately consider alternatives or consider economic costs correctly. Professional economists have produced a long list of careful analyses that suggest that resource development projects on public lands or funded with federal funds are frequently economically unjustified.[34] One of the best-known examples of such an analysis was conducted by Krutilla for Hells Canyon (case 4-1).

An example of the use of systematic analysis was the U.S. Forest Service RARE-II process. After placing the inventoried roadless areas into ten alternative packages of differing size, agency officials developed a recommended alternative based on a combination of two of them. They then considered thirteen additional criteria to adjust the proposal to its final form. Whereas this approach did not overcome basic data gaps and did not avoid individual judgment, it did attempt to make explicit the factors considered. Some excellent examples of systematic analysis of preservation decisions were provided by the Canadian Mackenzie Valley Pipeline Inquiry, by the TVA-U.S. Department of the Interior study on Tellico Dam, and by W.E. Phillips' study of the Tule Elk.[35]

Setting Preservation Priorities

In practical resource management, it is essential to set priorities for preservation. These priorities then serve as management guides for funding, for planning related resource uses, and for attempting to deal with conflicts over resource use. The purist might feel that setting priorities is an admission that one area is less important than another. But there seems to be no alternative. Consider a state agency charged with spending a million-dollar budget each year to foster natural area preservation. It can be assumed that it will be presented with proposals far exceeding its budget.

On which areas should the funds be spent? This very practical problem faces many administrators today, and it is one area in which systematic analysis may be helpful. An agency faced with setting preservation priorities should follow roughly the following steps.

First, the agency should identify the geographic scope and general objectives on which its priorities will be based. Is the aim to protect areas of national or local significance? To protect floodplains, swamps, or other areas critical in the hydrologic cycle? To provide scenic open space buffers, or to provide recreation?

Based on this analysis, inventory of existing resources fitting the criteria can be conducted. Such inventories are commonly conducted under the Nature Conservancy's state heritage programs.[36] A valuable analytical aid in this process is to delineate the area studied into meaningful ecological units, and then to determine the representation of these units in existing preserved properties.[37]

Individual properties may be ranked on the basis of availability to the agency—will owners sell or be willing to discuss arrangements for protective easements? Will the managing agency, in the case of public land, admit preservation into its management priorities for the area? In the process, it can be useful to rate the areas, even if only arbitrarily, on the basis of the degree to which they appear to be threatened by incompatible developments. Areas inventoried can then be further classified into priority classes based on qualitative or quantitive measures related to the original preservation goals. Since goals will often be multiple and conflicting, it may be desirable to rank the same properties according to entirely different criteria. Managers must then form some opinion of the balance between conflicting goals and reach actual funding decisions. Often, in cases like these, attempts are made to employ detailed point systems in which each important criterion receives, for example, one to five points. Priorities are based on the sum of the points given to all factors considered. This system can lead to a false sense of objectivity and can obscure rather than illuminate important trade-off choices. Precisely this objection was repeatedly levelled at the U.S. Forest Service's procedure for choosing the roadless areas included in its RARE-I program.

For RARE-II, the Forest Service developed a wilderness attribute rating scale, which assigned numerical values to dimensions of wilderness quality as defined in the Wilderness Act. The ratings were used to provide a general indication of priorities for wilderness designation and to assist in balancing a simple indicator of wilderness quality against indices of opportunity costs. In a comprehensive analysis such as RARE-II, there is no alternative to using summary measures to express and compare large amounts of information.

Considerable attention has been given to evaluating specific dimensions of wilderness value that should be considered in any priority rating process. Examples include analyses of viewer reaction to landscape aesthetics[38] and studies attempting to provide quantitative comparisons of river scenery.[39] Other approaches have been applied to other specialized resources.[40]

At some point, attention must be given to opportunity costs. Market prices of land or other resources may be inadequate guides, but basic financial information will be needed. Costs and budget constraints will force planners to address the trade-off between an area's uniqueness and its cost. Should the budget be spent where it will buy the most acreage or where it will contribute the most to some specific protection goal? This is never an easy question to answer, even when the goals of a given program are fairly narrow and clear—as is the case for existing programs dealing with the acquisition of wildlife areas and recreational and open space lands.

Summary

The mandate for preservation is based on a wide range of social benefits provided by undisturbed wildland. It is not simply based on narrow interests like backpackers or water utilities. Private property and markets will not, by their very nature, provide for adequate protection of wildlands. This is not due to private greed or shortsightedness, but due to basic economic facts. I summarize these as the publicness of wilderness services, the concern for the future of the preservation decision, which preserves a national heritage for the future, and the flexibility required of policy for wildlands.

The new economics of conservation offers a useful perspective for interpreting trends in resource consumption, real cost of resources, and the relative value of undisturbed natural environments. It is one of several tools that may be employed in implementing a systematic approach to analyzing preservation decisions. It is possible to evaluate in quantitative or qualitative terms most of the values at stake for a given wild area, although quantitative analysis has its opponents.[41] Such evaluations can never achieve unanimous consent among interested parties, but they do identify key assumptions and require critical analysis of alternatives. Finally, ranking systems of various kinds may be used to compare values that translate poorly into numbers or dollars. Ranking areas for priority cannot be avoided in a world of scarce administrative time and inadequate implementation funding.

Economic reasoning, thoughtful assessment of goals and options, and carefully examined empirical data can illuminate the path of the ultimate actor facing a preservation decision. But facts and analysis cannot wipe away the uncertainty about the impacts of decisions, the uncertainty about the future, and the deep value conflicts that characterize preservation decisions. Still less can they erase the high stakes in conflicting private interests and belligerent citizen and industry coalitions. Ultimately, there is no substitute for vigorous adversary discussion and for action by a sensitive and well-informed decision-maker.

Case 4-1. Whitewater Versus Kilowatts at Hells Canyon

As an example of a systematic approach to a preservation decision, consider the classic analysis of Hells Canyon provided by Krutilla and his coworkers.[a] *Hells Canyon is a dramatic reach of the Snake River along the Idaho-Oregon border, which includes the deepest canyon in the United States. Its wild country harbors important fishery and wildlife resources. Hells Canyon represents one of the only sizable reaches of the Columbia River system that remains undammed, and it contains considerable hydropower potential. In 1976, a large wilderness and national recreation area complex was created by Congress to protect the area, ending more than two decades of controversy and formal proceedings before the Federal Power Commission over various plans to dam the river there.*

Krutilla first studied the benefits claimed to arise from generating power in Hells Canyon. He found that they were significantly overstated by failure to take into account the fact that future technical change in steam power generation would reduce costs of conventional generation, thereby reducing the benefits of the hydro development. This is because the benefits of hydro dams are calculated as savings below the costs of generating electricity in steam plants. Considering technical change, Krutilla found that one of the dam proposals was not economically sound, without even considering the environmental damages of the dam. Another proposal, the High Mountain Sheep proposal, was found to have positive net benefit equal to around $150,000 per year.

Krutilla then asked "Does it appear that the measurable and nonmeasurable values of preserving the Hells Canyon in its present undeveloped state exceed, as a minimum, $150,000 as an initial year's annual value?"[b] *He then proceeded to evaluate directly the measurable losses that would result from damming Hells Canyon to construct the High Mountain Sheep project:*[c]

Quantified Losses (1976 estimate):

Water recreation	84,000 visitor/days at $5/day	$420,000

Hunting

Big game	7,000 at $25/day	175,000
Upland birds	1,000 at $10/day	10,000
Diminished value of hunting experience	29,000 at $10/day	290,000

Total quantified losses $895,000 ± 25%

Unquantified Losses

Unmitigated anadromous fish losses outside project area
Unmitigated resident fish losses
Option value of rare wild area
Others

On the basis of this analysis, Krutilla concluded that the directly measurable values threatened by High Mountain Sheep exceeded its potential economic benefits and that therefore Hells Canyon should remain wild. Note that it was not necessary to attempt to place a dollar value on aesthetic or ecological values of Hells Canyon.

By extension of this reasoning, it is possible to measure the amount of economic benefits that would be forgone as a result of barring any development project to preserve wilderness. That value then becomes the minimum value that must be placed on the nonquantified services of wilderness to justify preservation on a benefit-cost basis. This approach does not by itself, then, provide a means of quantifying all wilderness values. It does provide a way of defining issues much more clearly and identifying assumptions that are used by different parties to the debate.

[a] J.V. Krutilla and A.C. Fisher, *The Economics of Natural Environments,* (Baltimore: Johns Hopkins, 1975) chaps. 5, 6. This summary is highly simplified for brevity.

[b] Ibid., p. 133.

[c] Adapted from ibid., p. 136.

Notes

1. For reviews of these economic concepts as applied to land management, see J.V. Krutilla and J.A. Haigh, "An Integrated Approach to National Forest Management," *Environmental Law* 8 (Summer 1978): 373; and G. Hardin and J. Baden, *Managing the Commons* (San Francisco: W.H. Freeman, 1977), especially chaps. 3, 19-22. Also R.T. Page,

Conservation and Economic Efficiency (Baltimore: Johns Hopkins, 1977).

2. Public Land Law Review Commission, *One Third of the Nation's Land,* (Washington, D.C.: U.S. Government Printing Office, 1970).

3. R.A. Musgrave and P. Musgrave, *Public Finance in Theory and Practice* (New York: McGraw-Hill, 1973), especially chap. 3.

4. W. Stegner in Wildland Research Center, *Wilderness and Recreation,* Outdoor Recreation Resources Review Commission Report 3 (Washington: U.S. Government Printing Office, 1963) p. 36.

5. See the literature review by A.C. Fisher and F.M. Peterson, "The Environment in Economics: A Survey," *Journal of Economic Literature* 14 (March 1976): 1.

6. Musgrave and Musgrave, *Public Finance,* p. 80.

7. B. Weisbrod, "Collective Consumption Services of Individual-Consumption Goods," *Quarterly Journal of Economics* 77 (August 1967): 471.

8. For full discussion see A.J. Dasgupta and D.W. Pearce, *Benefit-Cost Analysis* (New York: United Nations, 1972), chap. 6; United Nations International Development Organization, *Guidelines for Project Evaluation* (New York: United Nations, 1972), chaps. 13, 14.

9. A.C. Pigou, *The Economics of Welfare,* 4th ed. (London: Macmillan, 1932), p. 25.

10. See, for example, R.T. Page, *Conservation and Economic Efficiency* (Baltimore: Johns Hopkins Press, 1977); J.W. Milliman, "Can People Be Trusted with Natural Resources?" *Land Economics* 38 (May 1962): 199; J. Seagraves, "More on the Social Rate of Discount," *Quarterly Journal of Economics* 84 (August 1970): 430; J. Somers, "The Demise of the Social Discount Rate," *Journal of Finance* 26 (May 1971): 565; W. Baumol, "On the Social Rate of Discount," *American Economic Review* 58 (September 1968): 788; S. Marglin, "The Social Rate of Discount and the Optimal Rate of Investment," *Quarterly Journal of Economics* 77 (February 1963): 95; and A.C. Fisher and J.V. Krutilla, "Resource Conservation, Environmental Preservation, and the Rate of Discount," *Quarterly Journal of Economics* 79 (August 1975): 358.

11. F. Ramsey, "A Mathematical Theory of Saving," *Economic Journal* 38 (December 1928): 543.

12. U.S. Water Resources Council, "Principles, Procedures, and Standards . . ." *Federal Register* 38 (September 10, 1973): part 3.

13. R.M. Solow, "The Economics of Resources and the Resources of Economics," *American Economic Review* 64 (May 1974): 10. Reprinted with permission.

14. A.C. Fisher et al., "The Economics of Environmental Preservation," *American Economic Review* 62 (September 1972): 605; K.J. Arrow and A.C. Fisher, "Environmental Preservation, Uncertainty, and

Irreversibility," *Quarterly Journal of Economics* 88 (June 1974): 312; and Krutilla and Fisher, *Economics of Natural Environments,* chaps. 3 and 4.

15. J.V. Krutilla, "Conservation Reconsidered" *American Economic Review* 57 (September 1967): 777. A mathematical formulation may be found in V.K. Smith, "The Effect of Technological Change on Different Uses of Environmental Resources," in J.V. Krutilla, ed., *Natural Environments* (Baltimore: Johns Hopkins, 1972). The most complete statement of the new economics of conservation is Krutilla and Fisher, *Economics of Natural Environments.*

16. U.S. Department of Agriculture, *Our Land and Water Resources* (Washington, D.C., Miscellaneous Publication 1290, 1974), p. 10.

17. J. Duffield, "Wilderness—A Political and Economic Analysis" (Ph.D. diss., Yale University, 1974) documents the decline of unroaded land area in the United States.

18. Duffield, "Wilderness" chaps. 5, 9.

19. See, for example, the chapter on aluminum in David Novick, *A World of Scarcity* (New York: John Wiley, 1976).

20. Real cost is the cost of a product stated in terms of a constant general price level, that is, adjusted for the effects of inflation. Major studies substantiating the long-run decline in real costs of resource extraction include: H.J. Barnett and C. Morse, *Scarcity and Growth* (Baltimore: Johns Hopkins, 1963); O.C. Herfindahl, *Copper Costs and Prices* (Baltimore: Johns Hopkins, 1959); M. Adelman, *The World Petroleum Market* (Baltimore: Johns Hopkins, 1972); L.C. Irland, *Is Timber Scarce? The Economics of a Renewable Resource,* Yale School of Forestry and Environmental Studies, Bulletin 83, 1974. See also, F. Banks, *Scarcity, Energy, and Economic Progress,* (Lexington, Mass.: D.C. Heath, 1977); and V.K. Smith, "Measuring Natural Resource Scarcity: Theory and Practice," *Journal of Environmental Economics and Management* 5 (1978): 150.

21. *Government and the Nation's Resources,* Report of the National Commission on Supplies and Shortages (Washington, D.C.: U.S. Government Printing Office, 1977), p. 16. Also, P.W. Guild, "Discovery of Natural Resources," in P.H. Abelson and A. Hammond, eds., *Materials: Renewable and Nonrenewable Resources,* (Washington, D.C.: American Association for the Advancement of Science, 1976).

22. Krutilla and Fisher, *Economics of Natural Environments,* chaps. 5, 6.

23. L.C. Irland, "Economic Issues Raised by the Federal Water Project Recreation Act," in U.S. Congress, Senate, Committee on Interior and Insular Affairs, *Studies of the Federal Water Project Recreation Act,* 94th Congress, 1st Session, December 1975, and sources cited therein.

24. See, generally, Wendell Beardsley, Dennis Schweitzer, and Douglas

Ljungren, "Measuring Economic Costs of Wilderness Land Allocation," in Jay M. Hughes and R. Duane Lloyd, eds., *Outdoor Recreation—Advances in Application of Economics* U.S. Department of Agriculture, Forest Service, General Technical Report WO-2, March 1977; and William McKillop, "Economic Costs of Withdrawing Timber and Timberland from Commercial Production," *Journal of Forestry,* 76 (July 1978): 414-417; J.G. Jones, W.G. Beardsley, D.W. Countryman, and D.L. Schweitzer, "Estimating Costs of Allocating Land to Wilderness," *Forest Science* 24 (September 1978): 410. Management costs and opportunity costs are discussed, with detailed case studies, in R.W. Guldin, "Economic Model of the Costs of Wilderness Recreation" (Ph.D. diss., Yale University, 1978).

25. Except when private individuals already own mineral rights. See the Beaver Creek example, case 6-1 in chapter 6.

26. For full analysis of valuation issues, see J.A. Sinden and A.C. Worrell, *Unpriced Values: Decisions without Market Prices* (New York: John Wiley, 1979). See also, W.E. Westman, "How Much are Nature's Services Worth?" *Science* 197 (2 September 1977): 960; and A.C. Fisher and F.M. Peterson, "The Environment in Economics: A Survey," *Journal of Economic Literature* 14 (March 1976): 1. A useful case study is provided in B. Ingle, "Corkscrew Sanctuary: Use of the Market for Evaluation," *Environmental Affairs* 3 (1974): 647. Also, R.C. Ainacher, R.D. Tollison, and T.D. Willett, "The Economics of Fatal Mistakes," *Public Policy* 20 (Spring 1974): 411, which applies economic reasoning to eagle preservation.

27. See, for example, R.W. Guldin, "Economic Model of the Costs of Wilderness Recreation" (Ph.D. diss., Yale University, 1978).

28. J. Knetsch, *Outdoor Recreation and Water Resources Planning* (Washington, D.C.: American Geophysical Union, 1974), pp. 117-118.

29. J. Knetsch and R. Davis, "Comparison of Methods for Recreation Evaluation," in M. Dorfman and R. Dorfman, eds., *Economics of the Environment* (New York: W.W. Norton, 1972).

30. U.S. Water Resources Council, "Principles, Standards, and Procedures," part 3.

31. M. Clawson and J. Knetsch, *The Economics of Outdoor Recreation* (Baltimore: Johns Hopkins, 1966); see also U.S. Department of the Interior, U.S. Fish and Wildlife Service, *1975 National Survey of Hunting, Fishing, and Wildlife-Associated Recreation* (Washington, D.C.: U.S. Government Printing Office, 1977). This is the fifth such survey conducted by USFWS since 1955; it contains extensive data on expenditures incurred by persons enjoying fish and wildlife-related pursuits. Also, J.A. Leitch and D.F. Scott, *A Selected Annotated Bibliography of Economic Values of Fish and Wildlife and Their Habitats,* Fargo, N.Dak.: Department of Agricultural Economics, North Dakota State University, Agricultural Economics Miscellaneous Report 27, August 1977.

32. J. Horvath, "Economic Survey of Southeastern Wildlife and Wildlife-Oriented Recreation," *Transactions of the 39th North American Wildlife and Fisheries Conferences,* Washington, D.C., 1974.

33. See, for theoretical support and computational detail, references cited in note 8.

34. See, for example, S. Hanke and R. Walker, "Benefit-Cost Analysis Reconsidered—the Mid-State Project," *Water Resources Research* 10 (October 1974): 898; R. Davis, L. Engle, and C. Gillen, "An Economic Perspective on the Small Watersheds Program," in *Benefit Cost Analysis of Federal Programs,* U.S. Congress, Joint Economic Committee, 92d Congress, 2d Session, 1973; J. Krutilla, "The Use of Economics in Project Evaluation," *Transactions of the 40th North American Wildlife and Natural Resources Conference* Washington, D.C., 1975, p. 374; D. Shapiro, "Can Public Investment Have a Positive Rate of Return?" *Journal of Political Economy,* no. 81, March-April 1973, p. 401; C. Stern, "Hydro-power vs. Wilderness Waterway: The Economics of Project Justification through the 1960's," *Journal of Leisure Research* 6 (Winter 1974): 46. Valuable case studies are presented in Krutilla and Fisher, *Economics of Natural Environments:* Hell's Canyon (chaps. 5, 6); molybdenum mining in the White Cloud Peaks (chap. 7); ski resort in Mineral King Valley (chap. 8); preservation of prairie wetlands (chap. 9).

35. Hon. Thomas R. Berger, *Northern Frontier, Northern Homeland Report of the Mackenzie Valley Pipeline Inquiry* (Ottawa: Supply and Services Canada, 1977); Tennessee Valley Authority and U.S. Department of Interior, *Alternatives for Completing the Tellico Project* (draft), Knoxville, Tenn., August 10, 1978; W.E. Phillips, *The Conservation of the California Tule Elk* (Edmonton, Alberta: University of Alberta Press, 1976).

36. New England Natural Resources Center, *Protecting New England's Natural Heritage,* Boston, 1973.

37. This was applied in the RARE-II inventory, using a national vegetation classification identifying 242 ecosystems. The classification was employed to identify any gaps in coverage of the proposed alternative mixes of recommended wilderness designations. U.S. Department of Agriculture, Forest Service, RARE-II Draft Environmental Statement (Washington, D.C.: 1979) pp. 11-13. An intensive application of this approach was employed by R.B. Pyle to identify preservation needs in the state of Washington. He used butterfly populations as an index of ecological differences and identified habitat preservation needs required to preserve Washington's Lepidopteran fauna: R.B. Pyle, "Ecogeographic Basis for Lepidoptera Conservation" (Ph.D. diss., Yale University, 1976). See also R.B. Pyle, "Conservation of Lepidoptera in the U.S.," *Biological Conservation* 9 (January 1976): 55.

38. See, for example, L.M. Arthur and R.S. Boster, *Measuring Scenic*

Beauty: A Selected Annotated Bibliography, U.S. Forest Service, Rocky Mountain Forest and Range Experiment Station, General Technical Report RM-25, 1976; T.C. Daniel and R.S. Boster, *Measuring Landscape Aesthetics: The Scenic Beauty Estimation Method,* U.S. Forest Service, Rocky Mountain Forest and Range Experiment Station, Res. Pap. RM-167, 1976); E.L. Shafer et al., *Recreation, Resources, and Right Decisions,* U.S. Forest Service, Northeastern Forest Experiment Station, Res. Pap. NE-293, 1974; G.H. Moeller, R. Mclachlan, and D.A. Morrison, *Measuring Perception of Elements in Outdoor Environments,* U.S. Forest Service, Northeastern Forest Experiment Station, Res. Pap. NE-289, 1974.

39. The classic articles are L.B. Leopold, "Landscape Aesthetics," *Natural History* 77 (October 1969): 36-45; L.B. Leopold, *Quantitative Comparison of Some Aesthetic Factors among Rivers,* U.S. Geological Survey, Circular 620, 1969; L.B. Leopold and M. Marchand, "On the Quantitative Inventory of the Riverscape," *Water Resources Research* 4 (August 1968): 709.

40. See Pyle, "Lepidoptera Conservation"; T. Gupta and J. Foster, "Economic Criteria for Freshwater Wetland Policy in Massachusetts," *American Journal of Agricultural Economics* 57 (February 1975): 40; P.R. Adams and G. Clough, "Evaluating Species for Protection in Natural Areas," *Biological Conservation* 13 (April 1978): 165.

41. Some authors have questioned the value and appropriateness of applying technical benefit-cost analysis to problems characterized by deep value conflict. For a useful review of methodological problems with full and up-to-date references, see Baruch Fischoff, "The Art of Benefit-Cost Analysis," Springfield, Virginia, National Technical Information Service, February 1977, #AD/A-041 526. A detailed case study of the use of analysis on a preservation problem is H.A. Feiveson, F.W. Sinden, and R.H. Socolow, *Boundaries of Analysis: An Inquiry into the Tocks Island Dam Controversy* (Cambridge, Mass.: Ballinger, 1976), especially chap. 4; for an articulate and informed polemic against the use of benefit-cost analyses for decision-making, see A. Lovins, "Cost-Risk-Benefit Assessments in Energy Policy," *George Washington Law Review* 45 (August 1977): 911-943.

5

Wilderness and Wood Supply

Most wilderness controversies have involved timber resources, and the timber supply issue has therefore generated more than its share of myth. This chapter treats the timber values of wilderness. It reviews the U.S. forest resource position, the impact of wilderness on timber supplies, and ways to resolve any conflicts that emerge.

Wilderness allocations need not pose significant threats to the nation's total supplies of wood products. The true issue is different. It arises from the fact that reduced resource supplies may place severe burdens of adjustment on local communities and individuals. It is not unusual for public projects—roads, flood control dams—to impose losses on individuals. What is unusual about the wilderness case is how little attention has been paid to means of mitigating those effects where they occur.

The U.S. Forest Resource Position

To understand the role played by wilderness decisions in the U.S. forest-products supply picture, it is necessary to briefly review the nation's timber supply position.

Historic Trends and Current Status

In colonial times, forest products were a prime source of export trade and employment. Up to the Civil War, timber was the economy's dominant building material and fuel. With the advent of wood pulp papermaking, the United States rapidly became the world's dominant producer and consumer of pulp and paper. Compared to other nations, the United States today has an extremely high level of per capita paper consumption, high use of wood in residential construction, and low use of wood as fuel.[1]

From 1962 to 1977, the United States' commercial forest land base declined by 23 million acres to about 488 million acres.[2] This decline reversed a previous rising trend that had continued for decades. About one third of the decrease was due to wilderness allocations; the remainder was due to competing land development. The trend is of special concern, since the most rapid losses are among the most valuable timberland. For example, in the bottomland hardwood forests of the Lower Mississippi Valley roughly 4 million acres were cleared from 1950 to 1969.[3] This represented a 36 percent decline in an ecosystem highly valuable as timberland, wildlife habitat, and green space. The Forest Service expects the forest land base to decline by about 5 million acres per decade for the next fifty years.

Despite recent losses of forest land, timber volumes have risen steadily since 1950. Before that time, inventories declined steadily under exploitive cutting, land clearing, uncontrolled wildfire, and insect and disease outbreaks. As late as 1944, total timber drain exceeded growth by 53 percent. The Forest Service's 1958 national timber inventory was the first timber review to report a stabilized inventory situation.[4] Between 1945 and 1970, total timber inventories (in cubic feet) rose by 38 percent. In 1970, the growth-cut ratio was 1.11 for softwoods and 1.8 for hardwoods. Total 1970 growth was 14 percent higher than in 1962.[5] What forces reversed the historic trend of forest liquidation? Significant factors included:[6]

1. The substitution of fossil fuels for firewood as a household and industrial fuel. In 1900, fuelwood accounted for 40 percent of total timber cut; by 1970, it was only 6 percent.

2. The long decline of timber demand from the housing recession of the late twenties until early World War II. This slackening of demand reduced harvesting pressure and permitted young forests established on cutover land enough time to grow to maturity.

3. Reliance on Canadian forests for a substantial share of our newsprint needs. As reliance on Canadian newsprint has declined, dependence on Canadian lumber has risen.

4. By the early fifties the benefits began to be felt from fire control and other custodial forest management programs established during the twenties.

5. Rapid technological change permitted the utilization of smaller trees, less desirable species, and the conversion of wood formerly wasted.

6. Of longer term importance has been the return of abandoned farmland to forest, a process that began in some regions before 1800. This trend has now run its course, and total forest area is declining.

The overall balance between demand and supply for a raw material is well summarized in the trend of its real price (the current price deflated by an index of all wholesale prices.)[7] Most forest products price trends gave evidence of increasing timber scarcity up to about 1950. From 1950 to 1970, real prices tended to decline and pointed to decisively improved timber resource supplies during the 1950-1970 period.[8] Since 1972, a historic record housing boom, and general inflation, have inflated lumber, plywood, and standing timber prices significantly. Prices are expected to stabilize, however, as housing activity moderates.

Over the long run, rising lumber and plywood prices have not had major effects on the price or production of housing. Despite this, Congress has repeatedly been urged to take measures to expand U.S. timber supplies to moderate inflation in prices of stumpage, lumber, and plywood and thereby promote the production of low-cost housing.[9] Analysis shows, however, that whereas rising wood prices do affect housing costs, they have not been as important as have land prices, taxes, and government controls, including building codes and land-use regulations.[10]

A useful measure of a nation's natural resource adequacy is its foreign trade position. Within the U.S. forest-products sector, offsetting trends have occurred. Lumber imports have risen over the past decade but so have log exports. Hardwood plywood imports have risen rapidly, now supplying roughly half of our consumption. At the same time, exports of paperboard have risen rapidly, and our degree of dependence on Canadian newsprint has declined. Considering all timber products together, our degree of dependence on imports (net imports as percent of annual consumption) has declined slightly since 1950.[11]

Supply and Demand Outlook

The current net growth of U.S. forests averages 38 cubic feet of merchantable stemwood per acre per year. This includes rapidly growing young stands as well as overmature stands in the West, which are losing merchantable volumes each year. The total net annual growth of U.S. forests is estimated at 18.6 billion cubic feet (bcf), a level comfortably above current consumption.[12] The relation between growth and harvest varies dramatically by region. In some areas, harvest exceeds growth, since high-volume old growth forests are being cut. In the South, fast growth of young stands provides a substantial surplus of growth over cut in most areas. In southern New England, the volume of wood removed in suburban land clearing exceeds the harvest for industrial purposes, but growth still exceeds cut by three to one.

Stephen Spurr and Henry J. Vaux recently assembled a careful estimate of the timber production potential of America's forests, based on a projected land base of 455 million acres by the year 2020.[13] Intensive management applied to the entire area would produce 34.6 bcf per year, or 2.6 times 1974 consumption. Because of economic constraints, however, they estimated that only 29.4 bcf would be produced because of high costs for some potential management practices. Considering additional constraints imposed by landownership and by public forest management policies, they suggested that the harvest level actually achievable would only be 19 bcf, which is only a marginal increase over the actual 1970 level.

What will be the future national requirement for wood products? The experts have offered numerous assessments of the future demand for wood in the United States.[14] Wood is one of the nation's leading raw materials on a tonnage basis. It appears in countless products used by consumers every day. All predictions expect the nation's consumption of wood products to rise significantly (table 5-1). In addition, potentially important new uses for wood include energy production and silvichemicals.

The past history of wood use and the outlook for major products present important questions. The U.S. Forest Service's medium projection foresees a near doubling of roundwood consumption to 2020, but the entire increase is due to growth in the use of pulpwood (table 5-2). This is because of the expected increase in per capita consumption of paper and board products. If this threefold increase in pulp and paper demand does not materialize, the future for wood consumption will be considerably different.

Comparing the prospects for demand and supply, analysts predict that substantial increases in the real price of wood products will be necessary to balance supplies and demands. For example, if the Spurr and Vaux projection of 19 bcf of annual wood harvest turns out to be correct by the year 2020, the Forest Service's projection of 22.1 bcf consumption will be impossible without liquidating inventory. Prices will have to rise more rapidly than expected in the Forest Service's medium projection to ration the available supplies. Is a rising real price for wood products really a social problem? That depends on who you ask. Higher prices for wood will aid forest landowners, will promote better forestry and more efficient conversion of logs into products, and will force users to economize on

Table 5-1
Total Roundwood Consumption and Projected Demand, 1974 to 2020
(*Billion Cubic Feet Per Year*)

	Low Projection	Medium Projection	High Projection
1980	15.5	16.6	17.8
2000	18.6	22.0	26.2
2020	21.2	27.8	37.3
1974 actual: 13.1			

Source: U.S. Department of Agriculture, Forest Service, *The Nation's Renewable Resources: An Assessment, 1975,* Forest Resources Report no. 21 (Washington, D.C.: U.S. Government Printing Office, June 1977), p. 154.

Note: The projections given assume different combinations of growth in population, GNP, and wood products prices.

Table 5-2

Roundwood Consumption in the United States by Major Use 1952 to 1970 and Projection to 2020, All Species

(*Billion Cubic Feet Per Year*)

Year	Total	Sawlogs	Veneer Logs	Pulpwood	Miscellaneous	Fuelwood
1952	11.9	6.1	0.4	2.7	0.7	2.0
1970	12.7	6.1	1.2	4.4	0.4	0.5
2020	22.1	5.5	2.0	13.8	0.3	0.5

Source: U.S. Department of Agriculture, U.S. Forest Service, *The Nation's Renewable Resources: An Assessment, 1975* (Washington, D.C.: U.S. Government Printing Office, 1977) p. 156.

Note: projection cited is the medium projection, assuming prices rising 1.5 percent/year for lumber, 1 percent/year for plywood, miscellaneous, and fuelwood, and 0.5 percent/year for paper and board.

wood. Higher prices will reduce our wood exports, will increase the costs consumers pay for products using wood, especially housing, and may make it more difficult for marginal processing firms to survive.[15]

One thing that is clear, however, is that if the nation can find ways—and I believe it can—to make do with a stable per capita level of paper consumption in the future, it will have ample capacity to supply its future wood needs.[16]

Whereas the indicators are mixed, it appears that the United States enjoys an abundance of forest resources that is exceeded among industrial nations only by Canada and the USSR. This basic forest abundance allows this nation the opportunity to consider devoting forests to uses other than commodity production.

Wilderness: Timber Values and National Economic Impact

Timber Values in Existing Wilderness

In 1977, there were 19.4 million acres of productive forest land in reserved status, plus 4.6 million formally deferred, awaiting preservation decisions. This was 4.6 percent of the national total of productive forest land (commercial forest land plus productive reserved forest). Formally reserved productive forest increased by 3.4 million acres over 1963 and 4.7 million acres over 1953. Of the total reserved acreage 43 percent is in the Rocky Mountains and 36 percent of it is in the East (table 5-3). By the late seventies the acreage reserved will undoubtedly increase further. The proportion of

Table 5-3
Acreage of Productive Reserved Forest Land: 1963, 1970, and 1977
(*million acres*)

Region	1963	1970	1977
North	4.1	4.3	5.1
South	1.3	1.7	1.9
Pacific Coast	3.5	3.3	3.8
Northern Rockies	5.8	6.0	6.6
Southern Rockies	1.4	1.9	1.8
West	10.7	11.2	12.4
United States Total	16.0	17.2	19.4

Source: U.S. Department of Agriculture, U.S. Forest Service, *Timber Trends in the United States* (Washington, D.C.: U.S. Government Printing Office, 1965), p. 76; U.S. Department of Agriculture, U.S. Forest Service, *Outlook for Timber* (Washington, D.C.: Government Printing Office, 1973), p. 9; U.S. Department of Agriculture, U.S. Forest Service, *Forest Statistics of the U.S., 1977*, review draft (Washington, D.C.: U.S. Government Printing Office, 1978), pp. 22-28.

Note: As of January 1, 1977, there were additional areas of deferred forest land: North, 153,200 acres; South, 100,800 acres; Pacific Coast, 880,000 acres (excluding Alaska and Hawaii); Northern Rockies, 1,975,300 acres; Southern Rockies, 1,208,000 acres. National total (lower 48): 4,626,200 acres.

Definitions: *Productive-reserved:* Productive public forest land withdrawn from timber utilization through statute or administrative regulations. *Productive-deferred:* National forest lands that meet productivity standards for commercial forest but are under study for possible inclusion in the wilderness system.

forest land in reserved status varies regionally (table 5-4). In the Rocky Mountain states fully 20 percent of the productive forest land is reserved. In the South the share is less than 2 percent.

Acreage data alone give little insight into the economic impact of current or prospective wilderness allocations. This is because of the diversity of forest conditions—species, stocking, growth rates, slopes—that control the value of timber on the stump. High lumber prices and modern technology are making higher altitudes and sparser stands economically accessible. Lodgepole pine, a species of high elevations in the Rockies and Cascades, for example, is becoming a major lumber species.

When the Wildland Research Center reviewed wilderness areas in 1960, it concluded that areas then reserved contained about 4.2 million acres of productive forest land and about 37 billion board-feet of timber.[17] This volume is roughly equivalent to one year's domestic lumber cut. For the additional 8.9 million acres of potential wilderness reviewed, fully half was found unproductive. Further, existing wilderness probably contains little standing timber that is merchantable under current conditions. Merriam appraised two potential timber sales on the Bob Marshall Wilderness using

Table 5-4
Area of Productive-Reserved and Productive-Deferred Forest Land, by Region, January 1, 1977

Region	Productive Reserved (1,000 acres)	Productive Deferred (1,000 acres)	Total Productive: Forest Plus Reserved and Deferred (million acres)	Reserved and Deferred as Percent of Total Productive Forest Land (percent)
New England	484.8	25.0	31.5	1.6
Mid-Atlantic	2,944.0	36.0	51.2	5.6
Lake States	990.6	36.0	51.0	2.0
Central States	718.1	56.2	42.3	1.7
South Atlantic	867.6	36.6	48.5	1.9
East Gulf	528.0	1.1	40.7	1.2
Central Gulf	370.7	18.5	51.4	0.7
West Gulf	104.7	44.6	49.7	0.3
Total East	7,008.5	254.0	366.5	2.0
Pacific Northwest	2,460.0	612.0	45.4	6.8
California	1,365.0	268.0	17.9	9.1
Northern Rockies	6,614.5	1,975.3	42.1	20.4
Southern Rockies	1,775.8	1,208.1	27.3	10.9
Total West[a]	12,408.6	4,372.2	132.7	12.6
Total United States	19,417.1	4,626.2	511.7	4.6

Source: U.S. Department of Agriculture, U.S. Forest Service, *Forest Statistics of the U.S., 1977* (review draft) (Washington, D.C.: U.S. Government Printing Office, 1978), pp. 22-28.

Regions: *New England:* CT, ME, MA, NH, RI, VT; *Mid-Atlantic:* DL, MD, NJ, NY, PA, WV; *Lake States:* MI, MN, ND, SD (East), WI; *Central:* IL, IN, IA, KS, KY, MO, NB, OH; *South Atlantic:* NC, SC, VA; *East Gulf:* FL, GA; *Central Gulf:* AL, MS, TN; *West Gulf:* AK, LA, OK, TX; *Pacific Northwest:* WA, OR; *North Rockies:* ID, MT, SD (West), WY; *South Rockies:* AZ, CO, NA, NM, UT.

[a]Alaska and Hawaii are ommitted from this portion of the table but are included in the U.S. total.

Forest Service methods.[18] He found negative stumpage values, indicating economically valueless timber. As a general conclusion, wilderness in existence as of the mid-seventies did not contain an economically important amount of valuable timber. The area of timber land devoted to wilderness from the twenties to the sixties was small compared to the acreage of forest cleared or otherwise withdrawn for urban, suburban, recreational, agricultural, industrial, and transportation uses.

Proposed Wilderness: Effects on the Land Base

The immediate effect of land use decisions is to change the land base available for timber management. Forest land on the national forests is already unavailable for sustained timber production on almost 40 percent of the acreage. In 1976, the Forest Service classified its acreage as follows:[19]

Commercial Forest	*Million Acres*
Standard	57.6
Special	8.1
Marginal	20.5
Unregulated	4.6
Total	90.8
Reserved and deferred forest	12.2
National forest system	182.8

The standard component is the acreage available for sustained wood growing without additional special measures. The special component requires additional measures, such as helicopter logging. The marginal component is not economically harvestable at present.

    The commercial forest land base is directly affected by wilderness allocations. The land identified as roadless in the Forest Service's recent roadless area review (RARE-II), for example, includes an estimated 26.5 million acres of commercial forest land. How much of this is in the standard component is not clear, but the area certainly represents a significant portion of the national forest land base. The continuous decline in national forest land available for timber-growing has been due to land-use planning, as well as to wilderness allocations. These declines have been of intense concern to the wood-using industry, especially in the West.[20] To look only at the proportion of the national forest land in each state that is now either dedicated to wilderness or is included in the RARE-II roadless area designations produces an alarming picture (table 5-5). This is especially true

Table 5-5
RARE-II Acreage Compared to Total Forest Area and Total Land Area, Selected States
(*thousands of acres*)

State	Total Wilderness 1978[a]	Total RARE-II Acreage	Percent of National Forest Land in Wilderness and RARE-II	Total Land Area in State[b]	Percent National Forest Wilderness and RARE-II of Total Land Area
Alaska	1,049	17,728	86	326,500	5
Colorado	1,795	6,623	53	66,400	12
Montana		6,808	51	93,200	9
New Hampshire	26	268	43	5,800	5
North Carolina	31	227	23	31,300	1

[a]Based on preliminary RARE-II tabulations, as summarized by the National Forest Products Association, *Wilderness Withdrawals and Timber Supply* (Washington, D.C., January 16, 1978), p. 14.

[b]Land areas from U.S. Department of Agriculture, U.S. Forest Service, *The Nation's Renewable Resources, An Assessment: 1975* (Washington, D.C.: U.S. Government Printing Office, 1977) pp. 15-16.

for those states, such as Idaho or Montana, that have little privately owned forest land. To place these figures in perspective however, the total acreage of commercial forest land needs to be considered. Further, if data on productive economic potential were available, they would probably show that in most cases little productive potential is included in the RARE acreage, when measured in terms of potential returns to investment in forest management.

In addition to a declining land base on public lands, the privately owned land available for timber-growing is declining as well. Each year, about 2 to 3 million acres of rural land are developed for roads, subdivisions, and factories, and forests are cleared for pasture and cropland. The U.S. Forest Service expects commercial forest land to decline by 25 million acres to the year 2020, a figure that some observers believe will prove to be an underestimate.

Of perhaps greater concern is the invisible erosion of the commercial forest base due to the booming market in rural land. Farms are being cut up and sold in one-acre pieces, awkwardly shaped parcels are being marketed for speculative resale, and the average period of ownership of small forest tracts is low. Spurr and Vaux identified these factors as important forces reducing the economically achievable output from American forests. Zivnuska suggested that a parcel of size of about 200 to 500 acres is a reasonable minimum for efficient forest management.[21] If so, then over half of the nation's 300 million acres of private nonindustrial forest land is probably not a part of the true commercial forest land base.

Effect on Timber Harvests

One class of wilderness allocations will have no effect whatever on the commercial timber supply. These are the areas created in the primitive areas and in the national parks and wildlife refuges. With unimportant exceptions, these lands are not now part of the nation's commercial forest land base. The nation's wilderness system, then, could grow by 24 million acres without affecting the timber supply at all.

In another category are timber stands that are included in allowable cut calculations for national forest or Bureau of Land Management (BLM) units. There are three classes of timberland in this position:

1. Accessible land of high growth potential. Withdrawal of such stands may reduce planned harvests by removing stands budgeted for current cut from the land base and may reduce the long-term allowable cut from the area affected.

2. Land of low growth potential supporting old-growth stands with high merchantable timber volumes. Such stands often occur on land of poor

site quality simply as a result of survival to a ripe old age. Designating such stands for wilderness involves giving up a one-shot timber mining opportunity, but it does not affect the long-term economic productivity of the affected area.

3. Merchantable stands on high sites that are not currently operable due to undeveloped markets, high road-building costs, or other factors. Their removal from the land base may not affect timber harvests directly but will reduce the future allowable cut and thus affect timber supply. In most western national forests, it is this indirect effect on the current allowable cut that is the issue, not the timber values of the lands proposed for wilderness.

Existing data do not allow us to estimate timber volumes falling in these three situations. Data have been provided, however, for national forest roadless areas and for the areas considered in eastern wilderness legislation.

In 1977 and 1978, the U.S. Forest Service conducted an intensive inventory of remaining national forest system roadless areas (RARE-II— see Chapter 8). The 62.5 million acres of roadless areas studied in RARE-II contain an estimated 26.5 million acres of commercial forest land. These lands were estimated to be capable of sustaining an annual allowable harvest of 3.075 billion board-feet, or a potential yield of about 6 billion board-feet under intensive management. This is substantial, compared to recent national forest harvests of 11 billion board feet.

The study areas proposed in the 1973 RARE-I review totalled 12.3 million acres. The allowable timber harvest on those 274 acreas was only 299 million board-feet per year—the areas were selected with timber value as a prime criterion so that they include a minimum of forgone timber values.[22]

These examples indicate the wide range of choice available in balancing demands for additional designated wilderness against potential reductions in timber supply. Fully 36 million acres of lands identified as roadless in RARE-II are of no commercial timber value, although they contain other significant resources.

On lands proposed for eastern wilderness, Forest Service studies show that timber and other values on the roughly 600,000 acres in question in the 1974 legislation are of small importance. On the nineteen areas proposed for instant status in Senate 3433, the gross land area involved was 252,000 acres. Timber harvest potentials on these nineteen areas totaled about 12 million board-feet per year or 2 percent of the allowable cuts on the forests affected.[23] The forty study areas proposed in Senate 3433 contained an annual allowable harvest of an additional 38 million board-feet per year. The total timber cut involved would be about 6 percent of the allowable harvest on the affected forests. In the East, the total RARE-II acreage (2.4 million) supports a nominal annual harvest level. Given the resource situation for eastern hardwood timber, wilderness designation of the RARE-II areas would not be economically significant. In most areas, substantial surpluses of growth exist. Considerable flexibility in management exists on most forests for temporarily compensating for any harvest reductions by harvesting outside of wilderness area. In some areas, however, local timber buyers could encounter difficulty in obtaining substitute timber from fragmented private landholdings.

Timber supply impacts of wilderness withdrawals, then, tend to be low on a per acre basis. This is because of the generally low biological productivity of most lands now being considered for wilderness. Further, high-elevation, steep lands are unattractive to loggers due to high roadbuilding and logging costs. Acreage figures, then, tend to overstate the importance of withdrawn lands to the nation's timber supply.

Effects on Wood Product Prices

Lumber and plywood prices are set in a highly competitive national market. The availability of imported softwood lumber from Canada helps limit price rises when demand is high. Lumber and plywood demand, in turn, are controlled primarily by the rate of new home construction, which in turn fluctuates in response to monetary and other forces in the economy. Prices fluctuate from year to year because it is impossible to maintain sufficient milling capacity to meet needs of occasional high-demand years. In such years, prices of lumber and plywood, and hence of standing timber, must rise to ration available supplies. Economists say that the supply of these products is inelastic in the short run. At the same time, lumber and plywood do not have close substitutes in home-building. When financing is available, builders start housing units, and they are willing to pay high prices to get the lumber and plywood they need. This makes the short-run demand for lumber and plywood relatively inelastic. Although short-run demand for lumber and plywood is inelastic, when a perspective of several years' duration is considered, many alternative sources of supply emerge. Price increases will set in motion a series of adjustments, which will expand the timber supply to compensate for harvests lost as a result of wilderness withdrawals.

As an example, 274 study areas selected in the first Forest Service roadless area review included 12.3 million acres of land. Since the areas were chosen to minimize withdrawal of commercial timber, the timber harvest supportable on that acreage was only 299 million board-feet per year.[24] The Forest Service estimated that allocating these lands to wilderness could have a short-run effect as high as a 1 to 5 percent increase in wood product prices. These studies report small impacts on timber harvests and prices from past wildland preservation proposals. To illustrate the extreme range of possibilities, let us examine the expected results when, in the mid-sixties, Congress, environmentalists, and industry were locked in conflict over a reduction in national forest harvests that could have reached 50 percent.

In the early seventies, a bitter controversy arose over clear-cutting on the national forests. An intensive effort by conservation groups to persuade Congress to ban clear-cutting on the national forests failed. But a lawsuit brought by the Izaak Walton League resulted in a court ruling that clear-cutting, as then practiced, was in conflict with the 1897 Forest Service Organic Act.[25] This was the famous "Monongahela Decision." The literal interpretation of this decision threatened to reduce national forest timber harvests substantially, until passage of the 1976 National Forest Management Act.[26] The debate over the potential impact of reduced national forest timber harvest spawned some detailed research, which is of interest here.

Professor Darius Adams of Oregon State University was asked by the U.S. Forest Service to construct a detailed computer model of the problem, building on his previous work.[27] Adams built a complex model depicting, in equation form, timber sale offerings by the Forest Service and by private owners, log flows, regional lumber and plywood output and prices, and imports and exports. He found that dramatic changes in national forest cut have only small effects on total national lumber and plywood production and prices, due to the compensating effects of changes in private timber harvests and net imports. From 1974 to 2000, national forest harvest is expected to be 20 percent of U.S. softwood harvest. Assuming that literal application of the Organic Act, under the Monongahela decision, would cut National Forest softwood output in half, national production would fall by 10 percent. Due to compensating increases and trade shifts, the actual resulting decline would be 4.8 percent for total U.S. production. Prices react more dramatically, rising by 12 percent compared to current policy for products and 24 percent for stumpage. The most important impact would be felt in the West, where the economic base for many mills and communities would disappear in short order. In the South, output would expand to fill the resulting market deficits.

The Bureau of Domestic Commerce, U.S. Department of Commerce, contracted with Data Resources Inc. (DRI), an economic consulting firm, for another analysis of the impact of the Monongahela decision.[28] That analysis presumed a 45 percent decrease in national forest softwood cut. The results showed that a 6 billion board-feet per year reduction in national forest cut would result in a net supply reduction of 3.9 billion board-feet per year due to compensating increases in private harvest and in trade patterns. A net loss in softwood lumber milling capacity of 4.7 billion board-feet would occur in the West; a substantial reduction in softwood plywood capacity would also occur. DRI found that a loss of 27,000 jobs would occur in the West, whereas jobs would increase by 6,000 in the East. Price increases to 1980 averaged 23 percent for lumber and 21 percent for softwood plywood.

Faced with these likely consequences, the Congress declined to tolerate a massive decline in national forest timber harvests. Following intensive debate, the Congress passed the 1976 National Forest Management Act, establishing tighter guidelines for timber production on the national forests, but avoiding large declines in harvest. These analyses by Adams and DRI, however, illustrate the possible consequences of large declines in national forest timber harvest, when imposed all at once. It should be noted that the RARE-II acreage supports an allowable cut potential of 3.075 billion board-feet, an amount half as large as the harvest declines analyzed by Adams and DRI. This suggests that immediate wilderness designation of all RARE-II areas, with no mitigating measures to offset impacts on timber supply, could have a noticeable effect on national wood products prices.

Resolving the Conflict

Three broad avenues of progress will allow the allocation of large areas of forest to wilderness without loss of significant wood production to the nation as a whole: growing more wood on the remaining highly productive commercial forest base, using the harvested wood more efficiently, and restricted backcountry management emphasizing natural timber growing practices and wildlife and watershed protection programs.

Growing More Timber

As demands increase and prices rise, more intensive management of the nation's forests will be undertaken. This increased management effort will also provide the means by which the nation and local areas will produce the wood formerly obtained from areas that will be devoted to wilderness preservation. Numerous appraisals of wood-producing potential have been made; only a few examples can be reviewed here.

In 1974, the U.S. Forest Service estimated that a program of forest management intensification could raise total wood output by as much as 13 billion board-feet per year by the year 2000. The program would cost $69 million per year and would assist in holding down wood prices to consumers.[29] In the state of Washington west of the Cascades, an intensified management program would produce an additional total output of 3 billion cubic feet over a twelve-decade period. In the southern loblolly pine-slash pine resource, total output could be doubled simply by assuring adequate pine regeneration and by lengthening rotation ages slightly to the age that maximizes mean annual wood growth.[30] These studies did not appraise the costs and returns of these programs, but the analysts clearly felt that they were attainable. Management intensification, however, is most economical on the most productive site (table 5-6). Large areas of forest land, especially in the national forests, do not possess high enough growth potential for economically improving their growth rates. Vaux cites Forest Service studies and his own research to suggest that 25 percent of the commercial forest on the national forests is economically submarginal for growing trees. He argues that timber on such submarginal sites should not be considered part of the timber supply.[31]

An example is seen on the Utah North Slope, adjacent to the High Uintah Primitive Area.[32] In this area, large areas of overmature and overstocked stands are degenerating due to bark beetle and dwarf mistletoe infestations. Of the National Forest land studied there, 60 percent was defined as commercial forest. More than three-fourths of this area, however, is "low site" or "very low site" land. Of the total 404,000 acres of commercial forest land, timber management could cover costs on only about 252,000 acres. This area would yield $266,000 per year in gross revenue in the second rotation after a massive management intensification effort. The Annual net revenue from the harvest would be only $32,000 after paying timber-growing and administrative costs. This is less than 13 cents per acre.

Table 5-6
Relation between Site Quality and Return on Investment in Timber-Growing in Oregon's Coast Range.

	Present Net Worth at 5 percent	Wood Volume Yield: Final harvest plus commercial thinnings, cubic ft./acre
Site I	983	14,895
Site II	809	12,618
Site III	539	10,003

Source: J.H. Beuter and J.K. Handy, *Economic Guides to Reforestation for Different Ownerships*, Oregon State University, Forest Research Laboratory, Research Paper 23, November 1974, tables 38, 42, 46, and 54.

Site I—average height of dominant and codominant trees at age one hundred is 200 feet; Site II—average height is 170 feet; Site III—average height is 140 feet.

The areas where wood-growing is least feasible economically are often high-elevation regions where growth rates are low and roading costs are high. Establishing regeneration may be difficult, and erosion problems can be serious. These areas also tend to be most highly prized as wilderness, for their scenery, wildlife populations, and ecologically sensitive landscapes. Clawson and others have seen in this fact the possibility that the nation can have its future timber needs supplied by intensive timber management on the highly productive lands. It could then release large areas wholly or partially to other uses. As an example, Clawson estimated that intensive forestry on only 180 million acres could produce a total wood volume 22 percent greater than the 1970 growth level, with no reliance on the remaining part of the land base.[33] It has been argued, in fact, that the capital that would be invested in roads and management in high-elevation de facto wilderness lands would produce more wood over time if it were invested instead on more productive lands elsewhere. In a study of six sample national forests, the U.S. Forest Service found that significant wilderness reservations could be made while sustaining recent harvests. In general, however, the reinvestment of road costs avoided by not developing wilderness could not maintain enough timber output to compensate for 100 percent withdrawal of all roadless lands.[34]

Herrick has examined the impact of intensified management in the Northeast on the land required for meeting expected future demands.[35] In most states, he finds that intensive management would allow expected wood needs to be produced on a fraction of the existing commercial forest land (figure 5-1).

Current trends in intensive forestry, such as the use of heavy machinery and of planted monocultures, protected by herbicides and insecticides, may produce environmental impacts of concern. But there are many ways to boost forest output without heavy dependence on such techniques.

Using Wood More Efficiently

The evidence suggests, then, that the nation's timber needs can be grown on the most productive fraction of the forest resource, while large areas can be spared for other uses. But the management required will be costly, and the experts have predicted rising prices. In most cases, the higher prices will be required to make intensified management possible. Rising prices will stimulate a series of adjustments, which will reduce demand for timber below the level that would exist if today's real price levels persisted into the future. In some cases, these adjustments will help achieve other resource management goals, such as economizing on energy and aiding in stand regeneration.

Higher wood prices will induce landowners, processors, and consumers to use wood more efficiently. The following opportunities appear especially promising:

1. More complete utilization of logging residue. Forest Service experts estimate that 1.6 billion cubic feet of logging residues are created each year, principally in the old-growth Douglas fir forests of the Pacific Northwest. There are many reasons for improving utilization of this resource.[36]

2. More complete utilization of processing wastes. Despite great progress in this area, large volumes of plant residues remain unused. In most mills, bark is used for fuel or for charcoal, while even sawdust and planer mill shavings are utilized for paper or particleboard.[37] One study estimated that by 1980 an additional 4.7 billion cubic feet of currently wasted wood fiber should be economically and technically recoverable.[38]

3. Improved building design. Use of prefab trusses and precut components such as studs raises the efficiency of wood use. Replacement of sheathing using random-length boards with plywood has materially cut wood waste in building.

Policy measures for fostering these trends are poorly studied and untested. In addition, it should be assured that such policies do not merely result in the substitution of other materials for wood. Wood, in fact, has a number of environmentally desirable features—its renewability and biodegradeability are only two. Wood construction materials are considerably more energy-efficient than competing metals. As compared to wood, competing materials consumed the following amounts of energy for equivalent functional strength:

Aluminum framing, exterior walls	20 times as much as wood
Aluminum studs, interior walls	12 times as much as wood
Steel studs, interior walls	8 times as much as wood
Aluminum siding	5 times as much as wood
Brick siding	25 times as much as wood

These facts show that the overall environmental desirability of wood as a construction material deserves to be considered in the national debate over wildland policy.[39]

4. Expanded recycling. Studies show that a much higher paper recycling rate is possible in this country. Our recycling rate, for example, is about half the rate in Japan. Recycling will reduce virgin fiber demand.[40]

5. Nonwood substitutes. Making paper from agricultural residues is an attractive possibility, especially in the tropics.[41] Bagasse (sugarcane refining waste) is already used for building board in this country. Other substitutes, such as aluminum studs or plastic paper, appear to be steps in the wrong direction ecologically.

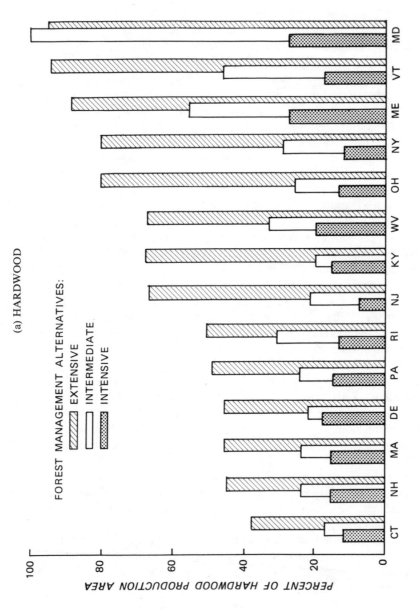

(a) HARDWOOD

Source: O. Herrick, *Impact of Alternative Timber Management Policies*, U.S. Department of Agriculture, U.S. Forest Service, Northeastern Forest Experiment Station, Research Paper NE-390, 1977.

Figure 5-1. Proportion of States' Commercial Forest Area Needed to Meet Timber Demands Projected at Rising Relative Prices, for Year 2000: (a) Hardwood (b) Softwood.

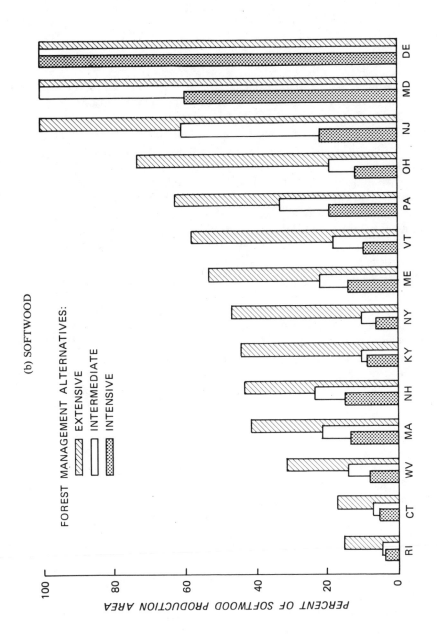

(b) SOFTWOOD

6. Eliminate unnecessary bleaching in paper-making. Production of unneeded whiteness causes significant fiber loss in bleached pulps.

Sensitive Backcountry Management

Decisions being faced today on about 26 million acres of commercial forest in the national forests, 400 million acres on BLM lands, and millions of acres in Alaska do not need to be faced in a black-and-white way. Analysis will undoubtedly show that sizable allocations of land to wilderness will be appropriate and justified, in providing the many benefits that arise from preserved wildlands.

The alternative to full wilderness designation need not be hydro dams, pine plantations, and copper mines. There is room for reasoned balancing of resource management goals with specific preservation needs. Over millions of acres of public land, there is wide scope for achieving goals for wildlife protection, watershed management, rangeland grazing, and limited timber production by carefully managing backcountry areas. These areas can produce a considerable amount of recreation in the forms of hiking, camping, fishing, and hunting and add to the backcountry experience for those unwilling or unable to hike into the alpine country within dedicated wilderness. The naturalistic management of forests on long rotations, with wide buffers near streams, and with restrictions on cutting in critical wildlife habitat and on slopes, can minimize the visual and ecological impact of logging. Restrictions such as these are being implemented generally on public forests, and they need only be tightened and adapted to high backcountry conditions. The use of highly intensive management systems in such areas would probably never be economically feasible anyway.[42]

Techniques for careful analysis of multiple-use trade-offs on an areawide basis are the only way to account for the changing values of different management approaches over time. Such techniques are now in rapid development, based on recent progress in the use of computer-based land management and planning models.[43] These models can be used to design economically sound programs of low-intensity management for backcountry areas.

On the 62.5 million acres of roadless lands reviewed in RARE-II, for example, 36 million acres of land could be devoted to nontimber purposes without affecting timber supply. This is 2.4 times the acreage of dedicated wilderness in the national forests as of April 1, 1978. One alternative discussed in the RARE-II DEIS would allocate 21 million acres to wilderness and an additional 19 million to study status but would reduce current programmed harvests by only 436 million board-feet.

At present, timber sales in high elevation regions of the central and southern Rockies and the Southwest earn negative net returns to the government, since timber sale preparation costs exceed the nominal stumpage revenues generated. Some critics, hoping in effect to force creation of additional wilderness, have urged that such deficit sales be stopped, since they are economically inefficient. In view of the dependence of area communities on forest products employment, and of the benefits to recreation and resource protection of the road systems financed by timber, such a conclusion may not be justified.

In sum, the case seems compelling for the creation of a land-use category intermediate between dedicated wilderness and the full-scale multiple use of the Standard Component. Such intermediate designations have in effect been used in the Sawtooth National Recreation Area and in designated management zones in areas such as the Boundary Waters Canoe Area, the Hells Canyon National Recreation Area, and the Alpine Lakes Wilderness. Sensitive designation of lightly managed backcountry units would allow the attainment of important preservation objectives but would permit limited production of timber from the same areas.

Summary

After decades of debate, only 5 percent of the nation's productive forest land was in wilderness by 1977. Production of timber is an important potential land use on much of the wildland that still awaits classification for use as wilderness, lightly managed backcountry, intensive resource management, or development. Sizable allocations of land to wilderness in national parks and wildlife refuges, on the public domain (BLM) lands, and in Alaska can be made with no effect on the national timber supply.

The Congress will decide the final allocation of these lands. In doing so, it should consider the following facts. First, much of the timberland at issue has low potential for yielding a return on investment in sustained-yield timber-growing. Such areas should be explicitly identified. Second, the commitment of all remaining unroaded forest to wilderness is probably not necessary to adequately fulfill the mandate for preservation. Third, in the case of the national forests, the impact of wilderness designation of all the RARE-II lands would be significant, especially if done all at once and with no offsetting mitigating measures. Fourth, a creative program of backcountry management can provide substantial protection for wildland values while still allowing controlled wood production, resource protection, wildlife habitat improvement, and developed recreation. Finally, a range of mitigating measures exist to reduce the impact of large timber supply reductions on local communities.

Notes

1. For detailed treatment of wood use in the U.S. economy, see National Research Council, Committee on Renewable Resources as Industrial Materials, *Renewable Resources as Industrial Materials* (Washington: National Academy of Sciences, 1976), p. 155 and, generally, chap. 5.

2. U.S. Department of Agriculture, U.S. Forest Service, *Outlook for Timber in the United States* (Washington, D.C.: U.S. Government Printing Office, 1973). Preliminary data for 1977 are released in U.S. Department of Agriculture, U.S. Forest Service, *Forest Statistics of the U.S. 1977* (Washington, D.C.: U.S. Government Printing Office, 1978).

3. H.T. Frey and H.W. Dill, *Land Use Changes in the Southern Mississippi Alluvial Valley, 1950-1969,* U.S. Department of Agriculture, Economic Research Service, Agricultural Economics Report 215, 1971; also, L.C. Irland, "Determining the Value of Forests . . . Southern Bottomland Hardwoods," in A.C. Main, ed., *Economics of Southern Forest Resources Management* (Baton Route, La.: School of Forestry and Wildlife Management, 1976), pp. 17-35.

4. U.S. Department of Agriculture, U.S. Forest Service, *Timber Resources for America's Future* (Washington, D.C.: U.S. Government Printing Office, 1953). A comprehensive listing of previous reports is found at p. 5. For more recent reports, see U.S. Department of Agriculture, U.S. Forest Service, *The Nation's Renewable Resources—An Assessment, 1975* Forest Resources Report 21, (Washington, D.C.: U.S. Government Printing Office, June 1977), p. 143.

5. U.S. Department of Agriculture, *Outlook for Timber,* p. 16.

6. L.C. Irland, *Is Timber Scarce?* Bulletin no. 83 (New Haven, Conn.: Yale School of Forestry and Environmental Studies, 1974), chaps. 4, 5.

7. V.K. Smith, "Measuring Natural Resource Scarcity, Theory and Practice," *Journal of Environmental Economics and Management* 5, (1978): 150-171.

8. Irland, *Is Timber Scarce?,* chap. 6.

9. U.S. Congress, Senate, Committee on Banking, Housing, and Urban Affairs, *Hearings on Lumber Prices,* 95th Congress, 1st Session, October 21, 1977. Also, Executive Office of the President, Council on Wage and Price Stability, *Lumber Prices and the Lumber Products Industry,* Washington, D.C., October 1977.

10. L.C. Irland, "Forest Products and the National Housing Goals," *Forest Products Journal* 24 (February 1974): 12-17; see also U.S. Department of Housing and Urban Development, *Final Report of Task Force on Housing Costs,* Washington, D.C., May 1978.

11. For further discussion on foreign trade, see U.S. Department of Agriculture, *Outlook for Timber,* chap. 4; J. Zivnuska, "Research in International Forest Economics," in Marion Clawson, ed., *Research in Forest Economics and Policy* (Washington, D.C.: Resources for the Future, 1977). Also, I. Holland, "Foreign Trade in Timber Products," in *Report of the President's Advisory Panel on Timber and the Environment* (Washington, D.C., 1973), and papers by Stone and Dickerhoof, Stone and Saeman, Holland, and Austin in *Forest Products Journal,* October 1977.

12. U.S. Department of Agriculture, *Nation's Renewable Resources,* p. 168.

13. S.H. Spurr and H.J. Vaux, "Timber: Biological and Economic Potential," in P.H. Abelson and A.L. Hammond, eds., *Materials: Renewable and Nonrenewable Resources* (Washington, D.C.: American Association for the Advancement of Science, 1976), pp. 158-162.

14. U.S. Department of Agriculture, *Nation's Renewable Resources,* p. 143ff. Also, L. Fischman, "Future Demand for U.S. Forest Resources," in M. Clawson, ed., *Forest Policy for the Future* (Washington, D.C.: Resources for the Future, 1974), pp. 21-86, and J.L. Keays, "Projection of World Demand and Supply for Wood in 2000," *TAPPI* 58 (November 1975): 90-95.

15. See, generally, U.S. Department of Agriculture, *Nation's Renewable Resources,* p. 143ff. R. Marty, "Softwood Sawtimber Supply and Demand Projections," in *President's Advisory Panel.*

16. These issues have occasioned considerable philosophizing. See, for example, papers by Row and by Duerr in F.J. Convery and C.W. Ralston, *Forestry and Long-Range Planning* (Durham, N.C.: Duke University School of Forestry and Environmental Studies, May 1977); C. Row, "Balancing Supplies and Demands," in M. Clawson, ed., *Research in Forest Economics and Forest Policy,* Research Paper R-3 (Washington, D.C.: Resources for the Future, 1977), pp. 81-158; R.S. Manthy, "Scarcity, Renewability, and Forest Policy," *Journal of Forestry* 75 (April 1977): pp. 201-205; and L.C. Irland, *Is Timber Scarce?*

17. Wildland Research Center, *Wilderness and Recreation,* Outdoor Recreation Resources Review Commission, Report 3 (Washington, D.C.: U.S. Government Printing Office, 1963) p. 76.

18. L.C. Merriam, "The Bob Marshall Wilderness Area of Montana—Some Socio-Economic Considerations," *Journal of Forestry* 62 (November 1964): 789-795.

19. U.S. Forest Service data, quoted in W.S. Bromley, *The Withdrawal of Commercial Forest Land from the Production of Timber* (New York: Fourdrinier Kraft Board Institute, August 1976).

20. American Forest Institute, *Wood and Wilderness—Can the National Forests Supply Both?* (Washington, D.C., April 1978); National

Forest Products Association, *Wilderness Withdrawals and Timber Supply* (Washington, D.C., January 16, 1978). See also American Forest Products Industries, Inc., *Government Land Acquisition* (Washington, D.C., 1964).

21. Spurr and Vaux, "Timber: Biological and Economic Potential"; and J. Zivnuska, "Forestry Investments for Multiple Uses among Multiple Ownership Types," in M. Clawson, *Forest Policy for the Future.*

22. U.S. Department of Agriculture, U.S. Forest Service, DEIS, *Roadless Area Review and Evaluation,* (Washington, D.C., 1978).

23. U.S. Congress, Senate, *Eastern Wilderness Areas Act of 1974* (S. Rept. 93-803, Cal. No. 771), p. 30.

24. U.S. Forest Service, DEIS, *Roadless Area Review and Evaluation,* (Washington, D.C., 1978).

25. "The Monongahela Decision": *Izaak Walton League* v. *Butz,* 367 F-Supp. 422 (ND W. Va., 1973). Sustained on appeal, *Izaak Walton League* v. *Butz,* 522 F. 2d, (4th Cir. 1975).

26. National Forest Management Act of 1976, PL94-588.

27. D.M. Adams, *Effects of National Forest Timber Harvest on Softwood Stumpage, Timber, and Plywood Markets,* Research Bulletin 15, (Corvallis, Oreg.: Oregon State University School of Forestry, 1977).

28. U.S. Department of Commerce, Bureau of Domestic Commerce, *Study of the Expected Impact on the Forest Products Industries of Assumed Nationwide Application of the Monongahela-Tongass Court Decisions,* 1976. A staff study, summarizing contract analyses by Data Resources, Inc. (DRI). See also a DRI study of the impact of RARE-II: C.E. Buchwalter, "RARE II: The Economic Effects of U.S. Softwood Supply Restrictions," National Forest Products Assn. Washington, D.C., August 1978.

29. The U.S. Forest Service analysis is based on detailed case studies of management intensification opportunities in the Northeast, Southeast, North Central, and Pacific Coast regions. See U.S. Department of Agriculture, *Outlook for Timber,* pp. 99-123. The price effects are reported in W. McKillop, *Economic Impacts of an Intensified Timber Management Program,* U. S. Forest Service Research Paper WO-23, Washington, D.C., 1974. For an alternative analysis, see M. Clawson, "Conflicts, Strategies, and Possibilities for Consensus in Forest Land Use and Management," in Clawson, *Forest Policy for the Future,* p. 159. At pp. 164-168, he presents data on the costs of achieving additional timber output through management intensification in the Pacific Northwest and the South.

30. Washington Department of Natural Resources, *Washington Forest Productivity Study,* Phase I Report, Olympia, Wash., (June 1975); S.G. Boyce, "How to Double the Harvest of Loblolly and Slash Pine Timber," *Journal of Forestry* 73 (December 1975): 761. For other examples, see S.G. Boyce, *Biological Potential for the Slash Pine*

Ecosystem, U.S. Forest Service, Southeastern Forest Experiment Station, Research Paper SE-141, Washington, D.C., October 1975; R. Gedney, D. Oswald, and R.D. Fight, *Two Timber Supply Projections in the Pacific Coast States,* U.S. Forest Service, Pacific Northwest Forest and Range Experiment Station, Resource Bulletin PNW-60, 1975; J.H. Beuter, K.N. Johnson, and H.L. Scheurman, *Timber for Oregon's Tomorrow,* Research Bulletin 19 (Corvallis, Oreg.: Oregon State University, School of Forestry, January 1976). See also, U.S. General Accounting Office, *Critique of Studies of Timber Scarcities in the Pacific Northwest* (Washington, D.C.: U.S. Government Printing Office, 1978).

31. H.J. Vaux, "Timber Resource Prospects," in W.A. Duerr, ed., *Timber: Problems, Prospects, Policies* (Ames, Iowa: Iowa State, 1973), p. 95; also H.J. Vaux, "How Much Land Do We Need for Timber Growing?" *Journal of Forestry* 71 (July 1973): 399.

32. S.B. Hutchison et al., *Timber Management Issues on Utah's North Slope,* U.S. Forest Service, Intermountain Forest and Range Experiment Station, Research Paper INT-23, 1965.

33. Clawson, *Research in Forest Economics;* and M. Clawson, *Forests: For Whom and For What?* (Baltimore: Johns Hopkins Press, 1976).

34. R.D. Fight et al., *Roadless Area—Intensive Management Tradeoffs on Western National Forests,* U.S. Forest Service, Washington, D.C., Revised October 1978.

35. Owen W. Herrick, *Impact of Alternative Timber Management Policies on Availability of Forest Land in the Northeast,* U.S. Forest Service, Northeastern Forest Experiment Station, Research Paper NE-390, 1977.

36. U.S. Department of Agriculture, U.S. Forest Service, *Report of the Close Timber Utilization Committee,* Washington, D.C., 1972; H.E. Young, "The Enormous Potential of the Forests," *Journal of Forestry* 73 (1975); E.C. Jahn, and S.B. Preston, "Timber: More Effective Utilization," in Abelson and Hammond, *Materials: Renewable and Nonrenewable Resources;* and J. Grantham, *Status of Timber Utilization on the Pacific Coast,* U.S. Forest Service, Pacific Northwest Forest and Range Experiment Station, General Technical Report PNW-29, 1974. H.G. Wahlgren and T.H. Ellis, "Potential Resource Availability with Whole-Tree Utilization," *TAPPI* 61 (November 1978): 37-39; P. Koch, "Five New Machines and Six Products Can Triple Commodity Recovery from Southern Forests," *Journal of Forestry* 76 (December 1978): 767-772.

37. Current product recovery from logs is well summarized by T.D. Fahey and R.O. Woodfin, Jr. in "The Cubics are Coming: Predicting Product Recovery from Cubic Volume," *Journal of Forestry* 76 (November 1976): 739-743. See also the paper by J. Saeman in *Report of the*

President's Advisory Panel on Timber and the Environment (Washington, D.C.: U.S. Government Printing Office, 1973); H.E. Young, "Forest Biomass Inventory: The Basis for Complete Tree Utilization," *Forest Products Journal* 28 (May 1978): 38-41; Environmental advantages of wood as a raw material are reviewed in National Academy of Sciences, *Renewable Resources for Industrial Materials,* report of Committee on Renewable Resources for Industrial Materials (Washington, D.C., 1976).

38. This is a huge subject. See, for an introduction, U.S. Environmental Protection Agency, *Fourth Report to Congress, Resource Recovery and Waste Reduction,* (Washington, D.C., 1977), especially chap. 2 and appendix B.

39. L.E. Lassen and D. Hair, "Potential Gains in Wood Supplies through Improved Utilization," *Journal of Forestry* 68 (July 1970): 404.

40. National Academy of Sciences, *Renewable Resources for Industrial Materials,* (Washington, D.C.: 1976), p. 154.
(Washington, D.C.: National Academy of Sciences, 1976), p. 154.

41. J.E. Atchison, "Agricultural Residues and Other Nonwood Fibers," *in* P. Abelson and A. Hammond, *Materials:* Renewable and Nonrenewable Resources.

42. This suggestion has been previously made by R.C. Lucas, in "Wilderness, A Management Framework," *Journal Soil and Water Conservation* 28 (July-August 1973), pp. 150-154.

43. An example for hardwood forest management in Stephen G. Boyce, *Management of Eastern Hardwood Forests for Multiple Benefits (DYNAST-MB)* U.S. Forest Service Research Paper SE-168, July 1977. Also summarized in Robert C. Biesterfeldt and Stephen G. Boyce, "Systematic Approach to Multiple-Use Management," *Journal of Forestry* 76 (June 1978): 342-345. See also, Steven Calish, Roger D. Fight, and Dennis E. Teeguarden, "How Do Nontimber Values Affect Douglas-fir Rotations?" *Journal of Forestry* 76 (April 1978): 217-221; Bruce Benninghoff and Coryell Ohlander, "Integrating Timber Harvest Scheduling Economics and Environmental Quality," *Journal of Forestry* 76 (June 1978): 348-351.

6

Wilderness and Minerals, Recreation, and Water

Forest products are only one of the important economic services provided by wildlands. Frequently in controversy has been the role of wild areas in providing minerals, recreation, and water. For minerals, exploration and development by conventional methods are clearly inconsistent with wilderness. In some cases, however, wilderness may have a more complex relation to society's supply of recreation opportunities or fresh water.

Mineral Resources

We have seen that mineral development on wilderness lands was so powerfully defended by mining interests that the Wilderness Act permitted mineral exploration and mining in wilderness—exploration until 1983 and production on valid claims at any time.

Mining can have severe environmental impacts, resulting from surface disturbance, leaching of toxic minerals into waterways, sedimentation, air and noise pollution, and disruption of wildlife migration.[1] The potential distruption of wild environments, and likely off-site effects, have produced considerable scientific, legislative, and administrative effort to ameliorate the impacts. Finally, wilderness designation has often been sought as a means of blocking mining altogether. Although the Wilderness Act does not bar mining, wilderness designation undoubtedly provides an additional barrier to mineral development (case 6-1).

Current Resources

Although much has been made of the nation's need for minerals and of the potential losses that would result from banning mineral exploration in wilderness, the record shows that few designated wilderness areas have contained significant mineral deposits. The Wildland Research Center gathered Bureau of Mines data for thirty-two national forest wilderness and primitive areas until 1960. They found siginificant mineral production in only five areas (High Sierra, Idaho Primitive Area, San Juan, Gila, and Mazatzal). Forest Service data for 1960 showed 225 patents covering about 11,000 acres, plus almost 7500 mining claims covering 140,000 acres.[2] An updating of this survey is badly needed.

The required mineral surveys under the Forest Service's primitive area studies have generated considerable information on the mineral resources of those lands. The resulting reports show a uniform pattern—most areas have been explored in the past but few patents or claims resulted. Few areas showed evidence of significant mineralization on examination of their geologic features. Few areas had ever produced significant mineral output.

A sizable resource of energy and other minerals is found, however, on the lands now being discussed for wilderness preservation. In the RARE-II lands, for example, eighty-one areas have existing fields of oil, gas, coal, or uranium, and many others have potential occurrences of these and other minerals (table 6-1). The areas of Bureau of Land Management land to be reviewed for wilderness undoubtedly will include mineral lands. In the debate over preservation in Alaska, mineral potential and access for pipeline and transportation corridors are major issues. In the proposals embodied in H R 39, substantial consideration was given to providing access to major known mineral deposits.

Economic Pressures

The fact that few minerals have been found in existing wilderness should not be a comfort to those interested in preserving wilderness. There are two reasons: First, very little of the land surface of the nation has ever been explored for minerals using sophisticated geophysical methods. Techniques such as geomagnetic prospecting, seismic shots, and satellite imagery are used to select promising targets for expensive core-drilling. As geological knowledge increases and exploration techniques improve, we can expect more mineral deposits to be discovered in remote areas. Second, debates over mineral access have slowed progress in designating wilderness areas and will continue to do so.

Additional pressure on wilderness mineral sources can be expected from

Table 6-1
Mineral Values on RARE-II Lands

Item	Number of Roadless Areas
Energy potential	588
Proven or producing mines	137
Producing fields, oil, gas, coal, or uranium	81
High potential for critical minerals	461
High potential for oil, gas, coal, or uranium	398

Source: U.S. Forest Service, RARE-II Draft Environmental Statement (Washington, D.C.: 1978) p. 17.

the same source—technological change—that was cited earlier as providing a way out of the Malthusian prospect. Cumulative technological change allows industry to extract useful products from ores of lower and lower grade. This process helps make recoverable many deposits that were not economic at previous cost/price relationships. For example, miners are now reworking old mine tailings to recover metals in rocks that were discarded as valueless a half-century ago. Mines long forgotten are being reopened.[3] Technological change, therefore, is a double-edged sword for wilderness. It provides society with alternative sources of needed raw materials. But it also increases the economic pressure to discover and extract minerals from wilderness areas.

These forces are generating a number of severe land use controversies in wild areas. For example:

1. In the 425,000-acre Glacier Peak Wilderness (Washington), Kennecott Copper Corporation holds extensive claims and plans to develop a large copper deposit.[4] Exploration has been conducted since 1937; potential production is estimated at 12,000 to 15,000 tons of copper yearly.[5]
2. In Oregon's Three Sisters Wilderness, about 1500 acres of claims are held by the U.S. Pumice Company for mining rock pumice. The claims include a section of the Pacific Crest National Scenic Trail.[6]
3. In the White Cloud Peaks in Idaho, a major molybdenum deposit is under consideration for development.[7]
4. Lawsuits have resulted from proposed mineral developments in the Boundary Waters Canoe Area in Minnesota. This area is one-third underlain by privately held mineral rights.[8]
5. Numerous active and proposed mineral developments affect remote national forest areas of potential wilderness quality: Beartooth Mountains, Montana (copper-nickel); Monongahela National Forest (coal); Ocala National Forest (oil and gas); Glacier National Park region (oil and gas); Osceola National Forest (phosphate); Northern Rocky Mountain Overthrust Belt (oil and gas).[9]
6. Whereas most national parks are not open to mining, five units of the park system contain claims that can legally be developed. Current mining of borates in Death Valley National Monument has generated considerable controversy. In 1976, Congress passed a law limiting further development of valid claims in six national park units.[10]

Minerals Policy

Access to federal lands for mineral exploration and development is governed by the general mining laws and their implementing regulations.[11]

The complex ownership structure of mineral rights can hinder land managers. There are specific areas such as national parks that are usually withdrawn from mining, and under large areas of privately owned lands, the federal government holds mineral rights. Conversely, there are significant acreages of federal land under which private parties hold mineral rights (generally on acquired lands in the eastern national forests). The laws provide two major modes of access to federal mineral resources: location under the General Mining Law of 1872 for hardrock minerals and leasing under the Mineral Leasing Act of 1920. Other authorities, applicable in special situations, will not be considered here.[12]

For minerals locatable under the 1872 law, a prospector may file a claim that entitles him to extract minerals from the public land. Surface disturbances are subject to reasonable regulation by the Forest Service and the BLM but development cannot be denied to a claimant holding a valid claim. The claimant is charged no rents or royalties for such use of federal land but is subject to diligence requirements. If the claimant decides to "go to patent" and obtain title to the mineral deposit and surface rights, he may do so for a modest per-acre fee.[13] For minerals leasable under the 1920 Act (principally coal, oil and gas, and oil shale), the BLM administers leasing on all federal lands, while the administering agency controls surface resource use. Lessees must pay annual rents, royalties on production, and lease bonuses on competitive sales.

Forest Service regulations on mining in wilderness were issued after passage of the Wilderness Act.[14] The regulations provide for access to claims, for notice to the Forest Service by claimants locating claims in wilderness, and for protection of surface resources. Persons desiring to prospect within Wilderness Areas must obtain Forest Service approval if they desire to use motorized vehicles. Since large areas of national forest land are considered to be de facto wilderness yet are outside designated wilderness, the regulations applied to nonwilderness lands are important as well. Forest Service concern with rising mineral activity was expressed in a memo to forest supervisors by Region 6 Assistant Regional Forester Leisz: "We believe that in this day of enlightenment there is no excuse for an individual through his ignorance of mining and prospecting practices to do unwarranted damage to valuable surface resources . . ."[15] The memo outlined recent cases giving the Forest Service leverage in protecting surface resources from mining disturbances. In 1973 the Forest Service issued regulations dealing with surface uses under the mining laws. The regulations were completed in 1974.[16] The principal requirement of these regulations is that operators file in advance a plan of operations to be approved by the Forest Service and modified as necessary to protect surface resources to the maximum extent consistent with the needs of the mining operation.

To improve methods of planning mining operations and to develop more effective reclamation practices, the Forest Service and BLM are jointly conducting a surface environment and mining (SEAM) program. The program is especially concerned with improving reclamation methods for disturbed areas and spoil banks in areas of low rainfall or otherwise harsh conditions.

Future needs for minerals, oil, and gas will continue to conflict with the requirements of preservation. Each individual situation will have to be judged on its own merits, in terms of the significance of the area affected, the alternative sources of the mineral involved, and reclamation opportunities. Resolving these questions will challenge resource managers, the public, and the Congress for generations to come.

Recreation

Wilderness areas are highly valued for hiking, hunting, and cross-country skiing, and recreational users have been the leading advocates of preservation. At times other recreationists such as downhill skiers and snowmobilers have opposed wilderness designation for particular areas. The RARE-II areas (62.5 million acres) provided 9 percent of total national forest system recreation use in 1977. The RARE-II study provided estimates of the potential motorized and developed recreation that would be foregone by full wilderness designation of the RARE-II areas.[17] In this section, social and economic characteristics of wilderness users are reviewed.

Recreational users of wilderness areas are a small proportion of the total population, and wilderness accounts for only a small portion of total outdoor recreation activity days in a typical summer. In the summer of 1972, the top five activities were picnicking, sightseeing, driving for pleasure, walking for pleasure, and outdoor swimming, not in pools. These pursuits accounted for an estimated 2.2 billion activity-days in that summer. In contrast, hiking, remote camping, and canoeing, not all of which actually occur in wilderness environments, totalled 120 million activity-days. The top five activities were enjoyed by 34 to 47 percent of the U.S. population in 1972, while hiking, canoeing and remote camping attracted 5 percent, 3 percent, and 5 percent each.[18]

With increased incomes, improved opportunities for effective use of leisure, improved transportation, and expanded facilities, all classes of outdoor recreation use have grown rapidly, and experts expect growth to continue. Past growth in activity has included the new users attracted to particular activities as well as increased participation by existing users.

Recreation participation varies by age group. Significant differences in participation are especially evident for wildland recreation activities (table 6-2). For remote camping, canoeing, and off-road motorcycling, rates are

Table 6-2
Age and Participation in Wildland Recreation
(*percentage of population 12 years and over*)

Activity	Age Class					
	12-17	*18-24*	*25-44*	*45-64*	*65+*	*Total*
Remote camping	8.2	6.9	6.3	2.4	0.3	5.0
Canoeing	4.4	4.9	3.5	1.2	0.6	4.0
Fishing	31.3	26.7	28.9	18.3	10.5	24.0
Hunting	15.0	18.0	14.0	9.0	4.0	12.0
Hiking with pack, mountain or rock climbing	12.7	8.4	5.2	2.1	0.3	5.0
Riding motorcycles off road	10.4	8.9	4.5	1.0	0.3	5.0

Source: T.C. Marcin and D.W. Lime, "Our Changing Population Structure: What Will It Mean for Future Outdoor Recreation Use?" in J.M. Hughes and R.D. Lloyd, eds., *Outdoor Recreation—Advances in Application of Economics*, U.S. Department of Agriculture, U.S. Forest Service, General Technical Report WO-2, March 1977, pp. 42-53.

Note: Based on combining data from 1965 and 1972.

above the average for age groups younger than 24 years; for fishing, hunting, and hiking, participation rates remain high in the 25-44 age group. Based on national data and studies in the Pacific northwest, Burch has developed a life cycle hypothesis of camping preferences. He defined three types of camping: easy-access or auto camping, combination camping (where users camp at developed campgrounds and take day hikes or short overnight excursions), and remote camping. He argues that participation in these camping types is affected by the family life cycle—marital status, age, presence of children: ". . . combination camping families represent the early stages of the family life cycle, easy-access camping families represent middle and post-retirement stages, and remote camping families represent those just beginning their families and in the contracting phase of the family life cycle."[19] If this holds true more generally for wilderness recreation, it could mean significant changes in use patterns as household formation and family patterns change in the future.

The life-cycle approach emphasizes the need to view past and future recreation trends in the context of changing demographic trends and individual attitudes. Extending this approach raises important questions. Many of the wildland recreation activities important to wilderness managers experienced rapid growth due to increasing numbers of young people—the post-World War II "baby-boom" age class. At the same time, the participation rate of this age class increased due to increased popularity of low-cost and convenient equipment. Will these individuals continue to visit wilderness areas and wild rivers as they grow older and their family circumstances change, or will their use patterns resemble those of today's older age groups?[20]

Wildland recreationists tend to be more highly educated and to earn more than the average for the U.S. population (tables 6-3 and 6-4). For example, a 1972 survey showed that 9 percent of remote campers had family incomes exceeding $25,000, whereas 12 percent of hikers and 9 percent of canoeists had equally high incomes. This contrasts with only 5.4 percent of the U.S. population in that year. Use patterns differed by income class. The annual activity days per participant were highest in the lower income classes for remote camping, whereas the reverse was true for hiking and canoeing (table 6-3). This pattern may be partially explained by the general relation of income to age and the availability of longer spans of effective leisure to younger individuals. Those with the most money have the least time to enjoy it. Also involved, no doubt, are family life-cycle changes and a decline in zest for wilderness camping with age.

Wilderness recreationists must not only be great hikers, they must also be great drivers. As table 6-4 shows, more than half of the users in the areas surveyed had travelled more than 250 miles to the area.

Whereas it is true that wilderness users are predominantly from higher-income groups, this is also true generally for all classes of outdoor recreation. Lower-income groups are underrepresented in most major types of outdoor recreation. Stankey has argued that the high incidence of high-income individuals among wilderness recreationists is not due to the cost of wilderness camping or to the use of wilderness areas by persons enjoying a greater amount of leisure than the average for the nation.[21] It is simply a matter of preferences. Further, as Burch points out, "all forest recreation groups are minorities. . . . a 'majority' ethos is an irrelevant factor in the allocations of public land for different recreational experiences."[22]

Water Resources

Existing wilderness areas are mostly in mountainous areas. These regions catch the snowfall that provides most of the surface water supply for nearby farms and cities. In the western states, by reason of their topography, they also include excellent reservoir sites. In the arid regions, steep canyons provide grand scenery and remote environments but at the same time make the best dam sites. These facts have led to conflict over water development between wilderness advocates and various groups intent on developing water resources. The U.S. Department of the Interior's Westwide Study identified twenty-two major stream reaches on which major conflicts are imminent.[23]

Table 6-3
Participation in Wildland Recreation by Family Income, Summer 1972

Family Income (dollars)	Camping in Remote Areas		Hiking with a pack; mountain- and rock-climbing		Canoeing		Percentage of U.S. population 12 years and over
	Percentage of Participants	Activity-days/participant	Percentage of Participants	Activity-days/participant	Percentage of Participants	Activity-days/participant	
Under 5,999	17	8.2	16	4.7	14	2.9	32.6
6,000-9,999	29	9.4	28	3.2	29	4.0	23.8
10,000-14,999	31	7.1	32	7.1	29	3.5	22.6
15,000-24,999	14	6.5	12	3.2	19	2.8	15.8
25,000+	9	4.6	12	8.1	9	8.3	5.4

Source: Robert C. Lewis, "Policy Formation and Planning for Outdoor Recreation Facilities," in J.M. Hughes and R.D. Lloyd, eds., *Outdoor Recreation—Advances in Applications for Economics*, U.S. Department of Agriculture, U.S. Forest Service General Technical Report WO-2, March 1977.

Note: Income classes are condensed from Lewis's table. Activity-days are the average of classes where condensed.

Table 6-4
Wilderness-User Characteristics
(*in percents for each category*)

	Adirondacks		Appalachian Trail Southern National Forests		Mount Marcy		Boundary Waters Canoe Area	High Sierra	U.S. Average
Occupation	Professional	54.6	Professional-Technical	60.3	Professional, Semi-professional	50	36	48	49
	Nonprofessional	29.6	Business	16.7	Self-employed, white-collar, farm	35	45	31	38
	Student[a]	15.8	Housewife	11.7	Wage-earner	8	17	16	10
			Skilled, nonskilled	6.2	Retired	1	1	6	2
			Retired/other	5.1	Student	20	13	6	
Income	5,000	10.1	5,000	9.7	5,000	33	27	9	
	5-9,999	34.3	5-9,999	24.07	5-5,999	39	33	44	
	10-14,999	37.4	10-14,999	22.5	10-19,999	26	34	34	
	15,000+	18.2	15-19,999	27.0	20,000+	3	6	12	
			20,000+	16.8					
Age	21	20.8	16-18	20.9	19-29	40	36	21	29
	21-29	27.5	19-24	27.4	30-49	48	54	59	54
	30-39	18.1	25-34	19.8	50+	12	10	20	17
	40-49	18.1	35-44	16.1					
	50+	15.5	45-54	9.2					
			55+	6.6					
Miles travelled	0-100					8	6	4	
	101-250					32	7	17	
	251-500					48	31	75	
	501+					12	56	4	

Source: E.L. Shafer and J. Mietz, "Aesthetic and Emotiona Experiences Rate High with Northeast Wilderness Hikers," *Environment and Behavior* 1 (December 1969): 187-197; Judith Buckley Murray, *Appalachian Trail Users in the Southern National Forests*, U.S. Department of Agriculture, U.S. Forest Service Research Paper SE-116, July 1974; Wildland Research Center, *Wilderness and Recreation—A Report on Resources, Values, and Problems*, ORPPC Study Report no. 3 (Washington, D.C.: U.S. Government Printing Office, 1962), p. 130.

[a]Student category overlaps with others where the students had jobs.

Today, there are major impoundments in Yosemite, Glacier, North Cascades, and Grand Teton National parks. In their inventory of federal wilderness areas larger than 100,000 acres, the Wildland Research Center found seventy-three dams or other structures within or influencing the inventoried areas. There were an additional twenty-two potential dam sites on national park lands, and there were twenty-five Federal Power Commission dam site reservations totaling nearly 600,000 acres within national forest wilderness.[24] These sites can be developed if a presidential finding is made that it is essential to the national interest.[25]

Water experts have expressed concern that wilderness management restrictions may restrict the use of permanent rain gages and stream-gaging weirs for measurement of precipitation and stream flow. Snow pack measurement on permanent snow-courses would not be restricted, although mechanized access would be. In addition, vegetation manipulation, snow fences, or other steps to increase water yields, alter the seasonal pattern of run-off, or reduce avalanche hazard would not be permitted.[26]

Protecting wildlands is a prime means of protecting water quality. High-quality water for agriculture, municipal and industrial uses, and fish and wildlife habitat is one of the most important services of wildland environments. The most serious potential disturbances of water quality are mining, road construction, and residential and commercial development. In addition, poorly managed livestock grazing can damage water quality. Forest management practices such as herbicide- and pesticide-spraying, logging on steep slopes without regard to drainages, and fire-fighting can degrade water quality. Felling trees, of itself, harms water quality little, although overstory removal can produce a temporary rise in nutrient levels in streams and can cause streamwater temperatures to rise. Skidding logs may scarify soil and disrupt organic matter, allowing erosion. In some areas, steep slopes are anchored by tree roots and may be subject to mass wasting after logging. In most cases, however, proper road construction and logging practices can minimize damage to water quality.[27]

In protecting water quality for municipal uses, forested watersheds are especially important. A U.S. Forest Service tabulation showed that eighteen major cities around the nation depend heavily on national forest lands for watershed protection.[28] In New England and elsewhere, many cities own large areas of forest land for the purpose of protecting water quality. Since recreation may degrade water quality (this has been hotly debated), some cities bar all kinds of recreation from their watersheds, although most permit logging.[29] In some instances, acts of Congress dedicate large areas of national forest land exclusively to watershed protection for the benefit of individual cities.

A strong drive to develop domestic energy sources has raised severe conflicts between energy development and wildland preservation, especially in the western states. Potential damage to water quality, destruction of acquifers, consumptive use of water in energy conversion or power generation, and possible water export through coal slurry pipelines have been highly controversial.[30]

Since the mid-fifties, it has been known that vast oil shale deposits exist in this region and that large quantities of water would be needed to process the shale into synthetic crude oil.[31] This fact has been a significant spur to water development in the Upper Colorado Basin and has delayed moves to include the Upper Green River in the Wild and Scenic River System. In the Flattops Primitive Area in the White River National Forest, a large area on the South Fork of the White River was removed from widlerness proposals to prevent conflict with proposed dam sites on that stream. The water stored in the reservoirs would supply the oil shale industry. Elsewhere in Colorado, the Denver Water Supply Board has opposed conservationist proposals for the Gore Range-Eagles Nest Wilderness. The largest proposals under consideration would interfere with the Board's plans for reservoirs and aqueducts in the area.[32]

A more subtle form of environmental change—weather modification— is now under study for augmenting water supplies in the arid Intermountain West. Despite objections from the Park Service and Forest Service, the Bureau of Reclamation intends to pursue its Project Skywater pilot studies over wilderness areas.[33] The Bureau estimates that weather modification could increase water supplies by 4 to 5 percent in the western states outside of the Columbia Basin.[34]

Overview

Dedication of wildland to wilderness produces difficult choices about the role of specific land areas in production of minerals, recreation, and water. The issues involve local and national interests, questions of quality and quantity, and serious problems of state-federal cooperation. Too often, wilderness classification is seen as a simple way to attempt to bar an unwanted development. In such cases, all-or-nothing alternatives seem to dominate the debate. Decision-makers may find that no amount of analysis can yield a clear answer and that important long-term options—in favor of development or preservation—are being foreclosed prematurely.

Case 6-1. Coal and Wilderness in Appalachia

In southeastern Kentucky's mountainous Daniel Boone National Forest lies a quiet valley drained by Beaver Creek. This is coal country, in the region where subsurface mineral rights are commonly owned by parties other than the owners of the land surface. When national forests were created in this area, large areas of surface rights were purchased, and the mineral rights remained in private hands. Beaver Creek was purchased by the federal government in 1937.[a]

The Eastern Wilderness Areas Act designated a 4,780 acre Beaver Creek Wilderness in this valley. One year later, the Greenwood Land and Mining Company, which claims the mineral rights in the area, submitted to the U.S. Forest Service a proposed prospecting plan. The Forest Service found that most of the proposed prospecting sites were acceptable on environmental grounds alone but that such prospecting and further development would be inconsistent with the Wilderness Act. When the Forest Service refused to allow the prospecting to be conducted, Greenwood sued the agency, arguing that the Forest Service lacks authority to prevent its planned prospecting activities.[b] *The Forest Service proposes to acquire the mineral rights.*

Conflicts between the government, as steward of the surface resources, and private mineral owners desiring to develop their properties are potentially significant in eastern wilderness. For example, the nineteen instant areas proposed in Senate 3433 of 1974 (which ultimately became the Eastern Wilderness Areas Act) affected private mineral holdings in eight instances, most importantly in West Virginia's Otter Creek area.[c] *In the nearby Dolly Sods area, the Nature Conservancy raised funds to acquire coal rights to prevent their development. The rights were later purchased by the government. In the RARE-II inventory, the states of West Virginia, Pennsylvania, Vermont, and New Hampshire contained fifty-three inventoried roadless areas. Of these, eighteen private mineral rights, worth an estimated $33 million.*[d]

The Forest Service will find itself for years considering claims for development of known or suspected mineral deposits in eastern wilderness areas. In some instances, the costs of purchasing privately held mineral rights will be so high as to make some of these areas the most expensive pieces of real estate, on a per-acre basis, in the national wilderness preservation system (NWPS). Inevitably, the question will be raised of whether greater wilderness benefits could not be obtained by including in the NWPS areas requiring lower dollar outlays per acre. On the other hand, prevention of mining in many of these areas will provide significant benefits in preserving water quality, recreation, and fish and wildlife habitat.

---

[a]W.E. Shands and R.G. Healy, *The Lands Nobody Wanted* (Washington, D.C.: Conservation Foundation, 1977), p. 208ff.

[b]U.S. Forest Service, *Final Environmental Statement, Mineral Prospecting in the Beaver Creek Wilderness, Daniel Boone NF, Kentucky,* (Atlanta, Georgia, 1978).

ᶜU.S. Congress, Senate, *Eastern Wilderness Areas Act of 1974,* (Cal. No. 771, Senate Rept. 93-803, 93d Congress 2d Session, May 2, 1974), p. 30.

ᵈU.S. Forest Service, *Supplement, Northern Appalachian and New England States,* to *RARE-II,* Draft Environmental Statement (Washington, D.C., 1978).

Notes

1. See, for example, papers on mining and reclamation in *Forests for People, Proceedings of the Society of American Foresters* Washington, D.C., 1977; U.S. Council on Environmental Quality, *Environmental Quality,* (Washington, D.C.: U.S. Government Printing Office, 1977), p. 87ff.; and U.S. Council on Environmental Quality, *Hardrock Mining on the Public Land* (Washington, D.C.: U.S. Government Printing Office, 1977). Also, R.A. Wright, *The Reclamation of Disturbed Arid Lands* (Albuquerque, N. Mex.: University of New Mexico Press, 1978); R.F. Hadley and D.T. Snow, *Water Resources Problems Related to Mining* (Minneapolis, Minn.: American Water Resources Association, 1974). On conflicts between oil and gas production and pipelining and wildlife and social values, see, Mr. Justice T.R. Berger, *Northern Frontier, Northern Homeland: Report of the MacKenzie Valley Pipeline Inquiry* 2 vols. (Ottawa: Supply and Services Canada, 1977).

2. Wildland Research Center, *Wilderness and Recreation,* Outdoor Recreation Resources Review Commission, Report 3 (Washington, D.C.: U.S. Government Printing Office, 1963) p. 109.

3. For a useful review, see papers in the section "Finding and Processing Minerals," in P.M. Abelson and A.L. Hammond, eds., *Materials: Renewable and Nonrenewable Resources* (Washington, D.C.: American Association for the Advancement of Science, 1976).

4. J.H. Hammond, Jr., "The Wilderness Act and Mining: Some Proposals for Conservation," *Oregon Law Review* 47 (June 1968): 447.

5. U.S. Department of Agriculture, U.S. Forest Service, Region 6, "Fact Sheet—Mining in Glacier Peak Wilderness," Portland, Oregon, n.d.

6. U.S. Department of Agriculture, U.S. Forest Service, Region 6, "Fact Sheet—Mining in the Three Sisters Wilderness," Portland, Oregon, Rev. 616-74.

7. J. Krutilla and A.C. Fisher, *Economics of Natural Environments* (Baltimore: Johns Hopkins, 1975), chap. 7.

8. U.S. Department of Agriculture, U.S. Forest Service, *Boundary Waters Canoe Area Management Plan and Environmental Statement,* Milwaukee, Minnesota, 1974. Mining in this area has produced a long sequence of litigation, see *Izaak Walton League* v. *St. Clair,* 353 F.S. pp. 698 (D. Minn. 1973); 497 F. 2d. 849, 853-53 (8th Cir. 1974). The issues were

resolved by the Omnibus Parks Act of 1978.

9. U.S. Congress, Senate, Committee on Interior and Insular Affairs, *Hearings on Mining Activities in the Custer and Gallatin National Forests in Montana,* 92d Congress, 1st session, August 18, 1971.

10. W. Greenburg, "Showdown in Death Valley," *Sierra Club Bulletin,* February 1976, p. 4. The law is PL 94-429, 90 Stat. 1342 (1976).

11. General Mining Laws are at 30 U.S.C. 21-54. Regulations for BLM administration are found in 43 C.F.R. 3400-3600. Also, P.R. Hagenstein, "Changing an Anachronism: Congress and the General Mining Law of 1872," *Natural Resources Journal* 13, (July 1973): 480. U.S. Council on Environmental Quality, *Hardrock Mining,* and R.C. Anderson, "Federal Mineral Policy—the General Mining Law of 1872," *Natural Resources Journal* 16 (July 1976): 602.

12. 30 U.S.C. 22; 30 U.S.C. 181; see U.S. Department of Agriculture, U.S. Forest Service, *Principal Laws Relating to Forest Service Activities,* Agricultural Handbook 453, (Washington, D.C.: U.S. Government Printing Office, 1974).

13. U.S. Bureau of Land Management, *Patenting a Mining Claim on Federal Lands* (Washington, D.C., 1970); U.S. Bureau of Land Management and U.S. Department of Agriculture, U.S. Forest Service, *Staking a Mining Claim on Federal Lands,* Washington, D.C., 1970.

14. 36 CFR 252, (28 August 1974).

15. Douglas R. Leisz, "Memo on Mining Claims to Supervisors," U.S. Forest Service, Region 6, Portland, Oregon, April 4, 1969.

16. 39 *Federal Register* 168. (August 28, 1974); U.S. Department of Agriculture, U.S. Forest Service, *Mining in National Forests—Regulations to Protect Surface Resources,* (CI Report no. 14, Washington, D.C., January 1975); F.E. Fergusson Jr., and J.L. Haggard, "Regulation of Mining Law Activities in the National Forests," *Land and Water Law Review,* 8 (1973): 391, and U.S. Congress, Senate, Committee on Interior and Insular Affairs, *Hearings To Amend the Wilderness Act (S-1010),* 93d Congress, 1st session July 18, 1973; G. Libecap, "Federal Mining Policy: The General Mining Law of 1872," *Natural Resources Journal* 18 (July 1978): 461.

17. U.S. Department of Agriculture, U.S. Forest Service, *RARE-II, Draft Environmental Statement,* (Washington, D.C.) pp. 14, 61.

18. R.C. Lewis, "Policy Formation and Planning for Outdoor Recreational Facilities," in J.M. Hughes and R.D. Lloyd, eds., *Outdoor Recreation—Advances in Application of Economics,* U.S. Forest Service, General Technical Report WO-2, 1977, p. 62-69. For a detailed review, see J. C. Hendee, G.H. Stankey, and R.C. Lucas, *Wilderness Management,* U.S. Department of Agriculture, U.S. Forest Service, Miscellaneous Publication 1365, 1978, chap. 13.

19. W.R. Burch, Jr., "Wilderness: The Life Cycle and Forest

Recreational Choice," *Journal of Forestry* 64 (August 1966): 609, reprinted with permission. For a stimulating review of the sociology of outdoor recreation, see N.H. Cheek, Jr. and W.R. Burch, Jr., *The Social Organization of Leisure in Human Society* (New York: Harper & Row, 1976); an extensive review of sociological data appears in chaps. 2 and 3.

20. W.F. Lapage, *Growth Potential of the Family Camping Market,* U.S. Forest Service, Northeastern Forest Experiment Station, Research Paper NE-252, 1973.

21. G.H. Stankey, "Myths in Wilderness Decision-making," *Journal of Soil and Water Conservation* 26 (September-October 1971): 183.

22. Burch, "Wilderness," p. 610, reprinted with permission.

23. U.S. Department of Interior, *Critical Water Problems Facing the Eleven Western States—Westwide Study* (Washington, D.C.: U.S. Government Printing Office, 1975), p. 27.

24. Wildland Research Center, *Wilderness,* p. 39.

25. Wilderness Act, Sec. 4 (d)(4).

26. See, for example, P.D. Ffolliot and D.B. Thorud, *Vegetation Management for Increased Water Yield in Arizona,* University of Arizona, Agr. Exp. Sta. Tech. Bulletin 215, 1974, in which the authors report that intensive vegetation management could increase total streamflow by 600,000 to 1.2 million acre-feet per year. This would require special measures on millions of acres to be achieved.

27. Land management impacts on water quality have been of increasing interest since the federal mandate to minimize nonpoint pollution (Sec. 208, PL92-500, Federal Water Pollution Control Act Amendments of 1972). From a vast literature, the following are useful: U.S. Council on Environmental Quality, *Environmental Quality—1978* (Washington, D.C.: U.S. Government Printing Office, 1978), p. 118ff; J.R. Karr and I.J. Schlosser, "Water Resources and the Land-Water Interface," *Science* 201 (21 July 1978): 229; E.S. Corbett, J.A. Lynch, and W.E. Sopper, "Timber Harvesting Practices and Water Quality in the Eastern U.S.," *Journal of Forestry* 76 (August 1978): 484; U.S. Forest Service, *Nonpoint Water Quality Modelling in Wildland Management,* U.S. Environmental Protection Agency, Environmental Research Laboratory, Athens, Georgia, EPA-600/3-77-036, April 1977.

28. U.S. Congress, Senate, Subcommittee on Public Lands, Committee on Energy and Natural Resources, *Management of Bull Run Reserve, Oregon,* Publication 95-58, July 26, 1977.

29. L.C. Irland and S.M. Levy, "Southern New England Water Supply Lands, Changing Values and Policies," *Journal of the New England Water Works Association* 91 (March 1977): 12; U.S. Council on Environmental Quality, *Recreation on Water Supply Reservoirs* (Washington, D.C.: U.S. Government Printing Office, 1975).

30. J. Harte and M. El-Gasseir, "Energy and Water," *Science* 199 (10 February 1978): 623.

31. See, for example, The Institute of Ecology, *Scientific and Technical Review of the . . . Oil Shale Final EIS,* Washington, D.C., 1973.

32. U.S. Congress, Senate, Committee on Interior and Insular Affairs, *Colorado Wilderness Areas,* June 11, 1973, p. 152.

33. U.S. Department of Interior, U.S. Bureau of Reclamation, *Position Paper on Weather Modification over Wilderness Areas,* (Washington, D.C.: U.S. Government Printing Office, 1974); see also U.S. Department of Commerce, Weather Modification Advisory Board, *The Management of Weather Resources,* vol. I, Washington, D.C., June 30, 1978.

34. U.S. Department of Interior, *Westwide Study,* p. 17.

7 Evaluating Local Economic Impacts

Allocating wildland to wilderness uses can have significant effects on the flows of raw materials used by nearby communities. Although water, wildlife, and minerals may be affected, most of the discussion has been over the effects of wilderness decisions on local timber supplies. This chapter reviews the issues, the methods used by economists to study these issues, and the methods available for mitigating any adverse effects that may occur.[1] It closes with a case study of the Redwood National Park.

Local economic impacts have been receiving increasing attention in U.S. Forest Service, National Park Service, and Bureau of Land Management (BLM) land-use planning. The high level of controversy over local impacts, and the demand for more thorough analysis of decisions in environmental impact statements, have led agencies to increase their staffs for performing such analyses and to improve the methods employed.[2]

Reduced Log Supply and Local Mills

The volumes of timber or other materials removed from commercial use do not provide a direct basis for estimating local economic impacts. The economic impact depends on the ability of the local processing industry to continue operations after the reduction in log supply. This is controlled by the availability of timber from other sources. The two possible sources are other public land and private land. In the short run, even if no private timber is available, it may be possible to sell nearby public timber to keep existing mills in operation and avoid job losses. In addition, private land owners may supply timber to meet mill demand. In many areas under consideration for wilderness, however, most forest land is publicly owned—alternate sources of private timber may not exist. The effect of public timber withdrawals on timber prices depends, therefore, on the elasticity of demand for public timber, or the degree to which price changes with changes in quantity supplied.[3]

The complexities of assessing the local timber supply effects of roadless area allocations to wilderness were explored in a 1978 case study of six western national forests.[4] That study considered the effects of 50 percent and 100 percent withdrawal of roadless lands in six national forests with and without reallocation of roading funds thus saved into intensive

119

management on the remaining managed acres. The relationships among potential yield (an estimate of ultimate long-range managed yield), programmed harvest (amount planned for cutting based on projected timber sale budgets), and actual recent harvest (amount cut based on past sales and purchaser cutting-decisions) are critical in the short run. The six forests studied received varying portions of estimated potential yield (67 percent on the Bridger-Teton; 15 percent on the Willamette) from inventoried roadless areas. Yet the reduction from actual recent harvests due to withdrawal of the roadless areas was in each case small.

As an example, consider the Willamette National Forest, in Oregon's Cascade Mountains, one of the Forest Service's leading timber-producing forests.[5] Its forests are highly productive Douglas-fir-Hemlock stands. Its statistics were as follows:

	Million cubic feet/year
Recent harvest	106
Programmed harvest	
All roadless in base	115.4
100 percent withdrawn, no reallocation of road funds	102.8
100 percent withdrawn with reallocation of road funds to silviculture	102.8
Potential yield	
All roadless in base	157.4
100 percent withdrawn	134.1

On the Willamette, reallocation of funds that would have been spent on roadless areas into intensive management produces no increased timber output over the case without reallocation, since the harvest is not limited by the budget for intensive management on that particular forest. Still, if the budget on which the programmed harvest is based is in fact made available, it will be possible to sustain the recent cut level, with only a slight decline, despite the allocation of 195,000 roadless acres to wilderness. The effect of the withdrawal would be the removal of an investment opportunity that could increase the forest's potential yield by 50 percent to 157.4 million cubic feet per year.

Economic Impact of Withdrawals

The volume of harvestable timber taken off the market does not measure the economic impact of withdrawals. The important consideration is the actual effect on jobs and incomes. A community's ability to absorb a reduced timber harvest is based on its degree of dependence on timber-using industry. Economists have applied input-output analysis and economic base studies to analyze the effect of changing resource supplies on local economics.

Timber Dependence

Dependence on timber industries varies widely across the United States. In the South, forest industries account for 13 percent of manufacturing employment and 2.4 percent of total personal income. In the Rocky Mountains, by contrast, lumbering alone provides 43 percent of Idaho's manufacturing jobs and 41 percent of Montana's. In New England, forest-related industry provides 2 percent of the region's nonfarm jobs and 6 percent of the manufacturing jobs. In Maine, wood industries provide 8 percent of the nonfarm jobs and account for fully 28 percent of manufacturing employment.[6] Maki and Schweitzer applied the economic base concept to evaluate the dependence of Douglas-fir region communities (western Oregon and Washington) on timber.[7] They found that 40 percent of the region's excess employment—jobs attributed to export of goods outside the region—was from the timber-related industry. Within the region, dependence on timber ranged from 2 percent in Seattle to 98 percent in Roseburg, Oregon. For most areas studied, timber dependence fell from 1959 to 1971. These data do not directly estimate the effect of a given reduction in log production, but they show the varying importance of forest industry among different communities.

In many areas, job losses in primary industries may understate local economic impact. This is because of the multiplier effect of expenditures and payrolls in primary industries. These outlays support jobs and incomes in service and supply sectors of the local economy.

Input-Output Models

To explore the relation between total economic activity and the growth or decline of individual industries, economists have developed input-output analysis. This is a mathematical technique that traces the rippling effects of a given change in output on all industries in a national or local economy.

An input-output model for a given area is constructed in several steps.[8] First, a set of economic sectors is defined that will include enough detail, subject to data availability, to answer the questions posed. For an analysis of tourism, for example, the lodging and service and retail sectors might be finely disaggregated. Next, detailed transactions data are obtained representing all financial flows, and inventory changes where necessary, between sectors in the area economy. This information is arrayed in a transactions matrix which enables the user to trace dollar flows from industry to industry (table 7-1).

Then, the transactions matrix is converted into a direct requirements matrix, which shows the percent of total input contributed by each sector to the output of a given sector (table 7-1). Mathematically inverting this table produces an inverse matrix that shows the total direct and indirect requirements of every sector from every other sector. This matrix incorporates all the multiplier effects created by the respending of income within the area. There are two types of models in this respect. Closed models treat the household and government sectors as internal to the model and, therefore, reflect the respending of household income. They take account of induced effects created by the circular flow of household incomes back into the community. Open models do not recycle household incomes through the economy but treat only first-round direct and indirect effects. Open models, therefore, underestimate the total economic effects of changes in basic sectors.

Input-output models can be used to trace the ultimate economic effects of changes in the final demand (What would happen if a lumber mill sold an additional 30 million board-feet per year of lumber cut in a given county?) or of changes in resource supply (What if the county's timber cut fell by 10 percent?).

To use these results correctly, some understanding of terminology is required. Input-output models are built up from transactions data. A common use of multipliers is to express, based on the inverse matrix, the relation between a dollar change in final demand for one sector and the total volume of business transactions in the geographic area studied. Multipliers are frequently expressed in terms such as "business income multiplier," "total output multiplier," or "sales multiplier." These are all equivalent concepts referring to gross financial flows within an area. They can provide a rough indication of total business activity and may be of use in forecasting such things as sales tax revenues. But they are not equivalent to multipliers depicting the effect of output changes on local household incomes.

Using the inverse table, the total effects on area business income or transactions volume can be estimated for a change in any given sector. For Douglas County, for example, a one-dollar output change in sawmilling in 1970 resulted in a $3.09 change in total county output (table 7-1). In contrast, the multiplier for retail and wholesale trade was only 1.70 and for automotive sales and service was 1.43 (these multipliers are not shown in table 7-1).

These multipliers illustrate the concept of leakage. The multipliers in a sense represent the intensity with which a given industry utilizes local labor

Table 7-1
Sample Columns from Input-Output Model for Douglas County, Oregon, for Sawmill Sector

Sector from which Purchases Made	Transactions (millions of dollars)	Requirements (dollars/dollar of output)	Inverse Matrix
Timber harvest and hauling	14.0	.33	.34
Financial services	5.4	.13	.17
Retail and wholesale trade	1.9	.04	.27
Auto sales and service	0.6	.01	.16
Households	9.5	.22	.53
Total	42.8	1.00	3.09

Source: R. C. Youmans et al., *Douglas County, Oregon* . . ., Oregon State University Agricultural Experiment Station, Circular 645, 1973, tables 3, 4, and 5.

Note: Columns do not add to totals due to selection of sample items only for presentation in this table.

and locally owned resources. In a field such as sawmilling, relatively intensive use of local labor is made. The output multiplier is therefore high. In retailing, a large part of the sales dollar reflects goods purchased from outside. Payments for such goods leave the county immediately, contributing to a high rate of leakage.

As a general rule, the smaller the area, the higher the leakage, and the lower the multiplier will be on changes in basic industry output or payrolls. This is because smaller areas are generally more dependent on outside regions for supplies and raw materials. An economy with a diversified, mature economic base will have higher output multipliers than a one-industry town. The diversified economy will be more self-sufficient and thus have a lower leakage rate. For this reason, multipliers developed from statewide models should not be used in studies of counties or subcounty areas.

The direct impact of an output change in a given sector on local household income is given by consulting the requirements matrix under households for the given sector. For example, in Douglas County in 1970, every dollar change in sawmill output resulted in 22¢ in payments to households in the form of wages and salaries (table 7-1). This shows the direct effect of a dollar change in sawmill output on local income before accounting for wage payments by other sawmill suppliers (loggers) and before accounting for respending effects.

The total direct and indirect impact on incomes per dollar of sawmill sales is given in the inverse matrix. Consulting this matrix, it is seen that a one-dollar change in sawmill sales results in a 53 cent change in Douglas County household income after accounting for multiplier effects.

Economic Base Models

An economic base model is essentially an input-output model collapsed into a highly aggregated form. The model is based on the proposition that the base or driving force of a local economy is its sales of products or services to outsiders.[9]

In preparing an economic base model, a county economy is divided into two sectors—industries substantially dependent on sales to outsiders and those dependent on the respending of incomes earned by local residents. The former industries are called the "basic" sector and the latter the "service" sector. Partitioning an economy into basic and service sectors requires considerable knowledge of its local structure and may require finely disaggregated data. For example, in some areas a significant portion of the sales in trade and service establishments are to tourists and hence represent basic income to the area. Any source of income from outside a given area can be considered basic income. Transfer payments such as social security and pensions should be included. Payments received by residents for capital assets (land) sold to nonresidents would qualify as basic income.

Economic base models are adequate for studying the aggregate impacts resulting from changes in basic incomes or employment. Their principal advantage is their low cost and ease of construction as compared to input-output models. The fact that they supply no detail on a sector by sector basis is no problem for many applications.

As an example, consider Garrison's results, used to analyze the economic impact of new industry in five Kentucky counties.[10] For Fleming County, the analysis for 1958 to 1963 showed:

	Thousands of Dollars
Basic income	
1. 1963	9,333
2. 1958	6,620
3. Increase	2,713
Total income	
4. 1963	13,469
5. 1958	9,499
6. Increase	3,970
Multipliers	
7. Ratio of (4) to (1)	1.44
8. Ratio of (5) to (2)	1.43
9. Ratio of (6) to (3)	1.46
Impact of new industry	
10. Local payroll of new plants	1,007
11. Impact on Total Income (10 x 9)	1,473
12. Indirect Impact (11 - 10)	466

This illustration shows in lines 7-9 the estimation of multipliers for 1958 and 1963 and an incremental multiplier comparing the changes from 1958-1963 in basic and total income. The incremental multiplier is used in the determination of total income effect in line 11.

Input-Output and Economic Base Models: Limitations

The principal limitation of input-output models is their cost in time and money. Although several attempts have been made to circumvent the costs of gathering direct transactions data from area business firms, they all have disadvantages. Sampling can be used to reduce data gathering costs but raises serious technical problems of its own. Adjusting state models to depict local areas has been done many times, and old models have been updated or even projected into the future, but these models are rarely verified later by checking the results back against reality.

Since production of input-output models for states and local areas has been busily pursued by a generation of students and professional economists, there are likely to be available models of similar areas to aid analysts working on a given problem.[11] Economic base models can generate multipliers useful in gauging aggregate economic impacts for employment and income. County areas are especially easy to handle due to ready availability of data in secondary sources.[12] For areas smaller than counties, however, data quality will rarely justify costly and sophisticated analytical methods.

A limitation of both input-output and economic base techniques is that they are linear models adapted to analyzing small changes in an existing economy whose structure remains fundamentally constant. They can help determine the impact of changes in livestock sales on an existing agricultural economy or the impact of higher lumber production on a rural milltown. They are less able to trace the effect of replacing a farm economy with a recreation-oriented economy. To do this would probably require building a new model of the hypothesized new economy.

Multipliers have frequently been abused by partisans in wildland allocation debates. They have been used to overstate the costs or benefits of particular decisions. Observers should examine assumptions used in such arguments carefully to assure that they are realistic in terms of local conditions. For example, consider a proposal to allocate to wilderness a tract capable of producing 100 million board-feet of timber per year. If alternate sources of timber can be found, it is incorrect to multiply the 100 million board-feet times the total payrolls per million board-feet to obtain the economic cost of the wilderness. Such a procedure is only correct if the lumber output and jobs in question would actually disappear as a result of the wilderness allocation.

Development Opportunities Forgone

In some cases, a wilderness proposal conflicts with a development proposal for the same area. Perhaps the best known example is the proposed ski development in California's Mineral King Valley, in which a 20-year controversy was finally ended in 1978 with the transfer of the land from Forest Service to Park Service control. Many rural areas today face declining employment prospects even if natural resource output is sustained. For example, in the Pacific Northwest region, timber industry employment fell by 3 percent from 1950 to 1965. Projections indicate that regional employment in forest industries will fall by 45 percent from its 1970 level of 121,000 by the year 2000.[13] Technological changes in agriculture and natural resource industries, then, may threaten the economic base of many established rural communities. The growing recreation industry based on public lands in the West offers the hope of an economic resurgence in these areas. But wilderness land allocations can remove the resource base for ski developments and other intensive-use facilities. The size of the opportunities forgone can be substantial.

Skiing is a multimillion dollar industry serving millions of persons each year. This market has grown rapidly in recent years. By adapting an existing input-output model, Standley studied the economic impact of the Vail ski complex on the Colorado economy.[14] He found that the complex involved a capital investment of $21 million over a six-year construction period. The economic impact of tourist use is substantial. In the 1967-1968 season, Vail was visited by 290,000 skiers. Nonresident skiers spent $29.44 per day, and resident skiers (30 percent of the total) spent $13.55 per day. The area thus generated total annual expenditures of $7 million. In areas facing potential developments on this scale, some residents are understandably hostile to wilderness reservations that might preclude development. Many areas, however, are finding that winter recreation is a mixed blessing. Rapid growth in construction and population can result in heavy tax loads on existing landowners and in a wide range of environmental and planning problems.[15]

Moreover, because of the high leakage associated with these expenditures, the income multipliers for tourist expenditures are very low. In cases where an area will generate growth in tourism after preservation, jobs related to wilderness management and tourist services may actually compensate for jobs lost in natural resource industries. But jobs in tourist service industries are poor substitutes for jobs in manufacturing. Pay levels are usually lower, and employment is often highly seasonal. This means that actual improvements in economic welfare resulting from recreational developments can be small.[16]

Policy Options to Mitigate Local Economic Impacts

Popular discussion often implies that the only way to mitigate adverse local economic impacts of designating a wilderness area is to forgo the wilderness area. This is not true. Numerous policy instruments are available that can reduce or compensate for the adverse impacts of public resource supply reductions.

A broad range of public programs testifies to congressional concern for the welfare of persons and communities affected by public programs:

1. Federal aid to school districts in areas impacted by concentrations of federal facilities such as military bases,
2. Relocation and adjustment assistance in highway, urban renewal, and flood control programs,
3. Sharing revenue from federal resource sales with local counties and states, to moderate the impact of public land ownership on local tax bases,
4. Federal aid to industries injured by relaxed trade restrictions.[17] Programs similar to these could be marshalled to assist areas that may be adversely affected by a federal resource withdrawal.

In addition, a range of economic development programs are available to areas with chronic and substantial unemployment. Programs of manpower development and training (Department of Labor), rural areas sewer grants (EPA), rural housing loans (USDA), and economic development loans (Department of Commerce) could be coordinated in areas affected by wilderness area designations.

Public agencies may be able to forestall local economic losses by judicious rearrangement of timber-cutting plans and timber prices to make up for reduced log supplies. The agency could arrange to temporarily overcut in a nearby area to keep a mill operating and maintain employment. Alternatively, timber at greater distance could be made available on a preference basis at lower-than-market prices to equalize delivered log costs with former supplies. In the Redwood National Park Expansion Act, the Forest Service was directed to study just such options to minimize impact on the local timber-processing industry.

Reduced local government revenues can be replaced by either raising timber revenue payments or by making special payments to compensate for lost taxes. These additional payments could be phased out as development replaces lost tax base.[18]

Lost development opportunities are more difficult to handle. Every small town believes it has the right to grow and resents interventions by government that thwart its opportunities. In cases where a massive development is to be forgone, little can be done. In other cases, however, it may be possible to find other, more environmentally acceptable, avenues for economic growth where justified to reduce chronic unemployment or low incomes.

Where timber is in substantial physical surplus on nearby private lands, as is usually the case in the East, it is necessary to overcome limits on the landowners' willingness to supply the timber for harvest. The limited economic supply may be addressed directly by a range of forestry programs.

Extension, technical assistance, and subsidies for management practices may be employed to make forest management and harvesting more attractive to owners. In addition, programs of education and regulation to minimize soil erosion caused by logging could go a long way toward reducing landowner reluctance to permit harvesting on their property.

Nationally, programs such as these have been in existence for years, but have made only limited progress, partly due to the limited funds and personnel applied to them.[19] A new interest in the problems of the nonindustrial private forests could lead to revitalization and improvement in these programs. The Carter Administration has made improvement in services for such forest ownerships an important policy objective. Professional groups and state agencies share this commitment.

Overview

Most of America's spectacular and ecologically significant undeveloped wildlands are now considered part of the raw material supply base for resource-dependent nearby communities. Those communities are sustained by the employment in logging and milling, mining, and grazing. They may also include important interests based on recreation, hunting, and other wilderness uses. But the relatively well-paying, seasonally stable resource industries remain important to their well-being. In addition, they may rely heavily on federal payments to them out of revenues received on federal lands for their public services.

Past debates over preservation decisions have relied on abundant rhetoric and limited analysis of local economic impacts. In most situations careful analyses of timber dependence, actual reductions in wood flows caused by preservation, alternative wood sources, and local multiplier relationships is helpful. Where necessary, mitigation measures to sustain log supplies to dependent mills will usually avoid adverse local impacts. Where this is impossible, additional measures, as applied in the Redwood Park case, can ease the economic transition for affected communities.

These communities face a future of declining employment as their basic industries mechanize.[20] Many of them suffer from chronic unemployment already. Their timber supply base will decline as a result of further harvesting restrictions applied in public land-use planning and of increasing subdivision and development of nearby private land. It is not surprising, therefore, that political leaders representing such communities see the social costs of allocating nearby public lands to wilderness uses as being unacceptable. In these situations, a high degree of sensitivity to the complex issues of protecting significant wild areas, of balancing national, local, and private interests, and of finding acceptable mitigating policies will be required. One of the major challenges of land-use policy in the future will be to provide for preservation of viable rural community economies based on wildlands, while protecting environmentally significant resources.

Case 7-1. Preservation and the Local Economy: Redwood National Park, 1968-1978

The redwood forests of California's rugged northern coast region have captured the imagination of visitors since the earliest explorers penetrated the region. The high commercial value of redwood timber, and the ease of harvesting and processing the large trees, make the old growth redwood stands a prized commercial resource. In the sixties, prices of $10,000 per acre and upwards were paid for well-stocked old growth lands.

By the mid-sixties the original 2 million acres of redwood forests had been reduced to about 300,000 acres, largely in state forests and industrial ownerships. A concerted drive began for preserving a significant example of redwood in a large national park along Redwood Creek. Following several years of hearings, debate, and economic studies, Congress established a compromise park of 58,000 acres. The park included only old stands of tall trees in the lower flats of Redwood Creek, which left the upper watershed in private ownership and open for logging. This small park did not meet the needs envisioned by Park supporters:

> *For all the trouble and expense, the park soon proved to be a disappointment to Congress, the Park Service, and the Public. Visitation was sparse . . . Even today, after all the publicity the Park has received, more people make the demanding climb up Mt. Whitney, the highest peak in the lower forty-eight states, then walk in eight easy miles to spend the night under the tallest trees in the world.*
>
> *There are good reasons for this. On any day but Sunday, one cannot make the hike without hearing dynamite blasts, the ripping noise of chain saws, and the sounds of giant trees falling, or without seeing clouds of dust raised by the logging trucks as they speed the timber out to the mills. Some ugly clear-cut patches can also be glimpsed up the slopes. This is hardly a pleasant way to experience the Redwoods.[a]*

Even the establishment of a small park was highly controversial in California's leading timber-producing county, where 24 percent of all employment depended on cutting trees, hauling them to mills, producing lumber and plywood, and shipping logs, chips, and products to buyers. Humboldt County's employment in wood products declined by one-third between 1959 and the early seventies, and many feared that reductions in timber supply would make matters worse. The employment outlook for the region was grim enough, with mechanization gradually displacing jobs and with the expected disappearance of heavily stocked old growth stands that would steadily reduce future timber harvest potential.

After the passage of the Redwood National Park Act in 1968, it became clear that continued logging on upstream private lands was accelerating natural erosion and threatening the redwood groves within the Park. Accelerated sedimentation caused the stream channels to fill in and widen, and reduced fish habitat. Higher runoff led to accelerated undercutting of banks and toppling of streamside trees. [b] *While geologists differed over the seriousness of these problems, conservation organizations filed lawsuits to reduce damage to Park resources caused by upstream logging. They worked to build support for expanding the Park.*

After much discussion, the Congress in March 1978 passed a bill calling for a 48,000 acre expansion of the Park, to protect areas most likely to damage the watershed if logged. Interior Department analysts estimated that the lands to be acquired contained a prodigious 1.6 billion board-feet of standing timber. The timber base for several mills would be severely affected. A consultant to the Economic Development Administration estimated that job losses might be as high as 715 jobs in the forest industry, and a total of 1,368 jobs counting multiplier effects in other sectors. This would amount to almost 4 percent of the jobs at a time of 15 percent unemployment. [c]

The park expansion proposals produced an outraged reaction among Humboldt County loggers, millworkers, businessmen, public officials, and affected landowners. The Louisiana Pacific Corporation, which stood to lose 27,000 acres, or 27 percent of its Humboldt County lands, vigorously opposed the expansion. [d] *A contingent of angry loggers drove twenty-three logging trucks across the country to stage a graphic protest at the Capitol—and they attempted to deliver an 8-ton peanut carved from redwood to the White House.*

The clear likelihood of employment losses and the angry response of Redwood region residents dependent on forest resources for their livelihood prompted some of the first serious consideration ever given to federal mitigation measures for job losses caused by a preservation decision.

The bulk of the text of the Park Expansion Act deals with complex provisions for mitigating economic impacts. [e] *The provisions begin from the premises that forest industry layoffs, with minor exceptions, until 1980 are "conclusively presumed to be attributable to the expansion of Redwood National Park" (Section 203). The act directs the secretaries of Interior and Agriculture to plan for watershed rehabilitation projects to repair eroded lands and provide employment. It provides for additional Park personnel and for job preferences for employees laid off by wood-using firms. The Secretary of the Interior is directed to cooperate with the secretaries of*

Agriculture, Commerce, and Labor to study appropriate mitigation measures, and the secretaries of Commerce and Labor are instructed to make full use of existing programs to aid employment in Humboldt County. In addition, the Secretary of Agriculture is directed to study potential changes in timber-harvesting policy on the adjacent Six Rivers National Forest to examine the feasibility of raising the national forest timber cut to replace log supplies lost to the Park expansion. Finally, the Act sets forth detailed provisions (Sections 203-212) for a system of unemployment benefits for affected workers and compensatory payments to local governments.

On signing the Expansion Act, President Carter expressed concern over these broad mitigation provisions. Only time will tell how successful the package is in maintaining the existing level of employment and economic well-being of Humboldt County residents. The total cost of the expansion, including mitigation measures, will not be known for years.

The mitigation package promises to minimize the adverse effect of the Park expansion on the local economy and to promote needed watershed stabilization work. It will thereby place a portion of the costs of any local impacts on the ultimate beneficiaries of the Park expansion, the federal taxpayers. At the same time, caution is required to prevent legitimate concern for needed mitigation measures from becoming a political logrolling tool to be used in buying local acquiescence in future preservation controversies, especially where local adverse effects are not as clearly demonstrable as in the Redwood Park expansion case.

---

[a]Marc Reisner, "The Tragedy of Redwood National Park," *NRDC Newsletter,* 6 (July/August 1977). Reprinted with permission. (A readable review of events leading to passage of the 1978 Act). For more detail, see D.A. Hudson, "Sierra Club versus Department of Interior: the Fight to Preserve Redwood National Park," *Ecology Law Quarterly* 7 (1979): 781.

[b]R.J. Janda, "Statement concerning pending Redwood National Park Legislation," U.S. Geological Survey, Menlo Park, California, processed. October 21, 1977. Reprinted in U.S. Congress, Senate, Committee on Energy and Natural Resources, *Redwood National Park (S. 1976),* Publication no. 95-85, 1977. This document contains a wealth of other information on the Park expansion.

[c]Greenacres Consulting Corporation, *Redwood National Park Proposed 48,000 Acre Expansion. Data Review and Analysis,* Prepared for Redwood Task Force for Economic Development, under a grant from Economic Development Administration, June 13, 1977. (Contains a full bibliography of previous studies on the economics of Redwood National Park and extensive economic data; also provides brief summary of federal programs that can serve as mitigation measures.) See also Gerald W. Dean et al., *Structure and Projections of the Humboldt County Economy,* California Agricultural Experiment Station, Giannini Foundation of Agricultural Economics, Research Report no. 318, July 1973.

[d]See, for example, Louisiana Pacific Corp, *1977 First Quarter Interim Report,* Portland, Oregon, May 6, 1977.

[e]Redwood Park Expansion Act, PL 95-250, March 27, 1978. 92 Stat. 163.

Notes

1. E.G. Schuster, *Local Economic Impact: A Decision Variable in Forest Resources Management* (Missoula, Mont.: Montana Forest and Conservation Experiment Station, 1976). This publication extensively reviews the agency mandate for concern with local economic impacts, summarizes methods, reviews literature, and provides a case study.

2. See Schuster, *Local Economic Impact;* B.R. Wall and D.D. Oswald, *A Technique and Relationships for Projections of Employment in the Pacific Coast Forest Products Industries,* (U.S. Department of Agriculture, U.S. Forest Service, Pacific Northwest Forest and Range Experiment Station, Research Paper PNW-189 1975); and references in notes 9 and 10.

3. W.J. Mead, *Oligopsony and Competition in the Douglas Fir Lumber Industry,* (Berkeley, Calif.: University of California Press, 1966) and T.A. Hamilton, *Stumpage Price Responses to Changes in Volume of Timber Sold,* U.S. Department of Agriculture, U.S. Forest Service, Pacific Northwest Forest and Range Experiment Station, Research Paper PNW-92, 1970.

4. R.D. Fight et al., *Roadless Area—Intensive Management Tradeoffs on Western National Forests,* U.S. Department of Agriculture, U.S. Forest Service, Pacific Northwest Forest and Range Experiment Station, October 1978.

5. Ibid., p. 5.

6. L.C. Irland, *Labor Trends in Southern Forest Industry,* U.S. Department of Agriculture, U.S. Forest Service, Southern Forest Experiment Station, Research Paper SO-81, 1972; A.K. Wilson and J.S. Spencer, Jr., *Timber Resources and Industries in the Rocky Mountain States,* U.S. Department of Agriculture, U.S. Forest Service, Intermountain Forest and Range Experiment Station, Research Bulletin Int-7, 1967; L.C. Irland, "Importance of Forest Industries to New England's Economy," *Northern Logger,* March 1975.

7. W.R. Maki and D.L. Schweitzer, *Importance of Timber-based Employment to the Douglas-fir Region, 1959 to 1971,* U.S. Department of Agriculture, U.S. Forest Service, Pacific Northwest Forest and Range Experiment Station, Res. Note PNW-196, 1973. See also, C. Schallau et al., "Economic Impact Projections for Alternative Levels of Timber Production in the Douglas-fir Region," *Annals of Regional Science* 3 (1969): 96, and E.F. Bell, *Estimating Effect of Timber Harvesting Levels on Employment in Western United States,* U.S. Department of Agriculture, U.S. Forest Service, Intermountain Forest and Range Experiment Station, Res. Note INT-237, 1977.

8. W. Miernyk, *Elements of Input-Output Analysis* (New York:

Random House, 1965). Also, W. Flick, "Input-Output Analysis for Forest Planning," in F.J. Convery, and C.W. Ralston, eds., *Forestry and Long Range Planning* (Durham, N.C.: Duke School of Forestry and Environmental Studies, 1977).

9. E. Nourse, *Regional Economics* (New York: McGraw-Hill, 1968).

10. C.B. Garrison, "The Impact of New Industry: An Application of the Economic Base Multiplier to Small Rural Areas," *Land Economics* 48 (November 1972): 329. For a convenient system applying economic base analysis to county data, see E. Hall, *The Regional Industrial Multiplier System,* U.S. Department of Agriculture, U.S. Forest Service, Southeastern Area, State and Private Forestry, Atlanta, Georgia, 1977.

11. See for example, J.M. Hughes, *Forestry in Itasca County's Economy,* Minnesota Agricultural Experiment Station, Misc. Rept. no. 95, 1970; D.W. Bromley, G.E. Blanch, and H.H. Stoevener, *Effects of Selected Changes in Federal Land Use on a Local Economy,* Oregon State University Agricultural Experiment Station, Bulletin 604, 1968; R.D. Fight and D. Darr, *Douglas County Oregon Potential Economic Impacts of a Changing Economic Base,* U.S. Department of Agriculture, U.S. Forest Service, Pacific Northwest Forest and Range Experiment Station, Research Paper PNW-179, 1974; R. Drake, S. Randall, and M. Skinner, "Evaluation of F.S. Programs in Northern New Mexico," Economic Resource Service, Natural Resource Economics Division, Berkeley, California, 1973; A.R. Dickerman and S. Butzer, "The Potential of Timber Management to Affect Regional Growth and Stability," *Journal of Forestry* 73 (May 1975): 268; F.L.C. Reed and Assoc., *The British Columbia Forest Industry* (Victoria, B.C. Department of Lands, Forests, and Water Resources, 1973); J.R. Gray and B.C. English, *Local Benefits of National Forest Resources in North-Central New Mexico,* New Mexico State University, Agricultural Experiment Station, Research Report no. 327, 1976; E.P. Lewis and D.T. Taylor, *Impact of Public Lands Policies on the Livestock Industry and Adjacent Communities, Big Horn County, Wyoming,* Wyoming Agricultural Experiment Station, Research Journal 116, June 1977; and R.T. Clark and R.R. Fletcher, *Economic Impact of Lumber Processing, Star Valley, Wyoming,* Wyoming Agricultural Experiment Station, B-620, March 1975.

12. For examples, see F. Convery, *Unit Planning and Local Economic Impacts,* Duke University School of Forestry, Tech. Paper no. 1, 1973; R.S. Boster, P.F. O'Connell, and Thompson, "Recreation Uses Change Mogollon Rim Economy," *Arizona Review* 23 (January 1974): 1.

13. Schallau, "Economic Impact Projections," and B. Wall, *Employment Implications of Projected Timber Output in the Douglas-fir Region, 1970-2000,* U.S. Department of Agriculture, U.S. Forest Service, Pacific

Northwest Forest and Range Experiment Station, Res. Note PNW-211, 1973.

14. S. Standley, "The Impact of the Vail Ski Resort," (Graduate School of Business Administration, University of Colorado, 1971).

15. For example, see J. Gilmore and R. Duff, *The Evolving Political Economy of Pitkin County: Growth Management by Consensus in a Boom Community,* (*Aspen, Colo.*) (Denver, Colo.: Denver Research Institute, 1974); T. Minger, "Impacts of a New Resort-town on a Natural-rural Environment: the Vail Experience" (Vail, Colo.: City Manager's Office, 1974); R. Stuart, *Impacts of Large Recreational Developments: The Gallatin Canyon Case,* Center for Interdisciplinary Studies and Montana Agricultural Experiment Station, Research Report 66, 1974, (The "Big Sky Study"). An especially detailed study of local impacts is provided in U.S. Department of Commerce, Economic Development Administration, *Final Environmental Statement, 1980 Olympic Winter Games, Village of Lake Placid, N.Y.,* Washington, D.C., January, 1977.

16. W. Beardsley, "The Economic Impact of Recreation Development: A Synopsis," in U.S. Department of Agriculture, U.S. Forest Service, *Recreation Symposium Proceedings,* Northeastern Forest Experiment Station, 1971; see also R.R. Nathan Association and Resource Planning Associates, *Recreation as an Industry,* Appalachian Regional Commission, Research Report no. 2, 1966; case studies are given in B.R. Payne, R. Cannon, and L.C. Irland, *The Second Home Recreation Market in the Northeast* (Washington, D.C.: U.S. Department of the Interior, Bureau of Outdoor Recreation, 1975); P.E. Polzin and D.C. Schweitzer, *Economic Importance of Tourism in Montana,* U.S. Department of Agriculture, U.S. Forest Service, Intermountain Forest and Range Experiment Station, Research Paper INT-171, 1975; and E.P. Lewis and G.E. Premer, *The Economic Value of Recreation and Tourism, Park County, Wyoming, 1976,* University of Wyoming, Agricultural Extension Service, B-664, March 1978.

17. Statutes mandating these programs are found at 12 U.S.C. sec. 1735 (1970); 42 U.S.C. sec. 3374 (Supp. IV, 1974); 23 U.S.C. sec. 581 et seq. (1970); 42 U.S.C. sec. 1455 (Supp. IV, 1974); 33 U.S.C. sec. 598 (1970); 16 U.S.C. sec. 500 (1970); 17 U.S.C. sec. 1981 et seq. (Supp. IV, 1974). See also provisions for Redwood Park, discussed in case 7-1.

18. See Advisory Commission on Intergovernmental Relations, *The Adequacy of Federal Compensation to Local Governments for Tax Exempt Federal Lands* (Washington, D.C.: U.S. Government Printing Office, 1978), p. 8 and generally chap. 3.

19. R.A. Sedjo and D. Ostermeier, *Policy Alternatives for Nonindustrial Private Forests* (Washington, D.C.: Society of American Foresters,

1971); and U.S. Department of Agriculture, *The Federal Role in the Conservation and Management of Private Nonindustrial Forest Lands* (Washington, D.C.: U.S. Government Printing Office, 1978).

20. See Wall, *Employment Implications;* also C.L. Bolsinger, *Timber Resources and the Timber Economy of Okanogan County,* U.S. Department of Agriculture, U.S. Forest Service, Pacific Northwest Forest and Range Experiment Station, Research Bulletin PNW-58, 1975; U.S. Department of Agriculture, U.S. Forest Service, *Final Environmental Statement: Twisp-Winthrop-Conconully Planning Unit Land Use Plan,* Okanogan National Forest, 1976.

8 Preservation Policy Issues

This review of American wilderness policy and its economic aspects shows that a number of unresolved policy issues await settlement. The basic issues were never faced directly by Congress, the administrative agencies, or the contending interests in the political struggle over wilderness. They are being dealt with, instead, on an ad hoc case-by-case basis. The issues discussed in this chapter are the future decisions that will determine the ultimate extent of our wilderness system and how it will be managed. To some degree at least, the economic principles and facts given in the previous four chapters will figure prominently in future discussions of these issues. The issues are the potential additions to the wilderness system and several practical and philosophical questions about wilderness land allocation.

Potential Additions to the National Wilderness System

Current case-by-case debates over specific areas are the expression of a basic policy conflict over the amount of the nation's resources that should be devoted to competing uses. Since wilderness as understood in current policy permits no extractive resource uses, the conflict is bitter. Areas can be made larger or smaller, but basically there is no way for the opposing groups to make compromises. The fundamental issue is the purpose and type of control that is to be exercised over resource use. The debates deal with hundreds of millions of acres of public domain lands administered by the Bureau of Land Management (BLM), with national forest roadless areas, and with the allocation of public land in Alaska.

Bureau of Land Management Lands

In Alaska, lands currently controlled by the BLM will be converted into park, forest, and wildlife refuge units in coming years. On those tracts, major wilderness areas will probably be established. Legislation submitted by the Secretary of Interior has provided for wilderness evaluations for both park service and wildlife service units created in Alaska.

On lands in the lower forty-eight states that will be retained in BLM control, the agency has preserved a small area in primitive status under

137

previous multiple-use and classification authorities. Under the 1976 Federal Land Policy and Management Act the Bureau plans a 15-year program of wilderness reviews covering a large acreage of roadless country, as reviewed in chapter 3.

National Forest Roadless Areas

The Wildland Research Center, surveying roadless tracts larger than 100,000 acres in area, found that about 7 million acres of de facto wilderness remained in national forests by 1960 (table 8-1). Under the 1964 Wilderness Act, national park and wildlife refuge unroaded units larger than 5,000 acres, plus roadless islands on the refuges, were to be surveyed for wilderness potential. On the national forests, however, only existing primitive areas were subject to mandatory review, but other roadless areas were not considered.

The Forest Service determined in 1967 to conduct a review of its 56 million acres of roadless areas for further study. This review got under way slowly, however. In February, 1971, Chief Cliff instructed the regional foresters to complete their reviews and public hearings by June 30, 1972. Data were collected to perform the so-called Roadless Area Review and Evaluation (RARE). The evaluation considered a range of criteria, including dispersal of areas, location of population centers, representation of a range of ecosystems, and obtaining wilderness acreage at the least opportunity cost in forgone resource values.[1]

When the draft environmental impact statement (EIS) was released in early 1973, a tremendous burst of outrage arose from environmental groups. The review had located a total of 1,449 roadless areas larger than 5,000 acres. Of these, it selected for study only 235 areas totaling 11 million acres. Many areas considered important by conservation groups were omitted. Many groups criticized the review as hasty and sloppy; the Forest Service admitted that it had been completed under tight time and budget constraints. The Sierra Club denounced the use of resource opportunity cost data in the evaluation, suggesting that the review had resulted in effect in a "woodless area inventory."[2] The Environmental Protection Agency (EPA) commented extensively on the draft environmental statement, noting in particular that wilderness reservations would have a favorable effect on water quality. The Attorney General's Office of California argued that the statement should actually discuss the impact of *not* selecting for study the 1,213 remaining areas.[3] The legislatures of Idaho and Wyoming, both of which states contain large areas of park and wilderness, memorialized the Secretary of Agriculture and the Forest Service to move cautiously in designating more wilderness.

Table 8-1
National Forest Roadless Area Inventories—Lands Outside Existing Designated Wilderness: 1960, 1973, 1978

Inventory	Year	Units	Millions of Acres
Wildland Research Center	1960		7
U.S. Forest Service, RARE-I	1973	274	56
U.S. Forest Service, RARE-II	1978	2,919	62

Sources: Wildland Research Center, 1962; U.S. Department of Agriculture, U.S. Forest Service, *Roadless Areas Review and Evaluation*, Washington, D.C., 1973; U.S. Department of Agriculture, U.S. Forest Service, *Final Environmental Statement, RARE-II*, Washington, D.C., January 1979.

The Forest Service, in response to the criticisms of the RARE review, corrected minor errors in its data and added a few areas to increase the total proposed for study to 274 areas totaling 12.3 million acres. The Roadless Area EIS provided no details as to the timetable to be established for study and recommendations on the final list.

In 1975, responding to the mandate of the Forest and Rangeland Renewable Resources Planning Act of 1974, the Forest Service presented a draft long-term program for national forest resources.[4] The program identified a range of opportunities for wilderness expansion, ranging from increases of 1.3 million to 25 million acres. The opportunity of devoting all 56 million roadless acres to wilderness was not discussed. Failure to consider that option left the program analytically incomplete and vulnerable to criticism.

During this period, two lawsuits affected Forest Service resource management and wilderness decision-making on the unroaded National Forest lands. These are the *Parker* case and the so-called de facto wilderness case, *Sierra Club* v. *Butz*.

In *Parker*[5] a group of individuals and environmental organizations brought suit to prevent the Forest Service from permitting timber-harvesting in an area adjacent to the Gore Range-Eagles Nest Primitive Area in Colorado. They asserted that the area should be studied for potential inclusion in the wilderness system before any timber-harvesting could be permitted. The Circuit Court ruled that areas contiguous to existing primitive areas, as long as they met minimum standards for wilderness quality, must be studied for their wilderness potential.[6] The U.S. Department of Agriculture officially believed that the decision in *Parker* was erroneous, and the Forest Service followed it only in the 10th Circuit.[7]

In the summer of 1972, the Sierra Club brought suit to halt all resource development activities in national forest roadless areas until environmental impact statements, wilderness studies, and public hearings had been completed.[8] The court granted a preliminary injunction barring resource development on 34 million acres of identified roadless areas. The Forest Service negotiated an out-of-court settlement, under which it agreed to file an environmental impact statement on any action affecting lands within the inventoried roadless areas.

As a result of the RARE review, existing Forest Service regulations, and the settlement in *Sierra Club* v.*Butz*, some protection of remaining roadless areas seemed assured. By 1974-1975, it appeared that the new study areas of the RARE review would be studied over an 8 to 10 year period and that further preservation initiatives on the national forests were unlikely.

The 1976 elections, however, carried into power the Carter Administration, which applied a strong environmental protection philosophy to public lands policy. President Carter attempted to halt a list of eighteen poorly justified water projects, supported expansion of Redwood National Park, and supported a strong preservation program for Alaska. He appointed former officials of environmental groups to senior policy posts. Assistant Secretary of Agriculture Dr. Rupert Cutler, a former Wilderness Society executive, believed that the pace set for allocation of the new study areas was too slow and the amount considered for wilderness too small. In addition, he saw the uncertain status of the entire roadless acreage as a barrier to multiple-use management and effective land use and timber harvest planning. He therefore initiated a new roadless area review, which was promptly dubbed RARE-II by all participants.

This review, conducted under difficult time and staff constraints, uncovered 2,919 areas totalling 62 million acres on national forests and grasslands, including a sizable acreage in the East.[9] A draft environmental statement issued in Spring 1978 discussed, in an often confusing manner, ten alternative allocations of the study areas among instant wilderness, further study, or return to multiple-use management. The statement did not offer a preferred alternative.

Predictably, RARE-II was condemned for doing too much and too little. Environmental groups fumed over parcels of wildland allegedly omitted.[10] Forest industry spokesmen foresaw vast resource lockups, doom for small lumber towns, and higher priced lumber for homebuilders.[11] Other observers saw that RARE-II was a basically political exercise that would raise expectations that could not possibly be fulfilled—and gloomily predicted a RARE-III before long.[12]

In January 1979, the Secretary of Agriculture announced his recommendations. He proposed to seek review based on RARE-II from governors and members of Congress before presenting a final proposal to Congress in late winter. His recommendation was to designate 15 million acres of instant wilderness (624 areas)—which would double the size of the existing national forest wilderness resource. He proposed 11 million acres (314 areas) for further study, and the immediate return of 36 million acres to multiple-use management. In the spring of 1979, the administration submitted final RARE-II proposals to Congress.

The RARE-II process assembled mountains of data, conducted over 200 public meetings, and established Wilderness Suitability Ratings for each tract identified. The masses of numbers, however, leave the reader feeling that something was missed somewhere. Meaningful contrasts among the numerous options seemed difficult to draw. At least, policy-makers were presented with something resembling a comprehensive view of the issue, which is certainly preferable to the alternative of area-by-area ad hoc decisions. But the results were predictable from the long-established pattern of federal wilderness decision-making. No one has ever cared enough about wilderness to provide funds and staff for the reviews and inventories. They were always (1964, RARE-I, RARE-II,) to be done by an already over-burdened staff. And, although most of the acreage is not immediately threatened, the work had to be done instantaneously, in a hasty manner ill befitting the seriousness of the decisions involved. In all, the situation does not do credit to those energetic individuals, inside and outside of government, who have claimed the mantle of wilderness protectors, saving wildlands for the public from the greedy special interests.

Wilderness in Alaska

Controversy has brewed for years over the "Forty Yellowstones"—the vast resource of public interest lands owned by the federal government in Alaska. The controversy has its roots in the tangled politics of Alaska statehood.[13] Under the Statehood Law of 1958, Alaska was entitled to select more than 103 million acres of land from the remaining public domain. These lands, plus tidelands granted under the same act, have provided the bonanza of oil lease bonuses and rentals since the Prudhoe Bay discoveries in the late sixties.

In 1971, another loose end in the statehood process was tied up. The Alaska Native Claims Settlement Act provided for the selection of 40 million acres of land plus a $1 billion cash settlement. The Act also provided, in Sections d-1 and d-2, that the Secretary of Interior may select lands of national interest for preservation in one of the four major federal land management systems—national parks, wildlife refuges, forests, and the wild and scenic river system. In December 1973, the Interior Department submitted its final d-1 and d-2 withdrawals to Congress—a total of 84 million acres (figure 8-1). The Sierra Club argued that more than

Source: U.S. Department of Agriculture, U.S. Forest Service.
Figure 8-1. U.S. Department of Interior Proposals for Alaska National
Interest Lands, 1973.

100 million acres should have been designated, an amount roughly
corresponding to the judgments of the Department's own experts as to the
amount of ecologically significant land in Alaska.[14] The largest single unit
the Club proposed was an 18.1 million acre Wrangell-Kluane International
Park, designed to protect mountain ranges and glaciers in South Central
Alaska.

In addition, conservation groups opposed the proposed allocation of 19
million acres to the Forest Service for multiple-use management. Even
though the Secretary's draft proposals noted that the Forest Service
expected to complete wilderness studies of these lands within three years,
conservationists feared uncontrolled resource development. Their
experiences in trying to oppose clear-cutting on the existing national forests,
and especially the lengthy litigation over the 50-year Champion International timber sale, lent substance to these fears. As a result, conservation

groups opposed a significant expansion of the Forest Service role in Alaska.

Congressional hearings proceeded annually after the Secretary's 1973 recommendation. Massive studies were produced in an atmosphere of tense interagency competition for a maximum stake in the nation's last frontier. In 1978, facing the end-of-year deadline for action, bills were introduced contemplating Alaska preservation systems ranging from about 30 million to 115 million acres (table 8-2).

When the Congress adjourned in December 1978, it was deadlocked over the Alaska Lands issue, and could not pass a bill by its own statutory deadline of December 18. In response, Secretary of the Interior Cecil D. Andrus withdrew 110 million acres of lands under existing authority. President Carter then designated 56 million acres of national monuments under the Antiquities Act of 1906. These moves, designed to provide interim protection until Congress could act, were bitterly denounced by development-oriented groups. In the early days of the 96th Congress, new Alaska bills were introduced.[15] At this writing, a large preservation package had passed the House, and was awaiting action in the Senate.

Wilderness Allocation Issues

Recurring themes in these debates are the balance between instrumental values of wildlands—commodity production—and amenity or intrinsic values. Previous chapters have reviewed the arguments about commodity production. Several more general issues, however, arise continually. These are: Does wilderness benefit a minority? Is wilderness consistent with multiple use? Is purity an essential property of wilderness? Should air pollution be allowed to degrade wilderness resources? These will be reviewed in turn.

Does Wilderness Benefit a Minority?

A perennial charge by wilderness opponents is that designating wildlands for wilderness benefits an exclusive minority, at the general public's expense. In chapter 1, values leading to the mandate for preservation were reviewed. It was found that protected wild areas do indeed benefit a wide range of people. Nonusers benefit from the protection of endangered species and wildlife habitat, from conservation of pure water sources, and preservation of cultural and scientific values. It is true that people who visit wilderness areas are a minority. But the beneficiaries are far more numerous than just the users. Wilderness advocates often righteously claim to represent the interests of the public as do the promoters of mining and

Table 8-2
Alaska Preservation Proposals: 1973-1978
(*millions of acres*)

	Society of American Foresters' Proposal	1974 Sierra Club	Interior Department 1973	U.S. Forest Service 1977	H R 39 1978	State of Alaska
National parks and monuments	14.890 (5 units, 2 additions)	44.0 (9 units)	32.26 (11 units)		64.1 (11 new units, 3 additions)	16.7
Wildlife refuges	20.902 (8 units, 2 additions)	58.9 (12 units)	31.59 (9 units)		46.4 (14 units)	15.3
Wild and scenic rivers	(9 streams instant, 15 study)	(13 streams)	(4 instant)		18 new; 15 study	
Multiple-use system	141.016 (19 units)	1.6 (2 units)	18.80	42.0	3.2	66.6
Total considered[a]	176.808	104.5	83.47		114.6 (much instant wilderness)	98.6 (includes 9.1 for special study)

Source: *Journal of Forestry*, July 1978, p. 401; E. Wayburn, "Great Stakes in the Great Land," *Sierra Club Bulletin*, September 1974; and U.S. Department of Agriculture, U.S. Forest Service, *New National Forests in Alaska*, Current Information Report no. 12, Washington, D.C. January 1977.
[a]Totals do not reflect individual items due to varying approaches to summarizing the data.

logging. These claims should not obscure the facts that large sectors of the public benefit from wilderness preservation and that use of publicly owned resources for commodity production is also in the public interest. The difficult task of balancing conflicting values is not aided by counting the downhill skiers, backpackers, or miners to see who is in the numerical minority.

Whereas wilderness areas supply a wide range of public benefits, they also supply specific private benefits to recreational users and water users. Recreationists, for example, benefit from free access to resources whose maintenance requires large annual outlays. Improved methods of charging user fees to recover these costs, reducing the subsidization of recreationists, should be implemented.

Is Wilderness Multiple Use?

The national forests are managed under a mandate to supply multiple wildland benefits to the public. These have been styled as timber, water, wildlife, recreation, range, and minerals.[16] The concept of multiple use assumes a harmony of resource uses and of user interests that rarely exists in practice. The concept, then, tends to mean what the speaker wants it to mean. Forest Service officers say, "What we do is multiple use." Environmentalists scorn "multiple abuse," saying, "you people cut too many trees. If you cut fewer trees, it would be multiple use." Industry spokesmen argue that using land for purposes inconsistent with logging and mining is not multiple use. In the Alaska debates, multiple use has come to be synonymous with commodity production.

Clearly, a sensible approach to multiple use does not require the production of every service on every single acre. A wilderness area produces a diversity of services and bars only a few activities. A ski resort or copper mine permits only a few uses on the acres it occupies. Timber-growing, contrary to the view held by some, is not necessarily a single-use and does not necessarily preclude wildlife, recreation, or other benefits.

The most serious consequence of the false wilderness versus multiple-use debate is that it creates an artificial and ultimately meaningless polarity of land uses. It bars the use of careful planning to create a large area of intermediate ground, in which backcountry values are given general protection, while low-intensity naturalistic silviculture, wildlife management, and recreation development are carried out.[17] In fact, the trade-off concept of "make up the timber lost by intensive management," may fall into this same trap. The ultimate result of huge wilderness areas, with pine plantations growing right up to their boundaries, would not seem to serve the true purposes of environmental protection.

How Untouched Must An Area Be To Qualify As Wilderness?

The issue of purity has received considerable discussion, especially for eastern wilderness. The debate contains several confusing threads, which will be briefly unraveled.

One question is the nature of boundaries and the propriety of internal enclaves or exclusions for nonconforming uses. The Forest Service has commonly drawn wilderness boundaries, or revised primitive area boundaries, to exclude commercially valuable resources. These decisions are often justified by the argument that certain rotting cabins, old roads, or other structures render the areas unsuitable for wilderness classification. Wilderness advocates have consistently opposed such thinking in hearings, articles, and public statements.[18]

The Park Service has submitted several wilderness proposals that were riddled with internal exclusions, providing locations for radio towers or weather stations. Private inholdings have also been excluded from wilderness status. This policy has been criticized as setting a dangerous precedent and permitting the managing agency excessive latitude.[19]

The Forest Service has performed its own balancing of interests in evaluating lands for wilderness suitability. The Forest Service justifies this position on the ground that the agency has a duty to consider local economic interests in making resource decisions. This is certainly true. But the wording of the 1964 Act, and the import of court decisions since, makes clear that Congress intended to reserve such balancing decisions for itself.

One common theme runs through the purity debate, enabling it to be correctly seen as a stand-in issue for other concerns. Purity is always taken with rigid seriousness by the development-oriented interests who oppose further wilderness designations. It is usually taken lightly by those who favor wilderness designations. These positions are easy to understand, when it is seen that in all cases purity is not the real issue.[20] The Forest Service, Park Service, and Fish and Wildlife Service endorse the purity position for another reason. The resource agencies, in opposing specific wilderness allocations, refer to several values. They refer to basic legislation authorizing their agencies to develop resources for public benefit. They argue that wilderness designation would restrict their freedom of action in complying with these legislative mandates. They also refer to the necessity for the use of professional judgment in resource decisions—a reflection of their commitment to professional norms and goals. It is the essence of a profession that it believes it knows what is best for its clients. Finally, they will note the fact that nearby local communities have a legitimate interest in resource uses on public lands and should not be economically injured by hasty or arbitrary action. The agencies simply seek to preserve their autonomy.

Environmentalists and wilderness advocates, in attacking the Forest

Service purity stand, found themselves taking curious positions. They were arguing that, well, timber-cutting, farming, or mining didn't really permanently destroy wilderness after all. See how fast areas could return to wilderness—in some cases in less than a century. See how much human intrusion could be tolerated—in southern Indiana, wilderness in the Hoosier National Forest was seriously proposed in a hilly area that contained working farms and more than two-dozen dwellings. At the same time, wilderness advocates in the West were arguing that tiny enclaves for rain gauges were serious evasions of the Wilderness Act, that temporary roads to carry out fire control or insect eradication work would permanently destroy wilderness, that trailside shelters or privies at campsites would be intolerable degradations of true wilderness.[21]

These examples could be multiplied at length by any careful reader of hearing transcripts, congressional debates, trade journals, and environmental magazines. They are assembled here not to make their writers appear foolish but to illustrate that the purity issue has simply become a stand-in for other value conflicts. There are basically three positions: (1) resource users, who desire access to as much public land as possible; (2) resource-managing agencies, who desire to preserve as much of their autonomy as possible; and (3) wilderness advocates, who desire to protect the largest possible amount of the nation's remaining wild lands.

The issues of boundary determination and purity have become intertwined in the specific debates discussed previously—the controversies over wilderness on BLM land, over national forest roadless areas, and over parks and wilderness in Alaska.

How Can Wilderness Be Protected from Air Pollution?

Threats to the visual character and environmental integrity of wild areas do not always come from bulldozers and loggers. Increasingly, threats of a more subtle character are affecting ecosystems in remote regions. In the sixties, it was realized that emissions from smelters were damaging vegetation in Montana's Glacier National Park and that this situation was not uncommon. Forests on ridges surrounding the Los Angeles Basin in southern California had suffered such damage for years.[22]

Visible browning of foliage is at least an obvious symptom of harm to vegetation. A far more subtle effect was noticed by scientists in the sixties and seventies. Researchers in New England observed that rainfall there was highly acid. They then found that the acidity of rainfall had increased in recent decades. On further study, it developed that acid precipitation—acid rain—had been intensively studied in Scandinavia, where it was thought to be responsible for reductions in fish populations and possible changes in forest soils.[23] Acid rain results from the airborne movement of sulfates from combustion of coal and other fossil fuels. The sulfates can make airborne water droplets significantly more acid than natural rainfall would be. The potential long-term effects of acid rain on wildland ecosystems are only beginning to be studied.

Wildlands cannot be preserved in their natural state, then, if they are downwind from major sources of air pollution. At a minimum, visibility may be reduced by nitrous oxides, and at worst, vegetation may be damaged by trace elements in fumes or by acid precipitation.

Amendments to the Clean Air Act, passed in 1970, declared a national policy to employ federal enforcement powers more vigorously to improve air quality.[24] The major effort was to be through state implementation plans and through regulations controlling automotive emissions. From the beginning, enforcement of the 1970 Amendments was a cauldron of controversy. Environmentalists objected to the EPA's failure to adopt stringent policies to prevent deterioration of air quality in regions where it was already high. Attempts by industrial groups and environmentalists to reform the significant deterioration policies led ultimately to the Clean Air Act Amendments of 1977.[25]

Under the 1977 Amendment, states are required to revise their state implementation plans to classify each air quality control region into two groups: attainment and nonattainment. Attainment areas that meet national standards for sulfur dioxide and total suspended particulates are designated as prevention of significant deterioration (PSD) areas. Three classes of PSD areas are then defined, each with specified degrees of latitude for permitting additional reductions in current air quality. The areas to be controlled most tightly are Class I, which consists of all international parks, national wilderness areas, and national memorial parks larger than 6,000 acres.[26] Detailed provisions cover the procedures to be employed in classifying regions into the three classes, for issuing permits, and for resolving differences between state and federal agencies.

The conflict between air quality and economic growth will be most intense in the Southwest and the northern Great Plains, where major increases in coal mining and electricity generation are planned. Potential air pollution impacts were the major cause for environmental opposition to the huge proposed Kaiparowits generating plant in southeast Utah, which was cancelled by the utility combine that planned it. In the Upper Colorado River Basin, plans for large oil shale development projects also conflict with air quality maintenance in a region with many wilderness areas and parks. In the RARE-II debate, wilderness opponents feared that the creation of still more Class I areas would hinder economic development further.

In these areas and elsewhere, the effectiveness of PSD policies will have a major impact on wilderness ecosystems and on the quality of the wilderness experience enjoyed by visitors. The task of balancing air quality against needs for additional energy and for economic growth in these regions—which tend to have low incomes and high unemployment—will be a severe challenge to our democratic institutions.

Overview

On hundreds of millions of acres of American wildland, the mandate for preservation remains to be fulfilled. These lands in Alaska, and on the national forests, national grasslands, and public domain lands, harbor significant conservation values. They also contain significant potential for production of wood, waterpower, and minerals. In a few years the nation will make decisions that will determine what lands will be preserved and what lands will be mined and roaded. The possibility of a lightly managed middle-ground status for much of this area has not yet been foreclosed, although at this writing it seems remote.

In determining the fate of this remaining wildland heritage, the Congress will have to consider arguments over whether wilderness benefits exclusively a minority. It does not. But one minority—recreationists—is currently being subsidized in an unnecessary way. Congress will be told that wilderness is—or is not—multiple use, and it should properly treat that question as a red herring. Similarly, there is considerable ambiguity in the view that wilderness must be, in some technical sense, pure. Finally, major national decisions about economic development and air quality control affect the existing and future wilderness system. The outcome of those decisions will have a major impact on the nation's wildland resource.

Notes

1. U.S. Department of Agriculture, U.S. Forest Service, *Roadless and Undeveloped Areas,* Final Environmental Impact Statement, Washington, D.C., 1973, p. 13.

2. "National Wilderness on the Line," *Sierra Club Bulletin,* March 1973, p. 9.

3. U.S. Department of Agriculture, *Roadless and Undeveloped Areas,* 1973, appendix 2.

4. U.S. Department of Agriculture, U.S. Forest Service, *The Forest Service Program for the Nation's Renewable Resources* (draft), Washington, D.C., August 1975.

5. 309 F. Supp. 593, 1 ERC 1163 (D. Colo. 1970), affirmed, 448 F. 2d 793, #3, ERC 1134 (10th Cir. 1971), cert. denied 405 U.S. 989, 3 ERC 1908 (1972).

6. This case reviewed in C. Wolcott, "Parker v. United States: The Forest Service Role in Wilderness Preservation," *Ecology Law Quarterly,* 3 (Winter 1973): 145.

7. W.C. Siegel, "Environmental Law—Some Implications for Forest Resource Management," *Environmental Law* 4 (Fall 1973).

8. *Sierra Club* v. *Butz,* 349 F. Supp. 934 (N.D. Cal., 1973).

9. U.S. Department of Agriculture, U.S. Forest Service *Roadless Area Review and Evaluation,* Draft Environmental Impact Statement, Washington, D.C., June 1978, with appendices. This document noted 2,686 areas; the final environmental statement summary (January 1979) included 2,919.

10. See, for example, B. Schneider, "Wilderness Through the Cracks," *American Forests* 84 (June 1978).

11. Useful sources for the industry viewpoint include Jay Gruenfeld, "David Is Goliath Now," *American Forests* 84, (June 1978): p. 14. Also, National Forest Products Association, *Wilderness Withdrawals and Timber Supply,* Washington, D.C., January 16, 1978; and American Forest Institute, *Wood and Wilderness, Can the National Forests Supply Both?* Washington, D.C., April 1978.

12. R. Day, "RARE-II, What Will it Buy?" *Journal of Forestry* 76 (April 1978): 204.

13. Letter from the Secretary of the Interior to the President, December 17, 1973 (transmitting draft bill creating management units from withdrawn d-2 lands). See also Joint Federal-State Land Use Planning Commission for Alaska, *Recommendations Concerning National Interest Lands,* Senate Committee on Interior and Insular Affairs, June 1974.

14. E. Wayburn, "Great Stakes in the Great Land," *Sierra Club Bulletin,* September 1974.

15. The Administration-supported bill was H R 39 (95th Congress, 2d Session, Report no. 95-1045, part 1, April 7, 1978), introduced by Rep. Udall, reintroduced again as H R 39 in the 96th Congress. The story is told in "Controversy over Alaska Lands Conservation," *Congressional Digest* 57 (December 1978): 289-314. Administrative protection is discussed in U.S. Department of the Interior, *Draft Environmental Supplement, Alternative Administrative Actions, Alaska National Interest Lands,* Washington, D.C., October 25, 1978. For additional reading on Alaska forest and wilderness issues, see U.S. Department of Agriculture, U.S. Forest Service, Alaska Region, *Tongass Land Management Plan,* Juneau, Alaska, June 1978; A.S. Harris and W.A. Farr, *The Forest Ecosystem of Southeast Alaska,* (U.S. Department of Agriculture, U.S. Forest Service, Pacific Northwest Forest and Range Experiment Station, General Technical Report PNW-25, 1974); *North American Forest Lands at Latitudes North of 60 Degrees* (Proceedings of Symposium, University of Alaska, Fairbanks, September 19-22, 1977). U.S. Congress, Office of Technology Assessment, *Analysis of Laws Governing Access to*

Federal Lands—Options for Access in Alaska (Washington, D.C.: U.S. Government Printing Office, February 1979).

16. Multiple Use-Sustained Yield Act of 1960; 16 USC 531, (1970). See, for a sampling of the large literature, classic analyses by J.F. Shanklin, *Multiple Use of Land and Water Areas,* ORRRC, Study Report 17, Washington, D.C., 1962, and by R.W. Behan, "The Succotash Syndrome: or Multiple Use—A Heartfelt Approach to Forest Land Management," *Natural Resources Journal* 7 (October 1967): 473-484. Also, P.R. Hagenstein, "The Public Land Law Review Commission and Its Approach to Land Use Conflicts," *Journal of Forestry* 70 (October 1972): 610-611; "Managing Federal Lands: Replacing the Multiple Use System," *Yale Law Journal* 82 (March 1973): 787.

17. See, for example, W. Shands and R. Healy, *The Lands Nobody Wanted* (Washington, D.C.: Conservation Foundation, 1977).

18. J. Foote, "Wilderness—A Question of Purity," *Environmental Law* 4 (1974): 255.

19. Foote, "Wilderness," p. 260.

20. See the debate in R. Costley, "An Enduring Resource," *American Forests* (June 1972), pp. 8-56, and R.W. Behan, "Wilderness Purism: Here We Go Again," *American Forests* (December 1972): pp. 9-11.

21. K. Haight, "The Wilderness Act: Ten Years After," *Environmental Affairs* 111 (1974): 299, has also noted this contradiction.

22. See, for example, W.H. Smith, "Air Pollution—Effects on the Structure and Function of the Temperate Forest Ecosystem," *Environmental Pollution,* 6 (1974): 111-129; W.H. Smith and L.S. Dochinger, eds., *Air Pollution and Metropolitan Woody Vegetation,* U.S. Department of Agriculture, U.S. Forest Service, Pinchot Institute for Environmental Forestry Research, 1975.

23. See G.E. Likens et al., *Biogeochemistry of a Temperate Forest Ecosystem* (New York: Springer, 1978), and U.S. Council on Environmental Quality, *Environmental Quality* (Washington, D.C.: U.S. Government Printing Office, December 1977), p. 195.

24. Clean Air Act, PL 91-604, (84 Stat. 1676), 31 December 1970.

25. See, generally, U.S. Council on Environmental Quality, *Environmental Quality* (Washington, D.C.: U.S. Government Printing Office, 1978), pp. 69-84.

26. PL 95-85, 91 Stat. 685; M. Reisner, "It's 1977: Why Don't We Have Cleaner Air?" *NRDC Newsletter,* March-June 1977. See also J. Whitaker, *Striking a Balance,* (Washington, D.C.: American Enterprise Institute, 1976), chap. 5; and B. Goldsmith and I.R. Mahoney, "Application of the 1977 Clean Air Act," *Environmental Science and Technology* 12 (February 1978): 144-149. An excellent legal review is provided in W. Perry Pendley and J. Michael Morgan, "The Clean Air Act of 1977: A Selective Legislative Analysis," *Land and Water Law Review* 13 (1978): 747.

Challenge of the Future: Wilderness Management

While debates still rage over large potential additions to the nation's wilderness system, management of the existing system must receive increasing attention. As the issue of wilderness allocation is settled in coming decades, the issue of wilderness management will become dominant. This chapter reviews five major concerns: resource management and protection, ecological and social aspects of recreational use, carrying capacity, policy options for managing visitor impacts, and several major management issues. The conclusion summarizes the importance of conflicting values in wilderness management.

Resource Management and Protection

Major issues of resource management and protection are dealt with in Sections 4 and 5 of the Wilderness Act. Mineral-prospecting and development are treated in chapter 6. Access to private holdings is provided for, and it is not at the moment a major issue. The Act requires that owners of inholdings be permitted access to their lands subject to reasonable regulation. Land exchange to eliminate inholdings is allowed. Inholdings may also be purchased as they become available by specific appropriation.

Natural forces alter ecosystems continuously. Beaches grow and recede, forests grow and change, and fires alter vegetation and damage man's property. Local attempts to resist beach erosion have been reconsidered by the National Park Service.[1] But forest and range protection presents more widespread conflicts. Wilderness boundaries do not affect wildfires, blowdowns, or insect and disease outbreaks. This fact has two implications. First, natural wilderness values—recreational, scientific, or watershed protection—can be damaged by catastrophic events originating outside the area. Should fire, insects, or disease outbreaks be fought at an area boundary or within the area to preserve wilderness values (see case 9-1)? On the other hand, fire, insect, and disease outbreaks originating within a wilderness area may threaten valuable resources outside of that area. Combatting these damaging agents usually requires vehicular access or other modifications of the terrain or the vegetation. In large blowdowns, which may cause bark beetle outbreaks, damaged trees must be cut and burned or hauled away. Fires are fought with heavy equipment or forces of firefighters who cut firebreaks through the vegetation. White pine blister rust is fought by eradication of *Ribes* (gooseberry), a shrub that serves as the pathogen's intermediate host.[2]

The Wilderness Act permits administrators to continue to maintain existing facilities and management practices—use of aircraft, for example—where already established. It also permits "such measures . . . as may be necessary in the control of fire, insects, and diseases, subject to such conditions as the Secretary deems desirable."[3] These words recognize the potential conflicts noted, but they provide no guidelines for concrete situations:

> . . . it is probable that these measures are authorized with the thought in mind that it would often be necessary to protect adjacent land outside of wilderness from the spread of fire and disease within wilderness boundaries. But when there is no danger of fire or disease spreading outside of a wilderness area, is there any limit on the control measures that may be used . . .?[4]

McCloskey notes that Forest Service regulations on this point take a conservative course, permitting controls only when damage will be "unacceptable."

An issue not addressed in the early discussion of wilderness resource protection is the fact that management on nearby lands can affect the lands within the areas. The most important example is fire. By exclusion of fire, the natural balance of plant communities is slowly altered by the forces of plant succession. Grasses, maintained by fires, give way to shrubby woodlands. Fire-regenerated species such as lodgepole pine are replaced by other species, more tolerant of shade but less tolerant of fire.

Management policy should be based on the purpose of the individual wilderness area—should the original vegetation be protected in its current condition, or should it be permitted to evolve under the impact of natural forces? Reservations exist that are intended to preserve remaining populations of plants, such as the ancient whitebark pines in California's mountains, or patches of old-growth white pine in New England. In such cases, prevention of their loss to fire may be a reasonable management goal. More commonly, the objective is protection of natural processes. In such cases, fires and disease outbreaks should be permitted to work their normal destruction, to regenerate new young forests over time.[5] In fact, both the National Park Service and the Forest Service are experimentally testing "let-it-burn" management policies on limited areas.[6] These experiments are testing the possibility of removing an artificial ecological factor—man's exclusion of fire.

Fire exclusion can have another serious effect. Without periodic light natural fires, fuel buildups occur, which can lead to more disastrous conflagrations later. Instead of frequent fires in low undergrowth and litter, disastrous crown fires, which kill the timber—and are much more difficult to control—become more likely.

A counterexample, however, can be cited. In some situations the unhindered working of natural processes will not promote the original goal of preservation. An example is the Sequoiah Forest of California (see case 9-2). Park officials have found that to perpetuate the Sequoiah, controlled burning is needed to permit sufficient regeneration. In this case, the purpose of the reserve is to perpetuate the large trees of a single species. Natural succession, which would supplant that species entirely, is unacceptable. But natural uncontrolled wildfire, endangering lives within the Park and threatening nearby resources, is not acceptable in most areas. Managed fire is being employed.

Another example is the Kirtland's warbler. This small bird lives in a very specialized habitat in only a few counties in Michigan. This habitat, a thinly stocked stand of young jackpine, is maintained by carefully controlled burning on national forest land. Normal plant succession would eliminate these stands and thus eliminate the warbler.

In sum, resource protection programs for wilderness areas must be based on the ecological role of fire, insects, disease, and other agents of change. The objectives of the management unit, human safety, and private property nearby must be considered. For these reasons, resource protection must be planned individually for each area. In some cases, simulation of natural processes, as with managed fire, will be required.

Wilderness Recreation: Ecological and Social Aspects

Although wilderness areas are established to protect natural environments in their untouched state, their principal use is usually in providing backcountry, low-density recreation experiences. This is not surprising given the growth in interest in backpacking and other wilderness pursuits. Recreation impacts have both ecological and social dimensions.

Ecological Impacts of Recreational Use

Recreational use of wilderness areas can have severe environmental effects. Since most existing wildernesses are in high mountain regions and in deserts, their plant life and soils tend to be easily damaged. Regrowth, because of the harsh physical conditions, can be slow. Specific impacts include[7]:

1. Trampling and erosion of trails. Hikers and packstock can trample and destroy vegetation that will not grow back in alpine areas, in areas of

poor drainage, or where soil porosity is destroyed. Where trails cross streams, erosion and bank failure can be accelerated.

2. Camping debris. Accumulations at campsites and along trails can create costly and disruptive disposal problems. Agencies hope that intensive "pack-it-out" programs will reduce this impact.

3. Campsites. Wilderness areas tend to develop famous campsites at important trail junctions, fishing spots, overlooks, or water supplies. These areas are quickly overused. Trampling can damage the plant community and even weaken large trees.

4. Wood supply. The popularity of campfires as part of the wilderness experience and the old styles of pioneering—using poles and saplings for improvised camp structures—can devastate the woods for a wide area surrounding a heavily used campsite. For this reason, stove-only camping is being required in more and more areas.

5. Water quality. Wildland recreation uses can cause water pollution through poor sanitation practices, dishwashing, and erosion.

Horseback trips with muletrain packstock can cause significant degradation through direct trampling and also through livestock feeding. In areas subject to heavy use by such parties, careful management is necessary to prevent overgrazing.

Varied techniques have been used to reduce the impacts of overuse. Most involve rationing access to favored campsites and the development of alternative routes and sites. Trails and campsites are often relocated away from sensitive lakesides and moved onto the drier uplands nearby. Occasionally, trail maintenance has been reduced to reduce use by increasing the difficulty of travel. Campsites and packstock-grazing areas are periodically closed and rotated where feasible. It has been found in the Boundary Waters Canoe Area that this policy cannot succeed in halting campsite deterioration, because it is not feasible to leave sites idle for sufficiently long periods.[8]

In the eastern mountains, steep terrain and sensitive mountaintop vegetation led trailbuilders to use shelters as campsites to concentrate use and to limit the area of ground disturbance. This policy has evolved to the point where meals and lodging are provided at selected locations in New Hampshire's White Mountains. The simple, open-front trail shelters remain an eastern institution, however, which is vigorously opposed by many western hikers.

In a few extreme cases, direct supervision of visitors has been attempted. Rangers require first-come-first-serve reservations at overused campsites. Those arriving too late must hike elsewhere. Limits on routes are often specified. One tool for accomplishing the necessary control is the mandatory wilderness permit. The permit serves the dual function of providing the manager with visitor use-data and helping to control visitor pressure on sensitive areas.[9]

Social Aspects of Wilderness Use

The previous section concentrated on the impact of overuse on the ecosystem. But there is another equally significant management issue—the impact of overuse on the quality of the wilderness experience. Many wilderness users seek remote areas to enjoy open lands in a relatively solitary setting. The term "relatively" is appropriate, since sociological studies show that the lone hiker is a rarity. The basic unit of wilderness recreation use is a group—from a couple to a scout troop.

Robert C. Lucas notes four prime imperatives in wilderness management from a social standpoint[10]:

1. Maintenance of a wide opportunity spectrum. This means maintaining a diversity of recreational opportunities ranging from developed campsites at roadheads to remote trailless expanses in the heart of wilderness areas.
2. Management of the wilderness periphery. The wilderness should be protected, as far as possible, from incursions at its margins that will be visible from within the area.
3. Management should strive to preserve visitor freedom of action. Methods of information, education, and development of additional trails and campsites within and outside of designated wilderness all play a part.
4. Management should emphasize the provision of opportunities for solitude.

Sociological research has shown that users perceive the quality of wilderness experience in terms of the number of encounters per day on the trail, the types of groups encountered, the condition of trails and campsites, and the opportunity for solitary camping.[11]

The quality of the wilderness experience, then, can be affected by management. Generally, steps that will increase the quality of the user's wilderness experience will also reduce unfavorable impacts on the natural environment. But steps to reach both of these goals must inevitably involve controls over the recreationist, even if only of a limited sort.

The fact that wilderness users are a diverse group with varying backgrounds and seeking different outdoor experiences leads to management conflicts. Should horses be banned from certain areas if they degrade mountain meadows and reduce the enjoyment of other users? Should motors be banned from the Grand Canyon or from the Boundary Waters Canoe Area because they are offensive to some of the users? These questions cannot be answered in a vacuum. In the absence of clear policy guidance from Congress, the agencies have answered them in varying ways, depending partly on local pressures.

George H. Stankey has suggested that the criterion for decisions in such

conflicts should be to follow the purist view—that choice will result in preservation of the natural resource and of the quality experience for all
users.[12] This represents a value judgment that the kind of experience desired
by the purist should be the only kind provided.

The move toward control of visitors as the solution to overuse has been
criticized by W.R. Burch, who argues that static concepts of use capacity
are not a sound basis for recreation management:

> Wildland management—except for commercial operations such as logging,
> grazing, and mining—seems to have always been custodial rather than
> service-oriented; consequently, barriers and channels and rules and restric-
> tions, and reservations and regulations, have emerged as the chief manage-
> ment tools of the profession. Unlike wildlife management, recreation
> management has never had a positive goal of seeing how many can be
> supported on a given range, or how various migratory patterns can be pro-
> tected, or how, through good management, the capacity of the habitat can
> be increased. People, as they say in business, are problems.[13]

This view urges that wilderness management should be aimed at
developing trail systems and use patterns so as to maximize the number of
people who can use a given area, while avoiding congestion and environmental impacts. This view is based on a different value orientation
than Stankey's purist approach.

As pressures on wilderness increase, it will become apparent that there
are some wilderness purposes—ecosystem preservation, wildlife habitat
protection—which are inconsistent with recreational use.[14] In some way,
those areas that are to be preserved for preservation's sake will have to be
delimited on the ground and protected from recreational incursions. A
major guide in the management process will be the concept of carrying
capacity.

Carrying Capacity

To aid wilderness managers in setting desired recreation-use levels for wild
areas, the concept of carrying capacity has been developed. Carrying
capacity has been adapted by wilderness managers from the concept
commonly applied to rangeland grazing—the maximum level of use sus-
tainable over time without degrading resource productivity. Such a notion
is biologically straightforward for dealing with the impact of Here-
ford steers on grassland—although experienced ranchers, range scientists, and administrators might (and often do) disagree on whether a
particular range is overgrazed. Carrying capacity has been adopted as a
convenient shorthand for a set of ideas that can be applied as well to the
management of people using wildlands for recreation.

Carrying capacity was defined by one of its early students as: " . . . the level of recreational use an area can withstand while providing a sustained quality of recreation. . . . If quality is to be sustained, it is important that values not be used up faster than they are produced. . . ."[15]

There are two kinds of Carrying capacity: ecological and social (see table 9-1). It is possible to find numerous examples of users exceeding the ecological carrying capacity of a given area; some have been discussed. Clearly, an ecological concept of carrying capacity is one of the basic management constraints that must be faced.

Measurement of ecological carrying capacity may be far from a simple matter. Obvious compaction, erosion, and vegetation damage may not be the only important concerns. A wider concept of ecological capacity would have to include the impacts of visitor use and occupancy on wildlife, through direct habitat damage as well as through disruption of feeding and migration patterns, and direct conflict for use of certain areas, as near ponds and streams. Ecological carrying capacity seen in this way clearly varies with season of the year and may vary from year to year, as does range livestock carrying capacity.

A more complex concept of carrying capacity has been proposed.[16] This is the concept of "design capacity." This concept employs measures of past site use, present condition, and past ecology and management measures. It then specifies a range of future use and management options to determine an optimum balance of use level, considering management cost and user demand in addition to the ecology of the site. This concept recognizes that management inputs, such as waterbars, huts, or campsite rotation can raise the use level at which a given level of site disturbance is sustained.

More recently, analysts have developed different concepts of social carrying capacity for wildlands. This concept is based on the notion that visitor interactions might set a social carrying capacity that differs from the ecological carrying capacity. As use of an area increases, encounters between users increase, and congestion rises at campsites and near entry points. So total benefits per user decline as total use increases. To assess total benefits from recreational use, therefore, it is necessary to account for the effect of both higher use and lower benefits per user. A case study of this approach has been conducted for Montana's Spanish Peaks Wilderness. By surveying users and statistically estimating how encounters and congestion affect their willingness to pay for wilderness use, Charles J. Cicchetti and V. Kerry Smith were able to estimate the level of use that produced the highest level of total user benefit.[17]

Studies of user preferences for different encounter levels and for encounters with different types of users (large groups, horses) have been widely used in providing guidance to management about social carrying capacity. But it seems unlikely that studies of social carrying capacity by themselves will answer all the questions confronting wilderness managers.

Table 9-1
Carrying Capacity Concepts

Concept	Definition
Rangeland—cattle	Grazing level sustainable indefinitely; no site degradation.
Recreation—ecological	
Site degradation	Use-level sustainable indefinitely; no site degradation.
Wildlife disturbance	Use-level possible without disruption of wildlife populations, migration, or habitat (for example, overfishing).
Recreation—social	
Economic	Use-level that maximizes aggregate net benefits to users, considering the decline in benefits per user as total use rises.
Preferences	Level at which expressed satisfaction of users appears at maximum.

There will remain a need for informed value judgments about the recreational objectives to be sought in a given area, and the best methods of achieving them. Informed estimates of ecological and social carrying capacity will be useful guides in this decision-making process.

Policy Options for Managing Visitor Impacts

To provide a coherent framework for analyzing the problems posed by visitor impacts, by social interactions of visitors, and by management needs on adjacent nonwilderness lands, an economic perspective may be helpful.

The perceived problem is that some wilderness areas are being overused in either ecological or sociological terms. This may be perceived in economic terms as a demand-supply disequilibrium. In effect, free availability of wilderness recreation has led to an excess of demand over supply, in effect changing the quality of the service provided. Options for dealing with the situation are two: supply-expanding programs and demand-constraining programs. Once a suitable carrying capacity concept has been chosen, these options can be used to prevent that capacity from being exceeded.

Expanding Supply

Following Burch's admonition, managers might consider programs to expand the effective supply of recreation opportunities. Specific steps might include:

1. Allocation of more land to wilderness. This is unlikely to solve the problem, since congested areas are near cities and much disputed roadless land is remote. In any event, allocating more land simply to mitigate congestion problems is a stop-gap that cannot meet escalating demand forever.
2. Hardening sites. Sites subject to heavy concentration of uses can be "hardened" by provision of privies, picnic tables, and even tentsites or huts. Wilderness purists tend to oppose such measures.
3. Improved information can expand the effective supply by advising users of areas that are congested and suggesting alternative areas that receive little use.
4. Trail development and roadhead planning. Many vast wildernesses are subject to severe crowding near the most popular roadheads, while thousands of acres remain empty. Improved access to existing wilderness areas could multiply the effective supply of wilderness recreation manyfold and could help reduce congestion at currently crowded areas. Since additional access roads would often cross existing roadless areas, they would likely be opposed by wilderness groups.
5. Improved backcountry opportunities. Development of additional trail and hut systems in lightly developed backcountry outside of existing wilderness deserves priority consideration. Such programs are described later.[18]

Perhaps as a result of the attitudes of the wilderness movement and administrators of wilderness areas, supply-expanding programs seem to have fared poorly in comparison with steps to constrain demand.

Constraining Demand

Overuse and congestion have usually been dealt with by demand-constraining programs. These programs aim to reduce congestion directly by restricting the user activities. Demand constraints can take two forms: user restrictions and rationing of access.

Restrictions on users can effectively increase the usability of wilderness and reduce congestion. Restrictions designed to spread use from peak periods—weekends and three-day holidays—to off-peak periods would significantly reduce congestion. Restrictions on camping, in use in some areas, can reduce perceived congestion by barring camping within 100 feet of a trail or 200 feet of a waterway. Such restraints work simply by spreading the users out.

Rationing of access has been used in extreme cases. It has taken the form, most frequently, of first-come-first-serve or reservation arrangements. A wide range of rationing options can be applied:

1. Selective trail nonmaintenance. This increases the difficulty of reaching some locations.
2. Cutting back roadheads. This has the same effect as selective trail nonmaintenance.
3. Requiring qualifications of fitness or wilderness knowledge. Some combination of these three methods is advocated by some wilderness purists who see wilderness as the domain for the strong.[19]
4. First-come-first-serve. Managers turn back visitors when an area becomes filled to "capacity," or reroute them to other locations.
5. Advance reservations. Both first-come-first-serve and reservations have significant administrative costs and impose costs on users. Reservations are used in national parks and in some eastern wilderness areas.
6. Random selection through a lottery. Hunting licenses for moose and other game are often distributed in this way. Rationing wilderness use through such a procedure would have equity advantages but could be complex and costly to administer.
7. Peak-load pricing. Demand in peak-use periods could be shaved by using entrance fees for only those days that experience congestion. Users might then be motivated to plan trips for off-peak periods.
8. Auctioning permits. The price system could be used to ration access and clear the market. This option is discussed later.

One imaginative proposal suggests using "risk zoning."[20] Under this concept an area would be divided into risk zones in which potential users would have equal probabilities of having permit applications rejected. This proposal would allow users themselves to express more accurately their preferences for solitude and wilderness. This is essentially a lottery method of rationing use.

In practice, combinations of all these methods will have to be employed. The optimal mix of methods must be determined based on the specific problems and opportunities offered by each distinct area. One barrier to improved wilderness management in the past has been differing perceptions of the resource on the part of managers and users. To overcome these differences, managers have begun conducting sample surveys to determine wilderness-user preferences. Also, quantitative models for predicting use pressure are being developed and tested.[21]

Developing effective and equitable programs combining opportunities to expand supply and constrain demand for wilderness recreation will be a major challenge to resource managers in the years ahead. As the conflicts over wilderness allocation subside, new conflicts over management will emerge. (See case 9-3, in which Maine's Baxter State Park presents an unusually rich mix of wilderness management choices.)

Four Management Issues

This section reviews four practical management problems: management of adjacent lands, trail management, wildlife management, and pricing.

Management of Adjacent Nonwilderness Lands

In mountainous areas, roads, timber cuts, and prescribed burns can be seen for miles, diluting the visitor's sense of isolation. This has generated demands for extensive scenic buffers around some wilderness areas. These demands strengthen the case for designing wilderness areas as far as possible around natural terrain units, to minimize the impact of inharmonious developments. Resource preservation may be made difficult or impossible by nearby management. The most prominent example is the impact of nearby logging on Redwood National Park. In the Grand Canyon, river fluctuations because of power generation schedules at Glen Canyon Dam have caused changes in stream fauna, shore vegetation, and beaches, and can affect recreational users as well.

On the other hand, lands not in wilderness status but thinly roaded and lightly utilized for timber or other extractive purposes deserve much more careful development as backcountry recreation areas. With access through existing roads and with carefully designed trails and shelter systems, these regions could provide a significant recreational resource for hiking, cross-country skiing, and camping. These areas would probably absorb considerable use pressure now being placed on designated wilderness areas:

> Backcountry areas could provide a quality primitive recreation experience desired by many people, for example, good hike-in fishing, which Wilderness provides somewhat incidentally and not always well. If people seeking this type of opportunity could find it better outside Wilderness, this could help free Wilderness to serve its own function . . . People who just want to hike should not be forced into Wilderness or related areas.[22]

In fact, just such an approach was recommended by the Conservation Foundation in a study of the eastern national forests.[23] The authors argued that a sensitive program of managing nonwilderness lands for multiple uses in such a way as to preserve a general backcountry atmosphere could help meet diverse needs for recreation and for timber and other wildland products on the East's small area of federal forest land.

Wilderness visitors often find unpleasant sights awaiting them at the gateways into the backcountry. Eloquent words have been written condemning the tacky miles of tourist development on both ends of the parkway through Great Smoky Mountain National Park, which will include one of the largest federal wildernesses in the East. A group studying national park management had harsh words for the Park Service's handling of this issue: " . . . We believe the Park Service has been much too tardy, timid, and reluctant in identifying and challenging external threats to the parks and aggressively working against these threats."[24] In all fairness, it must be noted that the Park Service has no policy levers with which to affect nearby development, outside of direct land purchase—an option already highly unpopular in the neighborhood of most parks. But the management of roadsides and related resources near major wilderness areas can be expected to become an increasing concern to land-managing agencies.

The most significant effort to address this issue is New York's Adirondack Park Agency. Created in 1971, the Agency's first task was to establish two management plans. The first, covering 2.3 million acres of state lands, provided for wilderness and primitive uses for much of the area. The most controversial plan, however, was the land use and development plan. This plan applied a scheme of development controls and land-use allocations to 3.7 million acres of privately owned land within the "blue line" designating the Park. This planning process was created to minimize the threats to the entire region posed by uncontrolled speculative land sales and recreational developments. As it sought to implement its plan through permits, the Agency found itself in a welter of lawsuits. An approach of this kind has been used in England's national parks, and it is the only way to protect rural economic and environmental values in scenic mountain regions.[25]

Becoming increasingly controversial is the problem of user transportation in and near wilderness areas. Controversial examples include the North Cascades Highway in Washington, the proposed airport expansion at Jackson Hole, and the proposed new highway in Great Smoky Mountain National Park.

Trail Management

One of the most important aspects of backcountry management is trail management. The backcountry trail systems accomodate the heaviest recreational uses by hikers and riders. Their design, management, and protection require constant attention and expense. Maintenance alone, in steep and unstable terrain, can cost thousands of dollars per mile annually (figure 9-1).

There are more than 100,000 miles of hiking trails in the United States,

Figure 9-1. Backcountry Trail, Grand Canyon National Park. (National Park Service Photo.)

of which about two fifths are on public land.[26] These trails are actively used by about 14 million persons each year—making hiking with a pack the nation's eighteenth largest outdoor recreational activity.

The major challenge in trail management is corridor protection. This may be no problem in dedicated wilderness, but it assumes considerable proportions outside of wilderness and on private land. On trails such as the Appalachian Trail (682 miles federal, 452 miles state, 866 miles private), protection is the biggest management problem. Trail sponsors employ a range of devices for this purpose, including written agreements, purchase of land, and purchase of easements.[27]

A joint U.S. Department of the Interior and U.S. Department of Agriculture study, *Trails for America,* appeared in 1967. This report documented existing trail systems, discussed major management problems, and recommended the establishment of a national trails system. The report gave detailed descriptions of the Appalachian, Pacific Crest, Potomac Heritage, and Continental Divide Trail proposals. It recommended establishment of Lewis and Clark, Oregon, North Country, Natchez Trace, and Santa Fe Trails. The report was instrumental in aiding the passage of the National Trails System Act of 1968.[28] The Act designated the

Appalachian and Pacific Crest Trails as initial components of the national trails system. It established three classes of trail—recreation, scenic, and connecting.

Sensitive planning of trails through backcountry outside of wilderness can be one of the most important positive steps taken in wilderness management. Careful layout of roadheads, trail-corridor protections, and possible use of floating trail systems can greatly multiply the effective use capacity of backcountry. It can provide a greater diversity of outdoor experiences and provide them closer to urban areas and at lower elevations, where they can be used a greater portion of the year. In view of the potential conflicts between wilderness and backcountry hikers and off-road vehicle users, trail planning for very different kinds of uses is essential.[29]

Wildlife Management

Wildlife populations may be incidental inhabitants of wilderness areas, as in most cases, or they may be the principal motive for their establishment, as is the case for the Tule Elk reserves and the California Condor reserves in California. Recreation may conflict with wildlife, as in the case of hikers and grizzly bears in Glacier Park, or wildlife populations lacking natural predation may endanger their own range through overgrazing. Whatever the case, wildlife management raises especially difficult problems for administrators. First, wildlife is controlled by state laws and agencies, leading to potential disagreements with administrators of the federal lands on which most wilderness areas exist.[30] Second, management of wildlife involves established constituencies with differing objectives, so that management programs are often highly controversial.

Perhaps the two best known examples are the Yellowstone Park elk herds, and the wild horses and burros of the Intermountain West.[31] In both cases, the herds have overpopulated their range, threatening severe ecological damage and losses to other resource uses, both within and outside of established wilderness units. The major factor in both cases is the lack of sufficient natural predation to keep populations in balance with their range, because of the elimination of wolves and mountain lions. In the case of the wild horses and burros, the option of killing the animals to control their population is barred by federal law.[32] In most cases, the option of habitat improvement is barred by policies of minimizing artificial disturbances of wilderness communities. Trapping and transplanting animals is an important management technique. From 1892 to 1963, 10,478 elk were removed from Yellowstone in this way.[33] Because of legal restrictions on hunting, it is the principal hope for managers of the wild horse and burro herds. Where permitted, hunting outside wilderness unit boundaries by the public may be of assistance. As a last resort, the Park Service has at times removed animals with its own staff of hunters. Although highly controversial, this practice was defended by the Secretary of the Interior's Special Advisory Board on Wildlife Management and was integrated into policy in the agency's 1969 policy handbook.

Pricing Wilderness Recreation

Managers have been reluctant to use pricing in the management of wilderness areas. This is so despite three important facts:

1. Giving away a valuable service results in overuse—ecological damage as well as congestion. This applies to appropriative water rights, range rights, or fishing rights, as well as to the right to use wilderness for recreation.
2. Free admission to wilderness areas subsidizes wilderness users by failing to require them to share in area operation and maintenance costs, or to share in any resource opportunity costs created by withdrawal of the area.[34]
3. Observers have noted a consistent bias in the congressional appropriations process against Forest Service activities that do not raise revenue.[35]

In view of these facts, pricing could play a potentially useful role in a mix of management policies. Charging fees would be feasible in most wilderness areas, since access points are typically few. In addition, the extension of the mandatory permit program would allow fee collection at the point of permit issuance. Fees could serve a useful role in restraining congestion—some users might, to avoid fees, use undeveloped backcountry outside of designated wilderness. Imaginative use of fees could allow peak-load or peak-area pricing to aid programs to redirect use away from heavily congested areas or time periods. Finally, fees could provide a revenue source capable of enhancing congressional support for funding maintenance expenses for wilderness areas and for accelerating the program of studies for areas still under study.

The first objection to charging fees for wilderness use is a practical one—it is against the clear intent of a decade's history of congressional policy on recreational use fees.[36] In the somewhat confused development of current policy, perhaps the only theme that is clear is that Congress does not desire that fees be charged for undeveloped areas.

This view may be characterized as "Davy Crockett economics." It asserts that government may charge for the use of the works of man (campsites) but not for access to the works of nature (wilderness). Such a view, of course, ignores the fact that wild areas sometimes have opportunity costs and that they demand significant expenditures in operation and maintenance costs. Another objection is found in the views of the recreational users. Many wilderness users appear to object to the idea of charging a fee for use of wild areas. Views vary, but there is a sense that charging for wilderness use is in a vague way immoral and inequitable.

Robinson has responded to the view that charging fees for wilderness use would be inequitable: "To all appearances the effect of providing free (or minimally priced) outdoor recreational opportunity on the federal lands is to shift wealth from a majority of the public to a minority who engage in outdoor recreation, and from relatively low income groups to the well-to-do.[37] In any event, Robinson argues, when compared to alternative means of rationing access, it is not clear that they are superior to pricing on equity grounds:

> The use of a fee to control access to a falcon eyrie is perhaps distasteful. But so too is an administrative edict that turns away those last in line. Again, putting equity aside, the only thing one can say of the latter is that it rewards the early riser and those who are fortuitously close to the site; neither person seems morally more deserving than the person who expresses his interest by the money he is willing to pay . . .[38]

Such views are hard to evaluate, but it is significant that "Davy Crockett economics" has been overcome in the wildlife field with a healthy effect on the availability of funds for wildlife conservation. As for the equity arguments, it seems unlikely that fees would be set at levels high enough to price users out of the market entirely. Few would advocate simply auctioning wilderness permits off to the highest bidders. All that is argued here is that pricing practices can be a useful tool in a mix of wilderness management practices, that they can help cover costs of wilderness management, and that they will reduce the subsidization of a minority.

Values in Wilderness Management

This chapter reviews the challenges faced by managers of wilderness areas. It summarizes measures that managers may take to see that recreation use remains within specified ecological and social carrying capacities. Many of the examples cited, however, show that determination of carrying capacities and appropriate management tools are not simple technical problems. They involve deep conflicts of values held by different groups of users and managers.[39] For ease of discussion, the values involved are shown in tabular form (table 9-2).

Table 9-2
Values in Wilderness Management

Value	Implication
Values referring to the resource	
Stewardship of utilitarian resources. (Subcase: Protect neighboring private or public commercial resources)	Control fire, insects, and disease to minimize direct destruction of existing timber, wildlife, and watershed protection values.
Unfettered operation of natural forces	Control damaging agents only at unit boundaries. Accept normal plant and animal succession (for example, reduction in deer population as forests mature).
Preserve existing plant or animal community	May dominate when considering endangered or rare species, or usually old-age classes (for example, Redwoods, old growth White Pine). May require exclusion of human uses.
Values referring to users	
Absolute wilderness	Minimize recreational use. Exclude all motorized equipment. No structures or signs.
Freedom of movement	Allow unhindered movement of users, regardless of social or ecological carrying capacity.
Access to users of different ages, incomes, or abilities	Develop convenient roadheads, huts, signs, and maximize development of adjacent backcountry for recreation.

Most decisions about wilderness management, although they may require biological or other technical information, are really decisions about values. In most cases of any practical importance, conflicting values about management goals will always occur. Such value conflicts cannot be resolved on a broad geographic basis by any central authority. They must be addressed in terms of the specific goals and conditions of a given land area. Each designated wilderness area will contain important natural features or processes and will play a particular role as a recreational resource. Intelligent management planning, with effective involvement of affected agencies and user groups, is required to develop appropriate management objectives and constraints for each area. An excellent review of policy options is provided by Stankey and Baden.[40]

For example, use of huts, tent platforms, and privies might be considered appropriate management in New Hampshire's White Mountains, but might be inappropriate in Colorado's Maroon Bells. Likewise, in areas of heavy recreational pressure, it might be found desirable to rely heavily on visitor management methods such as reservations, permits, and increased access routes to meet needs, where in other areas the ecological carrying capacity at low management investments would be the effective guideline. No one value or set of values can dominate every individual case.

As another example, managed natural fire might be considered mandatory in a wild area, to allow natural plant succession to occur uninterrupted. But if a principal purpose of the reservation is to protect an unusual and significant stand of a particular type, fire protection might be justifiable. Such an argument has been made in the case of unusual old growth spruce stands in Maine's Baxter Park. On the other hand, the Sequoiah National Park case is an example of direct and costly management intervention into plant succession to remedy artificial changes in vegetation caused by generations of fire exclusion.

Finally, an excellent case study in wilderness management is provided by the National Park Service's long-term struggle to control visitor use, protect fragile riverfront areas, and mediate conflicts between motor-powered and oar-powered rafting groups in the Grand Canyon.[41]

For a more detailed review of the field of wilderness management, the reader should consult Hendee, Stankey, and Lucas' major monograph, recently published by the U.S. Forest Service.[42]

Case 9-1. Chemical Spraying for Forest Insect Control

Before passage of the Wilderness Act, insect control activities in national parks and in national forest wilderness were extensive. Such activities included spraying of DDT for control of western spruce budworm and other defoliators. Since that time, greater emphasis has been placed on managing wilderness as a haven for operation of natural forces, including insects. In addition there has arisen a greater concern for the ecological impacts of wide-scale pesticide use. For example, spray programs using DDT in the Yellowstone region in the late fifties inflicted heavy damage on fish populations. Insecticides now employed have far less severe effects and are less persistent in the environment. But their use still constitutes an intervention into natural processes in the forest.

In many forest types, epidemics of native defoliating insects are a natural ecological force, which removes overmature forest stands and regenerates new forests. This is true of some bark beetles as well. The insect infestation serves the same function as fire, and it may in fact increase the likelihood of fire by producing areas of dry, dead trees that make highly flammable fuel for several years until they fall over and rot. Introduced insects may at times become important pests, as has the Gypsy Moth in the Eastern United States. In such a case, the usual arguments for the unhindered work of natural forces may not have the same persuasiveness. Introduced insects often lack natural enemies and can cause heavy devastation that may exceed damage done by native pests. In addition, sound quarantining practices may be able to slow their spread to uninfested areas.

In the mid-seventies a major outbreak of the western spruce budworm emerged in the forests on the east side of the Cascade mountains in Washington and Oregon. Several sizable spray projects were conducted to reduce timber damage and to prevent increases in fire hazard from dead timber. Because of the rugged terrain, helicopters were employed to apply the insecticides. In 1977, 90,000 acres within national parks and national forest wilderness were scheduled for spraying, on the basis that failure to spray would leave reservoirs of insects to reinfest nearby areas outside wilderness. Because of weather and other factors, the wilderness areas were not sprayed as planned. [a]

---

[a] Practices used in parks and forests in the fifties are summarized in Wildland Research Center, *Wilderness and Recreation,* Outdoor Recreation Resources Review Commission, Report 3 (Washington, D.C., U.S. Government Printing Office, 1963) pp. 287-298.

Case 9-2: Fire Management in Yosemite National Park

The conflict between the Wilderness Act's mandate to protect natural processes, and the traditional resource management approach to protecting natural resources is well illustrated by fire management in Yosemite National Park. The area's original mixed conifer forest was largely open and free of underbrush and was interspersed with small meadows. Walking or riding through the forest was easy, unhindered by undergrowth and dense regeneration. Park management emphasizing fire protection completely altered this community:

> Overprotection from natural surface fires permitted the forest floor to become a tangle of understory vegetation and accumulated debris. Shade-tolerant incense-cedar and white fir thickets increased and caused an unnatural ecological succession away from the less shade-tolerant ponderosa and sugar pines. . . . The early management decision to extinguish all natural fires has led to conditions which not only threaten to destroy those park values which were intended to be preserved but also modify the forest to an unnatural state. [a]

In Yosemite and elsewhere, the Park Service and the U.S. Forest Service are modifying their fire suppression policies, with the aid of complex scientific modelling techniques. The gradual shift to let-it-burn rules for selected areas has been made more difficult by the fact that the successional changes produced by barring fire have created highly flammable ecosystems, forests in which fires no longer harmlessly burn through litter but threaten to become unmanageable crown fires. In response, Park Service managers are testing the use of managed "prescribed burns" to reduce fuel loads and aid the return of the forest to its natural, unmanaged condition.

---

[a] J.W. Wagtendonk, *Refined Burning Prescriptions for Yosemite National Park,* National Park Service Occasional Paper no. 2, n.d., Washington, D.C., pp. 1-2.

Case 9-3: Managing a State-Owned Wilderness: Baxter State Park

In the center of Maine's north woods stands Mount Katahdin, the tallest peak in Maine, a scenic centerpiece of New England north of the White Mountains. This peak is the center of one of the nation's most unusual wilderness reservations—Baxter State Park, a preserve of 200,000 acres.

Mt. Katahdin is the northern terminus of the 2,000-mile Appalachian Trail. It is the largest single piece of publicly owned land in Maine. The Park was given as a private gift over a period of years by the late Governor Percival P. Baxter. It is held by the State as a trust for the benefit of all Maine citizens. The legal mandate for the Park's operation and protection is derived from Deeds of Trust drafted by Governor Baxter and then subsequently passed by the legislature as state law. By custom, certain other written expressions of his wishes have been used to interpret the Governor's policy intentions. Because of its nature as a legal trust created for the public benefit, the ultimate authority, as in all trusts, is the State court system. [a]

Thus, a major wilderness reserve—the largest in New England—was created not by state or federal, but by private, action. The Deeds of Trust passing title to the State provided for different management regimes in different portions of the Park. Most of the Park is to be kept "in its natural wild state," as a "sanctuary for beasts and birds." On a small portion, hunting is allowed. On about 28,000 acres, "scientific forestry" may be carried out.

When Baxter State Park was created, it was not in any sense an untouched region. Loggers had penetrated most of its area, removing valuable pine, spruce, and hardwoods. Their operations relied on haul roads over snow and horse teams skidding over snow, so that little visible effect occurred after regrowth. Little clear-cutting was done, as only large trees were valuable at that time. Most of the land was purchased by Governor Baxter from the Great Northern Paper Company, a major landowner in the region. Part of the heritage of this period is a series of sporting camps, developed campsites, trails, and a major "perimeter road" through the Park. These existing developments allowing ready access were sanctioned for permanent maintenance by the Deeds of Trust.

Rapid regrowth has made the logger's work nearly invisible over most of the Park. In its existence as a recreated wilderness, however, the Park's history has been controversial. At various times, the Park Authority has been sued to halt spraying for spruce budworm control within the Park and to halt the mechanized cleanup of a large volume of timber blown down by a winter windstorm. A ruling by the Attorney General's office that snow-mobile use off the main roadway during the winter was illegal under the Deeds of Trust touched off a storm of local protest. When the Authority allowed the Maine Forest Service to suppress a 3500-acre fire in the Park using mechanized equipment, a bitter public debate developed. In that fire, adjacent Great Northern Paper Company lands were damaged as well.[b]

After several decades of largely custodial management, the Park Authority has embarked on an overall Park management plan, developed in consultation with an advisory committee over a period of two years. In August 1978, the Authority adopted a policies and concepts plan, which will guide the preparation of detailed plans for managing the Park's four distinctive management zones. The Park has hired a forester, and work has begun to develop a management plan for the Scientific Forestry Management Area, which is intended to be a model of multiple-use forestry, producing revenue sufficient to cover management costs.

Governor Baxter's gift to Maine was left under terms allowing a considerable degree of policy latitude to its managers, the Park Authority. The legal mechanism of a trust is perhaps unique in the wilderness field. It provides explicitly the protection that many authors have argued for under the general public trust doctrine, and it has an automatic enforcement

*mechanism. Its future work in managing New England's largest wilderness
will be of great interest to all wildland managers.*

───────────

[a] Baxter State Park Authority, *Baxter State Park Plan, Sec. I: Policies and Concepts,* Milli-nocket, Maine, August 1978.

[b] Maine Forest Service, *Baxter Park Fire: Report of the Review Board,* Augusta, Maine, September 1977.

Notes

1. Robert Dolan, Bruce P. Hayden, and Gary Soucie, "Environmental Dynamics and Resource Management in the U.S. National Parks," *Environmental Management* 2 (May 1978): 249-258.

2. See Wildland Research Center, *Wilderness and Recreation,* Outdoor Recreation Resources Review Commission, Report 3 (Washington, D.C., U.S. Government Printing Office, 1963), pp. 292ff; U.S. Department of Agriculture, U.S. Forest Service, *1977 Environmental Statement—Addendum to the Final 1976 Cooperative Western Spruce Budworm Pest Management Plan,* Portland, Oregon, 1977.

3. Sec. 4 (d) 1 of The Act.

4. Michael McCloskey, "The Wilderness Act of 1964: Its Background and Meaning," *Oregon Law Review* 45 (June 1966): 310. Reprinted with permission.

5. U.S. Forest Service, *Fire in the Environment Symposium Proceedings,* Washington, D.C., 1972, especially papers by White and Rapoport. For a broad review on fire management, see Robert D. Gale, *Evaluation of Fire Management Activities on the National Forests,* U.S. Department of Agriculture, U.S. Forest Service, *Policy Analysis Staff Report,* Washington, D.C., 1977. Also, see papers about fire in *Western Wildlands,* Summer 1974. For a discussion of fire management in the Yellowstone-Grand Teton region see U.S. Congress, Senate Subcommittee on Parks and Recreation, Committee on Interior and Insular Affairs, *Management of National Parks,* 94th Congress, 1st session, 1976. B.M. Kilgore, "From Fire Control to Fire Management: An Ecological Basis for Policies," *Transactions of the 41st North American Wildlife and Natural Resources Conference,* Washington, D.C., 1976.

6. J.W. Wagtendonk, *Refined Burning Prescriptions for Yosemite National Park,* National Park Service Occasional Paper no. 2, Washington, D.C., n.d., pp. 1-2; see also S.R. Kessel, "Gradient Modelling: A New Approach to Fire Modelling and Wilderness Resource Management," *Environmental Management* 1 (1976): 39-48.

7. These examples are loosely drawn from the following sources: A.P. Snyder, "Wilderness Management, A Growing Challenge," *Journal*

of Forestry 64 (July 1966): 441-448; Ronald B. Taylor, "No Vacancy in the Wilderness," *Sierra Club Bulletin,* February 1973, pp. 25-27; K.L. Bell and L.C. Bliss, "Alpine Disturbance Studies: Olympic National Park," *Biological Conservation* 5 (January 1973): 25-32; B.E. Willard and J.W. Marr, "Recovery of Alpine Tundra. . . . after Damage by Human Activities," *Biological Conservation* 3 (April 1971): 181-190; M.A. Barton, "Water Pollution in Remote Recreational Areas," *Journal of Soil and Water Conservation* 24 (July-August 1969): 132-134. For an example of a controversial management failure, see U.S. Congress, Senate, Committee on Interior and Insular Affairs, *Closure of Crater Lake National Park,* 94th Congress, 1st session, 1976; Sidney S. Frissell, "Judging Recreation Impacts on Wilderness Campsites," *Journal of Forestry* 76 (August 1978): 481-483; James R. Gray, *Kinds and Costs of Recreational Pollution in the Sandia Mountains,* New Mexico Agricultural Experimental Station Bulletin 651, March 1977; T.E. Hinds, *Aspen Mortality in Rocky Mountain Campgrounds,* U.S. Department of Agriculture, U.S. Forest Service, Rocky Mountain Forest and Range Experiment Station, Research Paper RM-164, 1976; Ray W. Brown, Robert S. Johnson, and Douglas A. Johnson, "Rehabilitation of Alpine Tundra Disturbances," *Journal of Soil and Water Conservation* 33 (July-August 1978): 154-160, contains seventy-five useful references. See also bibliographies cited in note 8.

8. L.C. Merriam and C.K. Smith, "Visitor Impact on Newly Developed Campsites in the Boundary Waters Canoe Area," *Journal of Forestry* 72 (October 1974): 627-630. The vast literature on carrying capacity is listed in George H. Stankey and David W. Lime, *Recreational Carrying Capacity: An Annotated Bibliography,* U.S. Department of Agriculture, U.S. Forest Service, Intermountain Forest and Range Experiment Station General Technical Report INT-3, 1973. See also papers by Knudsen et al., and by Borden et al., in *Proceedings of the River Recreation Symposium,* U.S. Department of Agriculture, U.S. Forest Service, North Central Forest Experiment Station, General Technical Report NC-28, 1977. Several bibliographies conveniently cover the field: A.H. Conrad, *Wilderness Preservation, Planning, and Management: An Annotated Bibliography* (Monticello, Ill: Council of Planning Librarians, Exchange Bibliography 1516, 1978); Dorothy H. Anderson, Earl C. Leatherberry, and David W. Lime, *An Annotated Bibliography on River Recreation,* U.S. Department of Agriculture, U.S. Forest Service, North Central Forest Experiment Station, General Technical Report NC-41, 1978; G. Wall, *Impact of Outdoor Recreation on the Environment* (Monticello, Ill: Council of Planning Librarians, Exchange Bibliography 1363, 1977).

9. David W. Lime and Roland G. Buchman, "Putting Wilderness Permit Information to Work," *Journal of Forestry* 72 (October 1974):

662-626; see also J.W. Hendee and Robert C. Lucas, "Mandatory Wilderness Permits: Some Indications of Success," *Journal of Forestry* 72 (1974): 753-756; J.C. Hendee and Robert C. Lucas, "Mandatory Wilderness Permits: A Necessary Management Tool," *Journal of Forestry* 72 (April 1973): 206-209; V. Godin and R. Leonard, *Permit Compliance in Eastern Wilderness,* U.S. Department of Agriculture, U.S. Forest Service, Northeastern Forest Experiment Station Research Note NE-238, 1977.

10. Robert C. Lucas, "Wilderness: A Management Framework," *Journal of Soil and Water Conservation* 28 (July-August 1973): 150-154.

11. George H. Stankey, "A Strategy for Definition and Management of Wilderness Quality," in John V. Krutilla, ed., *Natural Environments* (Baltimore: Johns Hopkins University Press, 1975). Anthony Fisher and John V. Krutilla, "Determination of Optimal Capacity of Resource-Based Recreational Facilities," in Krutilla, *Natural Environments.*

12. Stankey, "Strategy for Definition." See also Glen O. Robinson, *The Forest Service* (Baltimore: Johns Hopkins University Press, 1975), p. 185.

13. W.R. Burch, Jr., "Adapting Forest Resources Management to Its Social Environment—Some Observations," Keynote Address, Canadian Institute of Forestry, Niagara Falls, Ontario, October 1974, pp. 11-12. Reprinted with permission. See also J. Alan Wagar, "Recreational Carrying Capacity Reconsidered," *Journal of Forestry* 72 (May 1974): 274-278.

14. Myron L. Heinselman, "Recreation and/or Nature Preservation," in U.S. Department of Agriculture, U.S. Forest Service, *Outdoor Recreation Research: Applying the Findings,* North Central Forest Experiment Station, General Technical Report NC-9, 1974).

15. J. Alan Wagar, "The Carrying Capacity of Wild Lands for Recreation," *Forest Science Monograph* 7 (1964): 3. Reprinted with permission.

16. V.B. Godin and R.E. Leonard, "Design Capacity for Backcountry Recreation Management Planning," *Journal of Soil and Water Conservation* 32 (July-August 1977): 161-164.

17. Charles J. Cicchetti and V. Kerry Smith, "Congestion, Quality Deterioration, and Optimal Use," *Social Science Research* 2 (1973): 31-40. Also see C. J. Cicchetti and V.K. Smith, *Costs of Congestion—An Econometric Study of Wilderness Recreation* (Boston: Lippincott-Ballinger, 1976). For another view, see H.J. Vaux, Jr. and N.A. Williams, "Costs of Congestion and Wilderness Recreation," *Environmental Management* 1 (1977): 495-503.

18. This suggestion has been urged by Lucas (note 10). Backcountry areas outside wilderness already receive considerable recreational use, to the extent that enterprising campers establish their own informal campsites:

J.C. Hendee, M.C. Hogan, and R.W. Koch, *Dispersed Recreation on 3 Forest Road Systems in Washington and Oregon,* U.S. Department of Agriculture, U.S. Forest Service, Pacific Northwest Forest and Range Experiment Station, Research Note PNW-280, October 1976.

19. See Robinson, *Forest Service,* p. 187 for a trenchant response to the strength-purists.

20. D. Griest, "Risk Zoning, a Recreation Area Management System," *Journal of Forestry* 73 (November 1975): 711. Also see George H. Stankey and J. Baden, *Rationing Wilderness Use,* U.S. Department of Agriculture, U.S. Forest Service, Intermountain Forest and Range Experiment Station, Research Paper INT-192, 1977. For a suggestive analysis of rationing procedures for other nonpriced public services, see D. Nichols, E. Smolensky, and T.N. Tideman, "Discrimination of Waiting Time in Merit Goods," *American Economic Review* 61 (June 1971): 312-323.

21. J.C. Hendee and R. Harris, "Foresters' Perception of Wilderness-User Attitudes and Preferences," *Journal of Forestry* 68 (December 1970): 759; B.W. Twight and W.R. Catton, Jr., "Politics of Images: Forest Managers vs. Recreation Publics," *Natural Resources Journal* 15 (April 1975): 297; H.E. Echelberger, D.H. Deiss, and D.A. Morrison, "Overused Unique Recreation Areas: A Look at the Social Problems," *Journal of Soil and Water Conservation* 29 (July-August 1974): 173; J. Murray, *Appalachian Trail Users in the Southern National Forests,* U.S. Department of Agriculture, U.S. Forest Service, Southeastern Forest Experiment Station, Research Paper SE-116, 1974); A.C. Fisher and J. Krutilla, "Determination of Optimal Capacity of Resource Based Recreational Facilities," in Krutilla, *Natural Environments;* A.J. Penz, "Outdoor Recreation Areas: Capacity and the Formulation of Use Policy," *Management Science* 22 (October 1975): 139; Cicchetti and Smith, *Costs of Congestion,* p. 112; R.C. Lucas and M. Shechter, "A Recreational Visitor Travel Simulation Model as an Aid to Management Planning," *Simulation and Games* 8 (September 1977): 375-384; G.H. Elsner, comp., *State-of-the-Art Methods for Research, Planning, and Determining the Benefits of Outdoor Recreation,* U.S. Department of Agriculture, U.S. Forest Service, Pacific Southwest Forest and Range Experiment Station, General Technical Report PSW-20, 1977; Gordon C. Rausser and R.A. Oliveira, "An Econometric Analysis of Wilderness Area Use," *Journal of the American Statistics Association* 71 (June 1976): 276-285.

22. Robert C. Lucas, "Wilderness: A Management Framework," *Journal of Soil and Water Conservation* 28 (July-August 1973): p. 153. Reprinted with permission.

23. W.E. Shands and R.G. Healy, *The Lands Nobody Wanted* (Washington, D.C.: Conservation Foundation, 1976).

24. Conservation Foundation, *National Parks for the Future*, Washington, D.C., 1972, p. 84. Reprinted with permission. See J. William Futrell, "Parks to the People: New Directions for the National Park System," *Emory Law Journal* 25 (1976): 283. Joseph L. Sax, "Helpless Giants: The National Parks and the Regulation of Private Lands," *Michigan Law Review* 75 (December 1976): 239-274, reviews legal issues thoroughly.

25. The Adirondack Park has spawned a vast literature, the best introduction being Frank Graham, Jr., *The Adirondack Park, A Political History* (New York: Knopf, 1976). See also the plans: *Adirondack Park Land Use and Development Plan,* March 6, 1973, and *State Land Master Plan,* June 1, 1972, (Ray Brook: Adirondack Park Agency). Related studies include D.H. Vrooman, "An Empirical Analysis of Determinants of Land Values in the Adirondack Park," *American Journal of Economics and Sociology* 37 (April 1978): 165-177; Peter H. Gore and Mark B. Lapping, "Environmental Quality and Social Equity: Wilderness Preservation in a Depressed Region, New York State's Adirondacks," *American Journal of Economics and Sociology* 35, (October 1976): 349. A highly controversial package of facilities for the 1980 Winter Olympics at Lake Placid was the subject of a 900-page environmental statement: U.S. Department of Commerce, Economic Development Administration, *Final Environmental Statement for 1980 Olympic Winter Games, Village of Lake Placid,* Washington, D.C., January 1977.

26. U.S. Department of the Interior, *Trails for America* (Washington, D.C.: U.S. Government Printing Office, 1966).

27. Patricia Solotaire, ed., *Protecting the Appalachian Trail in Maine* (Portland, Maine: Allagash Institute/University of Maine at Portland-Gorham, 1976).

28. P.L. 90-543 (82 *Stat.* 919).

29. On off-road vehicles, see Jean Albrecht and Diane Smith, *Environmental Effects of Off-Road Vehicles: A Selected Bibliography,* University of Minnesota, St. Paul, Forestry Library Bibliography Series no. 2, 1977; David Duncan and Ralph Maughan, "Feet vs. ORVs: Are There Social Differences Between Backcountry Users?" *Journal of Forestry* 76 (August 1978): 478-480; and Note, "Snowmobiles and the Environment," *Yale Law Journal* 82 (March 1973): 772-786; H.J. Plumley, H.T. Peet, and R.E. Leonard, *Records of Backcountry Use Can Assist Trail Managers.* U.S. Department of Agriculture, U.S. Forest Service, Northeastern Forest Experiment Station, Research Paper NE-414, 1978.

30. U.S. Council on Environmental Quality, *Evolution of Wildlife Law* (Washington, D.C.: U.S. Government Printing Office, 1978).

31. For elk, see reports of the *Special Advisory Board on Wildlife Management for the Secretary of the Interior, 1963-1968.* Reprinted by

Wildlife Management Institute, Washington, D.C., 1969; also Allen L. Lovaas, *People and the Gallatin Elk Herd* (Helena, Mont.: Montana Fish and Game Department, April 1970). On wild horses and burros, see Secretary of Interior and Secretary of Agriculture, *Report to Congress on Administration of the Wild Free Roaming Horses and Burros Act,* Washington, D.C., 1974; Linda Williams, "Constitutionality of the Free Roaming Wild Horses and Burros Act: The Ecosystem and the Property Clause in Kleppe v. New Mexico," *Environmental Law* 7 (Fall 1976): 137-152; and two annotated bibliographies by M. Zarn, T. Heller, and K. Collins, comps., *Wild, Free-roaming Burros,* Technical Note 297, and *Wild, Free-roaming Horses,* Technical Note 295, both published by the U.S. Department of the Interior, Bureau of Land Management, Denver, Colo., 1977.

    32. 16 *U.S.C.* Sec. 1331, et seq. (Suppl. I, 1971).

    33. Ibid., p. 11.

    34. J.H. Baden and R.W. Stroup, "Externality, Property Rights, and the Management of Our National Forests," *Journal of Law and Economics* 16 (October 1973): 303.

    35. See, generally, Richard Alston, *Forest-Goals and Decision-making in the Forest Service,* U.S. Department of Agriculture, U.S. Forest Service, Intermountain Forest and Range Experiment Station, Research Paper INT-128, 1972.

    36. Robinson, *The Forest Service,* 123ff provides the history of recreation fee policy.

    37. Robinson, *Forest Service,* pp. 141-142. Reprinted with permission.

    38. *Ibid.,* p. 144. Reprinted with permission.

    39. Further reflections on the role of values in wilderness management may be sought in Roderick Nash, "Wilderness Management: A Contradiction in Terms?" University of Idaho, Wilderness Research Center, Distinguished Lectureship no. 2, April 1978; Philip D. Levin, "Inward to Wilderness, Part III: An Ethical Wilderness," *Appalachia* 13 (2) (June 15, 1978): 25-44; Frank Fraser Darling and Noel D. Eichorn, *Man and Nature in the National Parks,* 2d ed. (Washington, D.C.: Conservation Foundation, 1969); Edward Abbey, *Desert Solitaire—A Season in the Wilderness* (New York: Simon and Schuster, 1968); Robert Marshall, "The Problem of the Wilderness," *Scientific Monthly,* 30 (February 1930): 141-148; William R. Burch, Jr., "In Democracy Is the Preservation of Wilderness," *Appalachia* 13 (December 1974): 90-101.

    40. Stankey and Baden, *Rationing Wilderness Use.*

    41. National Park Service, *Draft Colorado River Management Plan, and Draft Environmental Statement,* Grand Canyon, Arizona, 1977.

    42. J.C. Hendee, G.H. Stankey, and R.C. Lucas, *Wilderness Management,* U.S. Department of Agriculture, U.S. Forest Service, Misc. Publ.

1365, October 1978. On the management of a unique wilderness resource, see R.R. Stitt and W.P. Bishop, "Underground Wilderness in the Guadalupe Escarpment," *Bulletin of the Speleological Society* 34 (July 1972): 77.

10 Conclusions

"Like winds and sunsets, wild things were taken for granted until progress began to do away with them. Now we face the question of whether a still higher 'standard of living' is worth its cost in things natural, wild, and free."[1] Thus did Aldo Leopold provide an observation that could summarize this essay.

The mandate for preservation is based firmly on the instrumental and intrinsic values protected by wilderness. These values serve a wide range of citizens, not just the hikers who penetrate lonely valleys. There is every reason to believe that all wilderness values will be ever more highly prized in the future. But the mandate has as yet been imperfectly fulfilled. How it will be fulfilled presents citizens and policy-makers with perplexing questions. In closing, I will summarize issues, review the role of economics in preservation decision-making, and review the cultural significance of wilderness.

The Mandate: Issues

The economists propounding the new economics of conservation have argued that preservation of natural areas is frequently justifiable on the ground that the services such areas is provide will be ever more highly valued in the future, whereas the resource commodities they can supply will be available ever more cheaply. We can, truly, sacrifice our remaining wildlands for a mess of pottage. Further, wilderness preservation does not only serve a minority of recreational users but meets a wide range of needs.

The nation's present pattern of land use has evolved over the several centuries since European occupation of North America. Remaining wildland comprises several hundred million acres, an area comparable in size to the nation's cultivated farmland. Decisions about the future of this vast national patrimony will be made in the next decade. A land-use decision comparable to those made incrementally over centuries will be made in haste, by a political institution—the U.S. Congress—under heavy pressure from partisan interests and ill-disposed to invest time, talent, and funds in the study of alternatives. Yet the adversary process does seem to assure that major values involved can be considered.

The great questions of wilderness allocation will within a decade or two be settled—either by explicit decisions to reserve remaining lands or by the roadbuilders, miners, and loggers (see figure 10-1). The fate of Alaska's wildlands will be broadly settled in a few years. The 62 million acres of Forest Service roadless areas will be allocated to alternative uses—although probably not as soon as RARE-II's planners dream.

America can, in general, well afford the luxury of devoting substantial areas of wildland and water to preservation purposes. Our economy has the capacity to meet its needs for energy, wood, and minerals without plundering the last remaining wildlands. America will not be richer as a result of drilling the oil or smelting the ores under Alaska's mountains. It will be richer in a more important and lasting way by preserving unscarred those colossal regions.

W.R. Burch notes that our culture remains dominated by frontier values.[2] Our difficulties in making wilderness decisions stem largely from this fact. For preservation decisions are explicit choices about the limits to be placed on extractive economic activity, long supported by frontier themes in American culture.

The conflicting values come into sharper focus at the local level. Reduced local timber supplies can mean lost jobs, leading to unnecessary social conflict that stands in the way of implementing the mandate for preservation. The time has come to take a more mature approach to these conflicts, and to develop a richer tool-kit of measures for dealing with them. The complex and costly compensation provisions of the Redwood Park expansion program may indeed be a dangerous precedent, but they should rarely be necessary. More often, artful design of management alternatives can substantially accomodate preservation objectives and local economic needs.

A major issue has been the impact of preservation decisions on the national supply of wood products. Numerous studies show that a dramatic and immediate reduction in timber supply from public lands can indeed raise lumber prices. But major wilderness allocations can be made without such effects on wood supply. Increased emphasis on management of high-site lands in areas now roaded, and improved forestry on small private tracts, can significantly boost wood supplies in future decades. Total wood output can thus expand at the same time that large forest areas of low productivity are devoted to other uses. The true limits will not be the ultimate biological limits but the willingness of landowners to cut timber and invest in its culture.

This possibility of having our cake and eating it too should be supplemented by the opportunity for creative backcountry management that can permit low-intensity resource management, allow a diversity of recreation experiences, and still achieve many preservation goals. Consider the 62 million RARE-II acres. Probably half of this acreage could become wilderness without noticeable sacrifice of economically important resource

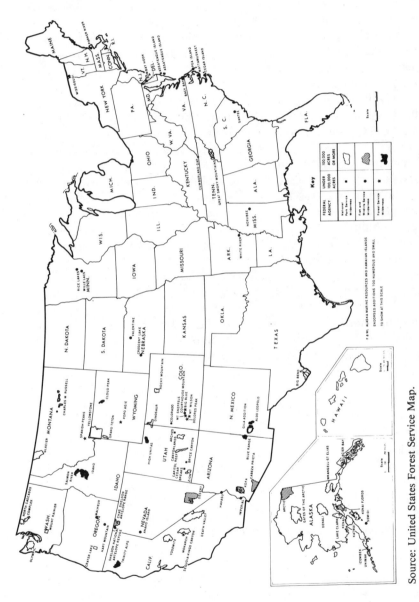

Source: United States Forest Service Map.
Note: Does not include RARE-II lands.
Figure 10-1. Administration-Endorsed Additions to The National Wilderness Preservation System, November 1, 1968.

development opportunities. This would instantly triple the size of the nation's wilderness system (outside of Alaska). The resulting area—45 million acres—could protect a significant resource of natural values. It should, however, take advantage of the few remaining opportunities to preserve low-elevation old growth timber stands as well as alpine rock fields. But would preserving the next 30 million acres really buy us a commensurate increase in preservation value? It is not easy to say. It is clear that sacrifices of alternative uses would be more noticeable, especially to affected nearby communities.

My judgment is that a special backcountry status should be created for these lands. Areas that, by reason of low site productivity, wildlife values, or soil fragility, should not be intensively managed belong here. Sound recreation planning could take much pressure off the designated wilderness areas. Naturalistic, nonintensive programs of silviculture would be developed and applied on these lands. A multiple-use program with timber, grazing, and mining as subordinate uses would develop. Fifty years from now, citizens might be inclined to devote these lands to wilderness, knowing that cutting units and roads would be expunged by natural forces in due time. The permanent despoliation that purist backpackers attribute to logging roads is an illusion when an appropriate time view is taken.

Farming, ranching, and small-scale forest-products production are rapidly vanishing ways of life in late twentieth-century America. The small rural communities of America's mountains and plains bear a close economic and moral relationship to the land that supports them. The nation has made it a policy objective to support employment opportunity in such communities. Creative solutions to the management of backcountry areas could contribute significantly to maintaining a stable employment base for such communities. A rural society based on selling gas, canned food, and lodging to tourists is economically fragile and has lost its relation to the land.

These issues are raised by questions of land-use allocation. But allocation is becoming an issue of the past. If the predictions of ever rising future wilderness use are correct, we can expect the management of existing wilderness areas to generate increasing controversy. Wilderness management is already a complex process—the Minnesota Boundary Waters Canoe Area is governed by forty pages of laws and regulations; the management plan for Arizona's Superstition Wilderness fills about seventy-five pages.[3] We can expect wilderness management to become even more complex in the future. We can hope that wilderness users and managing agencies will employ an intelligent mix of policies aimed at rationing access to wilderness, together with artful measures to increase the supply of backcountry experiences, inside and outside dedicated wilderness areas.

Instrumental and Intrinsic Values: The Role of Economic Analysis

Economic concepts are useful in stating the mandate for preservation of wilderness. Prominent concepts were the cultural values, the direct economic benefits such as recreation, and the role of wilderness in preventing various social diseconomies. In addition, a number of economic arguments have been used to suggest why private markets provide inadequately for wilderness preservation and why collective decision-making systems—government and private nonprofit organizations—are used to give effect to social values for preservation.

How can all these concepts and bits of information find use in an orderly approach to decision-making about wilderness allocation and management? There are a number of useful roles that economic analysis can play:

1. Economic concepts can guide analysts in studying the need and markets for commodities produced from lands proposed for wilderness classification. Economic analyses can show the prospective dynamics of demand and supply for a given product, estimate the likely costs of supply from alternate sources, and appraise the overall impact of forgoing development on the market for the commodity.

2. Economic analyses can clarify the overall impact of a given wilderness decision on the allocation of resources—the resource development opportunities forgone as well as values gained through increased recreation opportunity and reduction of potential environmental diseconomies such as water pollution.

3. Economic analysis can aid in describing the incidence of the costs and benefits of creating a given wilderness area. Effects on local economies can be analyzed. Costs of trail construction, maintenance, and wilderness patrolling can be estimated. Benefits flowing to various classes of users can be projected.

4. Systematic analysis can aid in setting preservation priorities.

Economic information has been used in a descriptive manner in many wilderness decisions—as for example, in the North Cascades Study Report, or the many wilderness reports filed by the U.S. Forest Service.[4] Most economists, however, would be skeptical of excessive reliance on benefit-cost approaches for making value choices in wilderness land allocation and management. In the recent resurgence of interest in benefit-cost analysis for environmental decisions, economists have been pointing out the severe limitations of benefit-cost analysis in making decisions characterized by deep value conflict.[5] At times, preservation controversies become embroiled in the technicalities of benefit-cost analysis. This has frequently occurred in the water development field, in which agencies present documented benefit-cost analyses in support of projects. Project opponents believe that they can improve their case by criticizing the agency economic justification for the project. This is often all too easily done. Yet it is clear that public works projects often have a broad range of purposes beyond simply contributing to the gross national product.

Economic logic by itself cannot resolve deep value conflicts over the uses to be made of the nation's remaining wildlands.[6] It is therefore unproductive to allow basic differences in values to be obscured in apparently technical debates over the correct level of the social discount rate or the correct technique for calculating hydropower benefits.

The traditional subject matter of economics has been dealing with instrumental values—deciding how much an undeveloped mineral deposit is worth to society. Such an evaluation has usually been made on the basis of simulating what an informed investor would pay, based on processing costs and expected prices of the metal produced. The prices are assumed to measure the value of the metal itself to society. In the appraisal of intrinsic values—the basic natural value of the valley sheltering the deposit— economics has lagged. In such apples-and-oranges situations, however, the analyst is not helpless. By carefully examining the situation, the consequences of different value judgments can be explored.

Considerable effort has been devoted to quantifying the intrinsic values of scenery, wildlife, recreation, and clean air and water. But such quantification will not really help settle society's conflicts over wilderness land allocation. Most techniques used so far embody the ethically unsatisfying assumption that the value of a mountain to society is simply what today's consumers will pay in dollars or in travel time to see it. So economics cannot overcome our difficulties in comparing "apples and oranges" in environmental decision-making. But it can help decision-makers by providing informed judgments about matters within its traditional sphere—resource demand and supply, opportunity costs, and the incidence of costs and benefits.

As Dr. Lewis Thomas has written, there are grounds for caution:

> The social scientists, especially the economists, are moving deeply into ecology and the environment these days, with disquieting results. It goes somehow against the grain to learn that cost-benefit analyses can be done neatly on lakes, meadows, nesting gannets, even whole oceans. It is hard enough to confront the environmental options ahead, and hard choices, but even harder when the price tags are so visible. Even the new jargon is disturbing: it hurts the spirit, somehow, to read the word *environments* when the plural means that there are so many alternatives to be sorted through, as in a market, and voted on. Economists need cool heads and cold hearts for this sort of thing, and they must write in icy, often skiddy prose.[7]

Cultural and Ethical Values

Wilderness is a cultural fact. The basic drive to preserve it may spring from deep roots of religion in early human cultures. As Erich Isaac writes, "On almost all levels of culture there are segregated, dedicated, fenced, hallowed spaces" that are seen as the property of God.[8] Terms employed by modern writers describing their reactions to wilderness often suggest the same attitude. Another source is economic history, as translated into cultural attitudes.

When Europeans explored the North American continent, it pleased them to think that they entered an uninhabited waste. Their culture defined it as wilderness. Chief Luther Standing Bear, of the Oglala Sioux, saw this clearly:

> We did not think of the great open plains, the beautiful rolling hills, and winding streams with tangled growth, as "wild." Only to the white man was nature a "wilderness" and only to him was the land "infested" with wild animals and "savage" people. To us it was tame . . . Not until the hairy man from the east came and with brutal frenzy heaped injustices upon us and the families we loved was it "wild" for us.[9]

The debate over wilderness preservation is a debate over values; it cannot be resolved in a market setting. The values are conflicting orientations toward nature. One orientation sees nature in instrumental terms—as a source of commodities, hiking opportunities, or research projects. The other orientation sees nature as intrinsically valuable, as contributing to wider and more durable human purposes than do aluminum billets or carloads of coal. Because the stakes are so high, the nation's preservation policies become a contest over whose values are to prevail—those of industry, those of preservationists, or those of the resource management agencies. Whose values? Chief Standing Bears', or those of the wheat market? The fact that deep conflict over values is at the heart of the debate over wilderness policy accounts for the predominance of righteous moralizing over analysis on the part of partisans on all sides. The tedious self-righteousness and endless ad hominem attacks on groups with differing views make much of the popular literature on wilderness policy difficult to read.

Individuals do sacrifice income to preserve wildlands for their intrinsic values—witness The Nature Conservancy's million-acre program. But the intrinsic values reach far into the future, so their preservation cannot be fully entrusted to the willingness of today's wealthy to finance it. Ultimately, the intrinsic value of the nation's wildland patrimony eludes economic appraisal.

But economics, as a science, must remain silent on how the conflicting values over wilderness allocations are weighed in decisions. We have seen that there is no generally accepted ethical philosophy on which society's stance toward nature can be based. It is also clear that we are distant from an accepted concept of what constitutes social justice. Whereas economists have devoted considerable attention to efficiency-equity trade-offs, they have only succeeded in more clearly defining the problem.[10]

Decisions to implement the mandate for preservation, then, are broad social value judgments made by an imperfect machinery of political institutions. Decisions to preserve wilderness are reflections of a nation's culture. The existence of wilderness provides a resource from which the young can learn values about nature and the old can refresh those values. Out of wilderness, Leopold says, man has hammered his civilization. In preserving wilderness, a civilization in turn expresses its values.

Notes

1. Aldo Leopold, *A Sand County Almanac* (New York: Oxford University Press, 1966), p. vii.

2. William R. Burch, Jr., *Daydreams and Nightmares: A Sociological Essay on the American Environment* (New York: Harper and Row, 1971), p. 156.

3. U.S. Department of Agriculture, U.S. Forest Service, *Boundary Waters Canoe Area Management Plan and Environmental Statement,* Milwaukee, Wisc., Region 9, 1974, pp. 38ff; U.S. Department of Agriculture, U.S. Forest Service, Tonto National Forest (Arizona), *Superstition Wilderness Management Plan,* Albuquerque, N. Mex., Region 3, 1972. See also National Park Service, *Draft Colorado River Management Plan,* October 1977, and *Draft Environmental Statement, Proposed Colorado River Management Plan,* DES-77-37 Grand Canyon, Arizona.

4. U.S. Department of the Interior, *North Cascades Study Report,* Washington, D.C., 1965. See also the sophisticated case studies in J. Krutilla and A. Fisher, *Economics of Natural Environments* (Baltimore, Md.: Johns Hopkins, 1975).

5. See, for example, D. Joskow, "Approving Nuclear Power Plants: Scientific Decision-making or Administrative Charade?" *Bell Journal of Economics and Management Science,* Fall 1974, p. 320; S. Hanke and R. Walker, "Benefit Cost Analysis Reconsidered: An Evaluation of the Mid-State Project," *Water Resources Research* 10 (October 1974): 898.

6. See items in note 5, and The Institute of Ecology, *Scientific and Policy Review of the Final Environmental Statement, Garrison Diversion Unit, N. Dakota,* (Washington, D.C.: 1975). For legal commentary, see:

D. Kumin, "Substantive Review Under NEPA: EDF v. Corps of Engineers," *Ecology Law Quarterly* 3 (1973): 173; E. Findley, "Planning of a Corps Reservoir Project," *Ecology Law Quarterly* 3 (1973): 42-59; note "Cost-Benefit Analysis and the NEPA of 1969," *Stanford Law Review* 24 (1972): 1092.

7. Lewis Thomas, *Lives of a Cell* (New York: Viking Penguin Inc., 1975), p. 121. Reprinted with permission.

8. Isaac Erich, "God's Acre," *Landscape* 14 (Winter 1964), p. 29, reprinted with permission.

9. Quoted in T.C. McLuhan, *Touch the Earth, A Self-Portrait of Indian Existence,* (New York: Promontory Press, 1971), p. 45.

10. R. Havemann, "Efficiency and Equity in Natural Resources and Environmental Policy," *American Journal of Agricultural Economics* 55 (December 1973): 868; A. Schmid, "Analytical Institutional Economics," *American Journal of Agricultural Economics* 54 (December 1972); and A.M. Okun, *Equality and Efficiency: The Big Trade-off* (Washington, D.C.: The Brookings Institution, 1977).

Documentary Appendix

Public Law 88-577
88th Congress, S. 4
September 3, 1964

An Act

To establish a National Wilderness Preservation System for the permanent good of the whole people, and for other purposes.

Be it enacted by the Senate and House of Representatives of the United States of America in Congress assembled,

Short Title

Section 1. This Act may be cited as the "Wilderness Act".

Wilderness System Established Statement of Policy

Sec. 2. (a) In order to assure that an increasing population, accompanied by expanding settlement and growing mechanization, does not occupy and modify all areas within the United States and its possessions, leaving no lands designated for preservation and protection in their natural condition, it is hereby declared to be the policy of the Congress to secure for the American people of present and future generations the benefits of an enduring resource of wilderness. For this purpose there is hereby established a National Wilderness Preservation System to be composed of federally owned areas designated by Congress as "wilderness areas", and these shall be administered for the use and enjoyment of the American people in such manner as will leave them unimpaired for future use and enjoyment as wilderness, and so as to provide for the protection of these areas, the preservation of their wilderness character, and for the gathering and dissemination of information regarding their use and enjoyment as wilderness; and no Federal lands shall be designated as "wilderness areas" except as provided for in this Act or by a subsequent Act.

(b) The inclusion of an area in the National Wilderness Preservation System notwithstanding, the area shall continue to be managed by the Department and agency having jurisdiction thereover immediately before its inclusion in the National Wilderness Preservation System unless otherwise provided by Act of Congress. No appropriation shall be available for the payment of expenses or salaries for the administration of the National Wilderness Preservation System as a separate unit nor shall any appropriations be available for additional personnel stated as being required solely for the purpose of managing or administering areas solely because they are included within the National Wilderness Preservation System.

Definition of Wilderness

(c) A wilderness, in contrast with those areas where man and his own works dominate the landscape, is hereby recognized as an area where the earth and its community of life are untrammeled by man, where man himself is a visitor who does not remain. An area of wilderness is further defined to mean in this Act an area of undeveloped Federal land retaining its primeval character and influence, without permanent improvements or human habitation, which is protected and managed so as to preserve its natural conditions and which (1) generally appears to have been affected primarily by the forces of nature, with the imprint of man's work substantially unnoticeable; (2) has outstanding opportunities for solitude or a primitive and unconfined type of recreation; (3) has at least five thousand acres of land or is of sufficient size as to make practicable its preservation and use in an unimpaired condition; and (4) may also contain ecological, geological, or other features of scientific, educational, scenic, or historical value.

National Wilderness Preservation System—Extent of System

Sec. 3. (a) All areas within the national forests classified at least 30 days before the effective date of this Act by the Secretary of Agriculture or the Chief of the Forest Service as "wilderness", "wild", or "canoe" are hereby designated as wilderness areas. The Secretary of Agriculture shall—

(1) Within one year after the effective date of this Act, file a map and legal description of each wilderness area with the Interior and Insular Affairs Committees of the United States Senate and the House of Representatives, and such descriptions shall have the same force and effect as if included in this Act: *Provided, however,* That correction of clerical and typographical errors in such legal descriptions and maps may be made.

(2) Maintain, available to the public, records pertaining to said wilderness areas, including maps and legal descriptions, copies of regulations governing them, copies of public notices of, and reports submitted to Congress regarding pending additions, eliminations, or modifications. Maps, legal descriptions, and regulations pertaining to wilderness areas within their respective jurisdictions also shall be available to the public in the offices of regional foresters, national forest supervisors, and forest rangers.

(b) The Secretary of Agriculture shall, within ten years after the enactment of this Act, review, as to its suitability or nonsuitability for preservation as wilderness, each area in the national forests classified on the effective date of this Act by the Secretary of Agriculture or the Chief of the Forest Service as "primitive" and report his findings to the President. The President shall advise the United States Senate and House of Representatives of his recommendations with respect to the designation as "wilderness" or other reclassification of each area on which review has been completed, together with maps and a definition of boundaries. Such advice shall be given with respect to not less than one-third of all the areas now classified as "primitive" within three years after the enactment of this Act, not less than two-thirds within seven years after the enactment of this Act, and the remaining areas within ten years after the enactment of this Act. Each recommendation of the President for designation as "wilderness" shall become effective only if so provided by an Act of Congress. Areas classified as "primitive" on the effective date of this Act shall continue to be administered under the rules and regulations affecting such areas on the effective date of this Act until Congress has determined otherwise. Any such area may be increased in size by the President at the time he submits his recommendations to the Congress by not more than five thousand acres with no more than one thousand two hundred and eighty acres of such increase in any one compact unit; if it is proposed to increase the size of any such area by more than five thousand acres or by more than one thousand two hundred and eighty acres in any one compact unit the increase in size shall not become effective until acted upon by Congress. Nothing herein contained shall limit the President in proposing, as part of his recommendations to Congress, the alteration of existing boundaries of primitive areas or recommending the addition of any contiguous area of national forest lands predominantly of wilderness value. Notwithstanding any other provisions of this Act, the Secretary of Agriculture may complete his review and delete such area as may be necessary, but not to exceed seven thousand acres, from the southern tip of the Gore Range-Eagles Nest Primitive Area, Colorado, if the Secretary determines that such action is in the public interest.

(c) Within ten years after the effective date of this Act the Secretary of the Interior shall review every roadless area of five thousand contiguous acres or more in the national parks, monuments and other units of the national park system and every such area of, and every roadless island within, the national wildlife refuges and game ranges, under his jurisdiction on the effective date of this Act and shall report to the President his recommendation as to the suitability or nonsuitability of each such area or island for preservation as wilderness. The President shall advise the President of the Senate and the Speaker of the House of Representatives of his recommendation with respect to the designation as wilderness of each such area or island on which review has been completed, together with a map thereof and a definition of its boundaries. Such advice shall be given with respect to not less than one-third of the areas and islands to be reviewed under this subsection within three years after enactment of this Act, not less than two-thirds within seven years of enactment of this Act, and the remainder within ten years of enactment of this Act. A recommendation of the President for designation as wilderness shall become effective only if so provided by an Act of Congress. Nothing contained herein shall, by implication or otherwise, be construed to lessen the present statutory authority of the Secretary of the Interior with respect to the maintenance of roadless areas within units of the national park system.

(d) (1) The Secretary of Agriculture and the Secretary of the Interior shall, prior to submitting any recommendations to the President with respect to the suitability of any area for preservation as wilderness—

(A) give such public notice of the proposed action as they deem appropriate, including publication in the Federal Register and in a newspaper having general circulation in the area or areas in the vicinity of the affected land;

(B) hold a public hearing or hearings at a location or locations convenient to the area affected. The hearings shall be announced through such means as the respective Secretaries involved deem appropriate, including notices in the Federal Register and in newspapers of general circulation in the area: *Provided,* That if the lands involved are located in more than one State, at least one hearing shall be held in each State in which a portion of the land lies;

(C) at least thirty days before the date of a hearing advise the Governor of each State and the governing board of each county, or in Alaska the borough, in which the lands are located, and Federal departments and agencies concerned, and invite such officials and Federal agencies to submit their views on the proposed action at the hearing or by no later than thirty days following the date of the hearing.

(2) Any views submitted to the appropriate Secretary under the provisions of (1) of this subsection with respect to any area shall be included with any recommendations to the President and to Congress with respect to such area.

(e) Any modification or adjustment of boundaries of any wilderness area shall be recommended by the appropriate Secretary after public notice of such proposal and public hearing or hearings as provided in subsection (d) of this section. The proposed modification or adjustment shall then be recommended with map and description thereof to the President. The President shall advise the United States Senate and the House of Representatives of his recommendations with respect to such modification or adjustment and such recommendations shall become effective only in the same manner as provided for in subsections (b) and (c) of this section.

Use of Wilderness Areas

Sec. 4. (a) The purposes of this Act are hereby declared to be within and supplemental to the purposes for which national forests and units of the national park and national wildlife refuge systems are established and administered and—

(1) Nothing in this Act shall be deemed to be in interference with the purpose for which national forests are established as set forth in the Act of June 4, 1897 (30 Stat. 11), and the Multiple-Use Sustained-Yield Act of June 12, 1960 (74 Stat. 215).

(2) Nothing in this Act shall modify the restrictions and provisions of the Shipstead-Nolan Act (Public Law 539, Seventy-first Congress, July 10, 1930; 46 Stat. 1020), the Thye-Blatnik Act (Public Law 733, Eightieth Congress, June 22, 1948; 62 Stat. 568), and the Humphrey-Thye-Blatnik-Andresen Act (Public Law 607, Eighty-fourth Congress, June 22, 1956; 70 Stat. 326), as applying to the Superior National Forest or the regulations of the Secretary of Agriculture.

(3) Nothing in this Act shall modify the statutory authority under which units of the national park system are created. Further, the designation of any area of any park, monument, or other unit of the national park system as a wilderness area pursuant to this Act shall in no manner lower the standards evolved for the use and preservation of such park, monument, or other unit of the national park system in accordance with the Act of August

25, 1916, the statutory authority under which the area was created, or any other Act of Congress which might pertain to or affect such area, including, but not limited to, the Act of June 8, 1906 (34 Stat. 225; 16 U.S.C. 432 et seq.); section 3 (2) of the Federal Power Act (16 U.S.C. 796(2); and the Act of August 21, 1935 (49 Stat. 666; 16 U.S.C. 461 et seq.).

(b) Except as otherwise provided in this Act, each agency administering any area designated as wilderness shall be responsible for preserving the wilderness character of the area and shall so administer such area for such other purposes for which it may have been established as also to preserve its wilderness character. Except as otherwise provided in this Act, wilderness areas shall be devoted to the public purposes of recreational, scenic, scientific, educational, conservation, and historical use.

Prohibition of Certain Uses

(c) Except as specifically provided for in this Act, and subject to existing private rights, there shall be no commercial enterprise and no permanent road within any wilderness area designated by this Act and, except as necessary to meet minimum requirements for the administration of the area for the purpose of this Act (including measures required in emergencies involving the health and safety of persons within the area), there shall be no temporary road, no use of motor vehicles, motorized equipment or motorboats, no landing of aircraft, no other form of mechanical transport, and no structure or installation within any such area.

Special Provisions

(d) The following special provisions are hereby made:

(1) Within wilderness areas designated by this Act the use of aircraft or motorboats, where these uses have already become established, may be permitted to continue subject to such restrictions as the Secretary of Agriculture deems desirable. In addition, such measures may be taken as may be necessary in the control of fire, insects, and diseases, subject to such conditions as the Secretary deems desirable.

(2) Nothing in this Act shall prevent within national forest wilderness areas any activity, including prospecting, for the purpose of gathering information about mineral or other resources, if such activity is carried on in a manner compatible with the preservation of the wilderness environment. Furthermore, in accordance with such program as the Secretary of the Interior shall develop and conduct in consultation with the Secretary of Agriculture, such areas shall be surveyed on a planned, recurring basis consistent with the concept of wilderness preservation by the Geological Survey and the Bureau of Mines to determine the mineral values, if any, that may be present; and the results of such surveys shall be made available to the public and submitted to the President and Congress.

(3) Notwithstanding any other provisions of this Act, until midnight December 31, 1983, the United States mining laws and all laws pertaining to mineral leasing shall, to the same extent as applicable prior to the effective date of this Act, extend to those national forest lands designated by this Act as "wilderness areas"; subject, however, to such reasonable regulations governing ingress and egress as may be prescribed by the Secretary of Agriculture consistent with the use of the land for mineral location and development and exploration, drilling, and production, and use of land for transmission lines, water-lines, telephone lines, or facilities necessary in exploring, drilling, producing, mining, and processing operations, including where essential the use of mechanized ground or air equipment and restoration as near as practicable of the surface of the land disturbed in performing prospecting, location, and, in oil and gas leasing, discovery work, exploration, drilling, and production, as soon as they have served their purpose. Mining locations lying within the boundaries of said wilderness areas shall be held and used solely for mining or processing operations and uses reasonably incident thereto; and hereafter, subject to valid existing rights, all patents issued under the mining laws of the United States affecting national forest lands designated by this Act as wilderness areas shall convey title to the mineral deposits within the claim, together with the right to cut and use so much of the mature timber therefrom as may be needed in the extraction, removal, and benefi-

ciation of the mineral deposits, if needed timber is not otherwise reasonably available, and if the timber is cut under sound principles of forest management as defined by the national forest rules and regulations, but each such patent shall reserve to the United States all title in or to the surface of the lands and products thereof, and no use of the surface of the claim or the resources therefrom not reasonably required for carrying on mining or prospecting shall be allowed except as otherwise expressly provided in this Act: *Provided,* That, unless hereafter specifically authorized, no patent within wilderness areas designated by this Act shall issue after December 31, 1983, except for the valid claims existing on or before December 31, 1983. Mining claims located after the effective date of this Act within the boundaries of wilderness areas designated by this Act shall create no rights in excess of those rights which may be patented under the provisions of this subsection. Mineral leases, permits, and licenses covering lands within national forest wilderness areas designated by this Act shall contain such reasonable stipulations as may be prescribed by the Secretary of Agriculture for the protection of the wilderness character of the land consistent with the use of the land for the purposes for which they are leased, permitted, or licensed. Subject to valid rights then existing, effective January 1, 1984, the minerals in lands designated by this Act as wilderness areas are withdrawn from all forms of appropriation under the mining laws and from disposition under all laws pertaining to mineral leasing and all amendments thereto.

(4) Within wilderness areas in the national forests designated by this Act, (1) the President may, within a specific area and in accordance with such regulations as he may deem desirable, authorize prospecting for water resources, the establishment and maintenance of reservoirs, water-conservation works, power projects, transmission lines, and other facilities needed in the public interest, including the road construction and maintenance essential to development and use thereof, upon his determination that such use or uses in the specific area will better serve the interests of the United States and the people thereof than will its denial; and (2) the grazing of livestock, where established prior to the effective date of this Act, shall be permitted to continue subject to such reasonable regulations as are deemed necessary by the Secretary of Agriculture.

(5) Other provisions of this Act to the contrary notwithstanding, the management of the Boundary Waters Canoe Area, formerly designated as the Superior, Little Indian Sioux, and Caribou Roadless Areas, in the Superior National Forest, Minnesota, shall be in accordance with regulations established by the Secretary of Agriculture in accordance with the general purpose of maintaining, without unnecessary restrictions on other uses, including that of timber, the primitive character of the area, particularly in the vicinity of lakes, streams, and portages: *Provided,* That nothing in this Act shall preclude the continuance within the area of any already established use of motorboats.

(6) Commercial services may be performed within the wilderness areas designated by this Act to the extent necessary for activities which are proper for realizing the recreational or other wilderness purposes of the areas.

(7) Nothing in this Act shall constitute an express or implied claim or denial on the part of the Federal Government as to exemption from State water laws.

(8) Nothing in this Act shall be construed as affecting the jurisdiction or responsibilities of the several States with respect to wildlife and fish in the national forests.

State and Private Lands within Wilderness Areas

Sec. 5. (a) In any case where State-owned or privately owned land is completely surrounded by national forest lands within areas designated by this Act as wilderness, such State or private owner shall be given such rights as may be necessary to assure adequate access to such State-owned or privately owned land by such State or private owner and their successors in interest, or the State-owned land or privately owned land shall be exchanged for federally owned land in the same State of approximately equal value under authorities available to the Secretary of Agriculture: *Provided, however,* That the United States shall not transfer to a State or private owner any mineral interests unless the State or private owner relinquishes or causes to be relinquished to the United States the mineral interest in the surrounded land.

(b) In any case where valid mining claims or other valid occupancies are wholly within a designated national forest wilderness area, the Secretary of Agriculture shall, by reasonable regulations consistent with the preservation of the area as wilderness, permit ingress and egress to such surrounded areas by means which have been or are being customarily enjoyed with respect to other such areas similarly situated.

(c) Subject to the appropriation of funds by Congress, the Secretary of Agriculture is authorized to acquire privately owned land within the perimeter of any area designated by this Act as wilderness if (1) the owner concurs in such acquisition or (2) the acquisition is specifically authorized by Congress.

Gifts, Bequests, and Contributions

Sec. 6. (a) The secretary of Agriculture may accept gifts or bequests of land within wilderness areas designated by this Act for preservation as wilderness. The Secretary of Agriculture may also accept gifts or bequests of land adjacent to wilderness areas designated by this Act for preservation as wilderness if he has given sixty days advance notice thereof to the President of the Senate and the Speaker of the House of Representatives. Land accepted by the Secretary of Agriculture under this section shall become part of the wilderness area involved. Regulations with regard to any such land may be in accordance with such agreements, consistent with the policy of this Act, as are made at the time of such gift, or such conditions, consistent with such policy, as may be included in, and accepted with, such bequest.

(b) The Secretary of Agriculture or the Secretary of the Interior is authorized to accept private contributions and gifts to be used to further the purposes of this Act.

Annual Reports

Sec. 7. At the opening of each session of Congress, the Secretaries of Agriculture and Interior shall jointly report to the President for transmission to Congress on the status of the wilderness system, including a list and descriptions of the areas in the system, regulations in effect, and other pertinent information, together with any recommendations they may care to make.

Legislative History

House Reports: No. 1538 accompanying H. R. 9070 (Comm. on Interior & Insular Affairs) and No. 1829 (Comm. of Conference).

Senate Report No. 109 (Comm. on Interior & Insular Affairs).

Congressional Record: Vol. 109 (1963): Apr. 4, 8, considered in Senate. Apr. 9, considered and passed Senate. Vol. 110 (1964): July 28, considered in House. July 30, considered and passed House, amended, in lieu of H. R. 9070. Aug. 20, House and Senate agreed to conference report.

Public Law 90-542
90th Congress, S. 119
October 2, 1968

An Act

To provide for a National Wild and Scenic Rivers System, and for other purposes.

Be it enacted by the Senate and House of Representatives of the United States of America in Congress assembled, That (a) this Act may be cited as the "Wild and Scenic Rivers Act".

(b) It is hereby declared to be the policy of the United States that certain selected rivers of the Nation which, with their immediate environments, possess oustandingly remarkable scenic, recreational, geologic, fish and wildlife, historic, cultural, or other similar values, shall be preserved in free-flowing condition, and that they and their immediate environments shall be protected for the benefit and enjoyment of present and future generations. The Congress declares that the established national policy of dam and other construction at appropriate sections of the rivers of the United States needs to be complemented by a policy that would preserve other selected rivers or sections thereof in their free-flowing condition to protect the water quality of such rivers and to fulfill other vital national conservation purposes.

(c) The purpose of this Act is to implement this policy by instituting a national wild and scenic rivers system, by designating the initial components of that system, and by prescribing the methods by which and standards according to which additional components may be added to the system from time to time.

Sec. 2. (a) The national wild and scenic rivers system shall comprise rivers (i) that are authorized for inclusion therein by Act of Congress, or (ii) that are designated as wild, scenic or recreational rivers by or pursuant to an act of the legislature of the State or States through which they flow, that are to be permanently administered as wild, scenic or recreational rivers by an agency or political subdivision of the State or States concerned without expense to the United States, that are found by the Secretary of the Interior, upon application of the Governor of the State or the Governors of the States concerned, or a person or persons thereunto duly appointed by him or them, to meet the criteria established in this Act and such criteria supplementary thereto as he may prescribe, and that are approved by him for inclusion in the system, including, upon application of the Governor of the State concerned, the Allagash Wilderness Waterway, Maine, and that segment of the Wolf River, Wisconsin, which flows through Langlade County.

(b) A wild, scenic or recreational river area eligible to be included in the system is a free-flowing stream and the related adjacent land area that possesses one or more of the values referred to in section 1, subsection (b) of this Act. Every wild, scenic or recreational river in its free-flowing condition, or upon restoration to this condition, shall be considered eligible for inclusion in the national wild and scenic rivers system and, if included, shall be classified, designated, and administered as one of the following:

(1) Wild river areas—Those rivers or sections of rivers that are free of impoundments and generally inaccessible except by trail, with watersheds or shorelines essentially primitive and waters unpolluted. These represent vestiges of primitive America.

(2) Scenic river areas—Those rivers or sections of rivers that are free of impoundments, with shorelines or watersheds still largely primitive and shorelines largely undeveloped, but accessible in places by roads.

(3) Recreational river areas—Those rivers or sections of rivers that are readily accessible by road or railroad, that may have some development along their shorelines, and that may have undergone some impoundment or diversion in the past.

Sec. 3 (a) The following rivers and the land adjacent thereto are hereby designated as components of the national wild and scenic rivers system:

(1) **Clearwater, Middle Fork, Idaho.**—The Middle Fork from the town of Kooskia up-

stream to the town of Lowell; the Lochsa River from its junction with the Selway at Lowell forming the Middle Fork, upstream to the Powell Ranger Station; and the Selway River from Lowell upstream to its origin; to be administered by the Secretary of Agriculture.

(2) **Eleven Point, Missouri.**—The segment of the river extending downstream from Thomasville to State Highway 142; to be administered by the Secretary of Agriculture.

(3) **Feather, California.**—The entire Middle Fork; to be administered by the Secretary of Agriculture.

(4) **Rio Grande, New Mexico.**—The segment extending from the Colorado State line downstream to the State Highway 96 crossing, and the lower four miles of the Red River; to be administered by the Secretary of the Interior.

(5) **Rogue, Oregon.**—The segment of the river extending from the mouth of the Applegate River downstream to the Lobster Creek Bridge; to be administered by agencies of the Departments of the Interior or Agriculture as agreed upon by the Secretaries of said Departments or as directed by the President.

(6) **Saint Croix, Minnesota and Wisconsin.**—The segment between the dam near Taylors Falls, Minnesota, and the dam near Gordon, Wisconsin, and its tributary, the Namekagon, from Lake Namekagon downstream to its confluence with the Saint Croix; to be administered by the Secretary of the Interior: *Provided,* That except as may be required in connection with items (a) and (b) of this paragraph, no funds available to carry out the provisions of this Act may be expended for the acquisition or development of lands in connection with, or for administration under this Act of, that portion of the Saint Croix River between the dam near Taylors Falls, Minnesota, and the upstream end of Big Island in Wisconsin, until sixty days after the date on which the Secretary has transmitted to the President of the Senate and Speaker of the House of Representatives a proposed cooperative agreement between the Northern States Power Company and the United States (a) whereby the company agrees to convey to the United States, without charge, appropriate interests in certain of its lands between the dam near Taylors Falls, Minnesota, and the upstream end of Big Island in Wisconsin, including the company's right, title, and interest to approximately one hundred acres per mile, and (b) providing for the use and development of other lands and interests in land retained by the company between said points adjacent to the river in a manner which shall complement and not be inconsistent with the purposes for which the lands and interests in land donated by the company are administered under this Act. Said agreement may also include provision for State or local governmental participation as authorized under subsection (e) of section 10 of this Act.

(7) **Salmon, Middle Fork, Idaho.**—From its origin to its confluence with the main Salmon River; to be administered by the Secretary of Agriculture.

(8) **Wolf, Wisconsin.**—From the Langlade-Menominee County line downstream to Keshena Falls; to be administered by the Secretary of the Interior.

(b) The agency charged with the administration of each component of the national wild and scenic rivers system designated by subsection (a) of this section shall, within one year from the date of this Act, establish detailed boundaries therefor (which boundaries shall include an average of not more than three hundred and twenty acres per mile on both sides of the river); determine which of the classes outlined in section 2, subsection (b), of this Act best fit the river or its various segments; and prepare a plan for necessary developments in connection with its administration in accordance with such classification. Said boundaries, classification, and development plans shall be published in the Federal Register and shall not become effective until ninety days after they have been forwarded to the President of the Senate and the Speaker of the House of Representatives.

Sec. 4. (a) The Secretary of the Interior or, where national forest lands are involved, the Secretary of Agriculture or, in appropriate cases, the two Secretaries jointly shall study and from time to time submit to the President and the Congress proposals for the addition to the national wild and scenic rivers system of rivers which are designated herein or hereafter by the Congress as potential additions to such system; which, in his or their judgment, fail within one or more of the classes set out in section 2, subsection (b), of this Act; and which are proposed to be administered, wholly or partially, by an agency of the United States. Every such study and plan shall be coordinated with any water resources planning involving the same river which is being conducted pursuant to the Water Resources Planning Act (79 Stat. 244; 42 U.S.C. 1962 et seq.).

Each proposal shall be accompanied by a report, including maps and illustrations, showing among other things the area included within the proposal; the characteristics which make the area a worthy addition to the system; the current status of landownership and use in the area; the reasonably foreseeable potential uses of the land and water which would be enhanced, foreclosed, or curtailed if the area were included in the national wild and scenic rivers system; the Federal agency (which in the case of a river which is wholly or substantially within a national forest, shall be the Department of Agriculture) by which it is proposed the area be administered; the extent to which it is proposed that administration, including the costs thereof, be shared by State and local agencies; and the estimated cost to the United States of acquiring necessary lands and interests in land and of administering the area as a component of the system. Each such report shall be printed as a Senate or House document.

(b) Before submitting any such report to the President and the Congress, copies of the proposed report shall, unless it was prepared jointly by the Secretary of the Interior and the Secretary of Agriculture, be submitted by the Secretary of the Interior to the Secretary of Agriculture or by the Secretary of Agriculture to the Secretary of the Interior, as the case may be, and to the Secretary of the Army, the Chairman of the Federal Power Commission, the head of any other affected Federal department or agency and, unless the lands proposed to be included in the area are already owned by the United States or have already been authorized for acquisition by Act of Congress, the Governor of the State or States in which they are located or an officer designated by the Governor to receive the same. Any recommendations or comments on the proposal which the said officials furnish the Secretary or Secretaries who prepared the report within ninety days of the date on which the report is submitted to them, together with the Secretary's or Secretaries' comments thereon, shall be included with the transmittal to the President and the Congress. No river or portion of any river shall be added to the national wild and scenic rivers system subsequent to enactment of this Act until the close of the next full session of the State legislature, or legislatures in case more than one State is involved, which begins following the submission of any recommendation to the President with respect to such addition as herein provided.

(c) Before approving or disapproving for inclusion in the national wild and scenic rivers system any river designated as a wild, scenic or recreational river by or pursuant to an act of a State legislature, the Secretary of the Interior shall submit the proposal to the Secretary of Agriculture, the Secretary of the Army, the Chairman of the Federal Power Commission, and the head of any other affected Federal department or agency and shall evaluate and give due weight to any recommendations or comments which the said officials furnish him within ninety days of the date on which it is submitted to them. If he approves the proposed inclusion, he shall publish notice thereof in the Federal Register.

Sec. 5. (a) The following rivers are hereby designated for potential addition to the national wild and scenic rivers system:

(1) Allegheny, Pennsylvania: The segment from its mouth to the town of East Brady, Pennsylvania.

(2) Bruneau, Idaho: The entire main stem.

(3) Buffalo, Tennessee: The entire river.

(4) Chattooga, North Carolina, South Carolina, and Georgia: The entire river.

(5) Clarion, Pennsylvania: The segment between Ridgway and its confluence with the Allegheny River.

(6) Delaware, Pennsylvania and New York: The segment from Hancock, New York, to Matamoras, Pennsylvania.

(7) Flathead, Montana: The North Fork from the Canadian border downstream to its confluence with the Middle Fork; the Middle Fork from its headwaters to its confluence with the South Fork; and the South Fork from its origin to Hungry Horse Reservoir.

(8) Gasconade, Missouri: The entire river.

(9) Illinois, Oregon: The entire river.

(10) Little Beaver, Ohio: The segment of the North and Middle Forks of the Little Beaver River in Columbiana County from a point in the vicinity of Negly and Elkton, Ohio, downstream to a point in the vicinity of East Liverpool, Ohio.

(11) Little Miami, Ohio: That segment of the main stem of the river, exclusive of its tributaries, from a point at the Warren-Clermont County line at Loveland, Ohio, upstream to the sources of Little Miami including North Fork.

(12) Maumee, Ohio and Indiana: The main stem from Perrysburg, Ohio, to Fort Wayne,

Indiana, exclusive of its tributaries in Ohio and inclusive of its tributaries in Indiana.

(13) Missouri, Montana: The segment between Fort Benton and Ryan Island.

(14) Moyie, Idaho: The segment from the Canadian border to its confluence with the Kootenai River.

(15) Obed, Tennessee: The entire river and its tributaries, Clear Creek and Daddys Creek.

(16) Penobscot, Maine: Its east and west branches.

(17) Pere Marquette, Michigan: The entire river.

(18) Pine Creek, Pennsylvania: The segment from Ansonia to Waterville.

(19) Priest, Idaho: The entire main stem.

(20) Rio Grande, Texas: The portion of the river between the west boundary of Hudspeth County and the east boundary of Terrell County on the United States side of the river: *Provided,* That before undertaking any study of this potential scenic river, the Secretary of the Interior shall determine, through the channels of appropriate executive agencies, that Mexico has no objection to its being included among the studies authorized by this Act.

(21) Saint Croix, Minnesota and Wisconsin: The segment between the dam near Taylors Falls and its confluence with the Mississippi River.

(22) Saint Joe, Idaho: The entire main stem.

(23) Salmon, Idaho: The segment from the town of North Fork to its confluence with the Snake River.

(24) Skagit, Washington: The segment from the town of Mount Vernon to and including the mouth of Bacon Creek; the Cascade River between its mouth and the junction of its North and South Forks; the South Fork to the boundary of the Glacier Peak Wilderness Area; the Suiattle River from its mouth to the Glacier Peak Wilderness Area boundary at Milk Creek; the Sauk River from its mouth to its junction with Elliott Creek; the North Fork of the Sauk River from its junction with the South Fork of the Sauk to the Glacier Peak Wilderness Area boundary.

(25) Suwannee, Georgia and Florida: The entire river from its source in the Okefenokee Swamp in Georgia to the gulf and the outlying Ichetucknee Springs, Florida.

(26) Upper Iowa, Iowa: The entire river.

(27) Youghiogheny, Maryland and Pennsylvania: The segment from Oakland, Maryland, to the Youghiogheny Reservoir, and from the Youghiogheny Dam downstream to the town of Connellsville, Pennsylvania.

(b) The Secretary of the Interior and, where national forest lands are involved, the Secretary of Agriculture shall proceed as expeditiously as possible to study each of the rivers named in subsection (a) of this section in order to determine whether it should be included in the national wild and scenic rivers system. Such studies shall be completed and reports made thereon to the President and the Congress, as provided in section 4 of this Act, within ten years from the date of this Act: *Provided, however,* That with respect to the Suwannee River, Georgia and Florida, and the Upper Iowa River, Iowa, such study shall be completed and reports made thereon to the President and the Congress, as provided in section 4 of this Act, within two years from the date of enactment of this Act. In conducting these studies the Secretary of the Interior and the Secretary of Agriculture shall give priority to those rivers with respect to which there is the greatest likelihood of developments which, if undertaken, would render them unsuitable for inclusion in the national wild and scenic rivers system.

(c) The study of any of said rivers shall be pursued in as close cooperation with appropriate agencies of the affected State and its political subdivisions as possible, shall be carried on jointly with such agencies if request for such joint study is made by the State, and shall include a determination of the degree to which the State or its political subdivisions might participate in the preservation and administration of the river should it be proposed for inclusion in the national wild and scenic rivers system.

(d) In all planning for the use and development of water and related land resources, consideration shall be given by all Federal agencies involved to potential national wild, scenic and recreational river areas, and all river basin and project plan reports submitted to the Congress shall consider and discuss any such potentials. The Secretary of the Interior and the Secretary of Agriculture shall make specific studies and investigations to determine which additional wild, scenic and recreational river areas within the United States shall be evaluated in planning reports by all Federal agencies as potential alternative uses of the water and related land resources involved.

Sec. 6. (a) The Secretary of the Interior and the Secretary of Agriculture are each authorized to acquire lands and interests in land within the authorized boundaries of any component of the national wild and scenic rivers system designated in section 3 of this Act, or hereafter designated for inclusion in the system by Act of Congress, which is administered by him, but he shall not acquire fee title to an average of more than 100 acres per mile on both sides of the river. Lands owned by a State may be acquired only by donation, and lands owned by an Indian tribe or a political subdivision of a State may not be acquired without the consent of the appropriate governing body thereof as long as the Indian tribe or political subdivision is following a plan for management and protection of the lands which the Secretary finds protects the land and assures its use for purposes consistent with this Act. Money appropriated for Federal purposes from the land and water conservation fund shall, without prejudice to the use of appropriations from other sources, be available to Federal departments and agencies for the acquisition of property for the purposes of this Act.

(b) If 50 per centum or more of the entire acreage within a federally administered wild, scenic or recreational river area is owned by the United States, by the State or States within which it lies, or by political subdivisions of those States, neither Secretary shall acquire fee title to any lands by condemnation under authority of this Act. Nothing contained in this section, however, shall preclude the use of condemnation when necessary to clear title or to acquire scenic easements or such other easements as are reasonably necessary to give the public access to the river and to permit its members to traverse the length of the area or of selected segments thereof.

(c) Neither the Secretary of the Interior nor the Secretary of Agriculture may acquire lands by condemnation, for the purpose of including such lands in any national wild, scenic or recreational river area, if such lands are located within any incorporated city, village, or borough which has in force and applicable to such lands a duly adopted, valid zoning ordinance that conforms with the purposes of this Act. In order to carry out the provisions of this subsection the appropriate Secretary shall issue guidelines, specifying standards for local zoning ordinances, which are consistent with the purposes of this Act. The standards specified in such guidelines shall have the object of (A) prohibiting new commercial or industrial uses other than commercial or industrial uses which are consistent with the purposes of this Act, and (B) the protection of the bank lands by means of acreage, frontage, and setback requirements on development.

(d) The appropriate Secretary is authorized to accept title to non-Federal property within the authorized boundaries of any federally administered component of the national wild and scenic rivers system designated in section 3 of this Act or hereafter designated for inclusion in the system by Act of Congress and, in exchange therefor, convey to the grantor any federally owned property which is under his jurisdiction within the State in which the component lies and which he classifies as suitable for exchange or other disposal. The values of the properties so exchanged either shall be approximately equal or, if they are not approximately equal, shall be equalized by the payment of cash to the grantor or to the Secretary as the circumstances require.

(e) The head of any Federal department or agency having administrative jurisdiction over any lands or interests in land within the authorized boundaries of any federally administered component of the national wild and scenic rivers system designated in section 3 of this Act or hereafter designated for inclusion in the system by Act of Congress in authorized to transfer to the appropriate secretary jurisdiction over such lands for administration in accordance with the provisions of this Act. Lands acquired by or transferred to the Secretary of Agriculture for the purposes of this Act within or adjacent to a national forest shall upon such acquisition or transfer become national forest lands.

(f) The appropriate Secretary is authorized to accept donations of lands and interests in land, funds, and other property for use in connection with his administration of the national wild and scenic rivers system.

(g) (1) Any owner or owners (hereinafter in this subsection referred to as "owner") of improved property on the date of its acquisition, may retain for themselves and their successors or assigns a right of use and occupancy of the improved property for noncommercial residential purposes for a definite term not to exceed twenty-five years or, in lieu thereof, for a term ending at the death of the owner, or the death of his spouse, or the death of either or both of them. The owner shall elect the term to be reserved. The appropriate Secretary shall pay to the owner the fair market value of the property on the date of such acquisition less the fair market value on such date of the right retained by the owner.

(2) A right of use and occupancy retained pursuant to this subsection shall be subject to termination whenever the appropriate Secretary is given reasonable cause to find that such use and occupancy is being exercised in a manner which conflicts with the purposes of this Act. In the event of such a finding, the Secretary shall tender to the holder of that right an amount equal to the fair market value of that portion of the right which remains unexpired on the date of termination. Such right of use or occupancy shall terminate by operation of law upon tender of the fair market price.

(3) The term "improved property", as used in this Act, means a detached, one-family dwelling (hereinafter referred to as "dwelling"), the construction of which was begun before January 1, 1967, together with so much of the land on which the dwelling is situated, the said land being in the same ownership as the dwelling, as the appropriate Secretary shall designate to be reasonably necessary for the enjoyment of the dwelling for the sole purpose of noncommercial residential use, together with any structures accessory to the dwelling which are situated on the land so designated.

Sec. 7. (a) The Federal Power Commission shall not license the construction of any dam, water conduit, reservoir, powerhouse, transmission line, or other project works under the Federal Power Act (41 Stat. 1063), as amended (16 U.S.C. 791a et seq.), on or directly affecting any river which is designated in section 3 of this Act as a component of the national wild and scenic rivers system or which is hereafter designated for inclusion in that system, and no department or agency of the United States shall assist by loan, grant, license, or otherwise in the construction of any water resources project that would have a direct and adverse effect on the values for which such river was established, as determined by the Secretary charged with its administration. Nothing contained in the foregoing sentence, however, shall preclude licensing of, or assistance to, developments below or above a wild, scenic or recreational river area or on any stream tributary thereto which will not invade the area or unreasonably diminish the scenic, recreational, and fish and wildlife values present in the area on the date of approval of this Act. No department or agency of the United States shall recommend authorization of any water resources project that would have a direct and adverse effect on the values for which such river was established, as determined by the Secretary charged with its administration, or request appropriations to begin construction of any such project, whether heretofore or hereafter authorized, without advising the Secretary of the Interior or the Secretary of Agriculture, as the case may be, in writing of its intention so to do at least sixty days in advance, and without specifically reporting to the Congress in writing at the time it makes its recommendation or request in what respect construction of such project would be in conflict with the purposes of this Act and would affect the component and the values to be protected by it under this Act.

(b) The Federal Power Commission shall not license the construction of any dam, water conduit, reservoir, powerhouse, transmission line, or other project works under the Federal Power Act, as amended, on or directly affecting any river which is listed in section 5, subsection (a), of this Act, and no department or agency of the United States shall assist by loan, grant, license, or otherwise in the construction of any water resources project that would have a direct and adverse effect on the values for which such river might be designated, as determined by the Secretary responsible for its study or approval—

(i) during the five-year period following enactment of this Act unless, prior to the expiration of said period, the Secretary of the Interior and, where national forest lands are involved, the Secretary of Agriculture, on the basis of study, conclude that such river should not be included in the national wild and scenic rivers system and publish notice to that effect in the Federal Register, and

(ii) during such additional period thereafter as, in the case of any river which is recommended to the President and the Congress for inclusion in the national wild and scenic rivers system, is necessary for congressional consideration thereof or, in the case of any river recommended to the Secretary of the Interior for inclusion in the national wild and scenic rivers system under section 2(a) (ii) of this Act, is necessary for the Secretary's consideration thereof, which additional period, however, shall not exceed three years in the first case and one year in the second.

Nothing contained in the foregoing sentence, however, shall preclude licensing of, or assistance to, developments below or above a potential wild, scenic or recreational river area or on any stream tributary thereto which will not invade the area or diminish the scenic, recreational, and fish and wildlife values present in the potential wild, scenic or recreational river area on the date of approval of this Act. No department or agency of the United States shall, during the periods hereinbefore specified, recommend authorization of any water resources project on any such river or request appropriations to begin construction of any such project, whether heretofore or hereafter authorized, without advising the Secretary of the Interior and, where national forest lands are involved, the Secretary of Agriculture in writing of its intention so to do at least sixty days in advance of doing so and without specifically reporting to the Congress in writing at the time it makes its recommendation or request in what respect construction of such project would be in conflict with the purposes of this Act and would affect the component and the values to be protected by it under this Act.

(c) The Federal Power Commission and all other Federal agencies shall, promptly upon enactment of this Act, inform the Secretary of the Interior and, where national forest lands are involved, the Secretary of Agriculture, of any proceedings, studies, or other activities within their jurisdiction which are now in progress and which affect or may affect any of the rivers specified in section 5, subsection (a), of this Act. They shall likewise inform him of any such proceedings, studies, or other activities which are hereafter commenced or resumed before they are commenced or resumed.

(d) Nothing in this section with respect to the making of a loan or grant shall apply to grants made under the Land and Water Conservation Fund Act of 1965 (78 Stat. 897; 16 U.S.C. 4601-5 et seq.).

Sec. 8. (a) All public lands within the authorized boundaries of any component of the national wild and scenic rivers system which is designated in section 3 of this Act or which is hereafter designated for inclusion in that system are hereby withdrawn from entry, sale, or other disposition under the public land laws of the United States.

(b) All public lands which constitute the bed or bank, or are within one-quarter mile of the bank, of any river which is listed in section 5, subsection (a), of this Act are hereby withdrawn from entry, sale, or other disposition under the public land laws of the United States for the periods specified in section 7, subsection (b), of this Act.

Sec. 9. (a) Nothing in this Act shall affect the applicability of the United States mining and mineral leasing laws within components of the national wild and scenic rivers system except that—

(i) all prospecting, mining operations, and other activities on mining claims which, in the case of a component of the system designated in section 3 of this Act, have not heretofore been perfected or which, in the case of a component hereafter designated pursuant to this Act or any other Act of Congress, are not perfected before its inclusion in the system and all mining operations and other activities under a mineral lease, license, or permit issued or renewed after inclusion of a component in the system shall be subject to such regulations as the Secretary of the Interior or, in the case of national forest lands, the Secretary of Agriculture may prescribe to effectuate the purposes of this Act;

(ii) subject to valid existing rights, the perfection of, or issuance of a patent to, any mining claim affecting lands within the system shall confer or convey a right or title only to the mineral deposits and such rights only to the use of the surface and the surface resources as are reasonably required to carrying on prospecting or mining operations and are consistent with such regulations as may be prescribed by the Secretary of the Interior or, in the case of national forest lands, by the Secretary of Agriculture; and

(iii) subject to valid existing rights, the minerals in Federal lands which are part of the system and constitute the bed or bank or are situated within one-quarter mile of the bank of any river designated a wild river under this Act or any subsequent Act are hereby withdrawn from all forms of appropriation under the mining laws and from operation of the mineral leasing laws including, in both cases, amendments thereto.

Regulations issued pursuant to paragraphs (i) and (ii) of this subsection shall, among other things, provide safeguards against pollution of the river involved and unnecessary impairment of the scenery within the component in question.

(b) The minerals in any Federal lands which constitute the bed or bank or are situated within one-quarter mile of the bank of any river which is listed in section 5, subsection (a) of this

Act are hereby withdrawn from all forms of appropriation under the mining laws during the periods specified in section 7, subsection (b) of this Act. Nothing contained in this subsection shall be construed to forbid prospecting or the issuance or leases, licenses, and permits under the mineral leasing laws subject to such conditions as the Secretary of the Interior and, in the case of national forest lands, the Secretary of Agriculture find appropriate to safeguard the area in the event it is subsequently included in the system.

Sec. 10. (a) Each component of the national wild and scenic rivers system shall be administered in such manner as to protect and enhance the values which caused it to be included in said system without, insofar as is consistent therewith, limiting other uses that do not substantially interfere with public use and enjoyment of these values. In such administration primary emphasis shall be given to protecting its esthetic, scenic, historic, archeologic, and scientific features. Management plans for any such component may establish varying degrees of intensity for its protection and development, based on the special attributes of the area.

(b) Any portion of a component of the national wild and scenic rivers system that is within the national widerness preservation system, as established by or pursuant to the Act of September 3, 1964 (78 Stat. 890; 16 U.S.C., ch. 23), shall be subject to the provisions of both the Wilderness Act and this Act with respect to preservation of such river and its immediate environment, and in case of conflict between the provisions of these Acts the more restrictive provisions shall apply.

(c) Any component of the national wild and scenic rivers system that is administered by the Secretary of the Interior through the National Park Service shall become a part of the national park system, and any such component that is administered by the Secretary through the Fish and Wildlife Service shall become a part of the national wildlife refuge system. The lands involved shall be subject to the provisions of this Act and the Acts under which the national park system or national wildlife system, as the case may be, is administered, and in case of conflict between the provisions of these Acts, the more restrictive provisions shall apply. The Secretary of the Interior, in his administration of any component of the national wild and scenic rivers system, may utilize such general statutory authorities relating to areas of the national park system and such general statutory authorities otherwise available to him for recreation and preservation purposes and for the conservation and management of natural resources as he deems appropriate to carry out the purposes of this Act.

(d) The Secretary of Agriculture, in his administration of any component of the national wild and scenic rivers system area, may utilize the general statutory authorities relating to the national forests in such manner as he deems appropriate to carry out the purposes of this Act.

(e) The Federal agency charged with the administration of any component of the national wild and scenic rivers system may enter into written cooperative agreements with the Governor of a State, the head of any State agency, or the appropriate official of a political subdivision of a State for State or local governmental participation in the administration of the component. The States and their political subdivisions shall be encouraged to cooperate in the planning and administration of components of the system which include or adjoin State- or county-owned lands.

Sec. 11. (a) The Secretary of the Interior shall encourage and assist the States to consider, in formulating and carrying out their comprehensive statewide outdoor recreation plans and proposals for financing assistance for State and local projects submitted pursuant to the Land and Water Conservation Fund Act of 1965 (78 Stat. 897), needs and opportunities for establishing State and local wild, scenic and recreational river areas. He shall also, in accordance with the authority contained in the Act of May 28, 1963 (77 Stat. 49), provide technical assistance and advice to, and cooperate with, States, political subdivisions, and private interests, interests, including nonprofit organizations, with respect to establishing such wild, scenic and recreational river areas.

(b) The Secretaries of Agriculture and of Health, Education, and Welfare shall likewise, in accordance with the authority vested in them, assist, advise, and cooperate with State and local agencies and private interests with respect to establishing such wild, scenic and recreational river areas.

Sec. 12. (a) The Secretary of the Interior, the Secretary of Agriculture, and heads of other Federal agencies shall review administrative and management policies, regulations, contracts, and plans affecting lands under their respective jurisdictions which include, border upon, or are adjacent to the rivers listed in subsection (a) of section 5 of this Act in order to determine what actions should be taken to protect such rivers during the period they are being considered for potential addition to the national wild and scenic rivers system. Particular attention shall be given to scheduled timber harvesting, road construction, and similar activities which might be contrary to the purposes of this Act.

(b) Nothing in this section shall be construed to abrogate any existing rights, privileges, or contracts affecting Federal lands held by any private party without the consent of said party.

(c) The head of any agency administering a component of the national wild and scenic rivers system shall cooperate with the Secretary of the Interior and with the appropriate State water pollution control agencies for the purpose of eliminating or diminishing the pollution of waters of the river.

Sec. 13. (a) Nothing in this Act shall affect the jurisdiction or responsibilities of the States with respect to fish and wildlife. Hunting and fishing shall be permitted on lands and waters administered as parts of the system under applicable State and Federal laws and regulations unless, in the case of hunting, those lands or waters are within a national park or monument. The administering Secretary may, however, designate zones where, and establish periods when, no hunting is permitted for reasons of public safety, administration, or public use and enjoyment and shall issue appropriate regulations after consultation with the wildlife agency of the State or States affected.

(b) The jurisdiction of the States and the United States over waters of any stream included in a national wild, scenic or recreational river area shall be determined by established principles of law. Under the provisions of this Act, any taking by the United States of a water right which is vested under either State or Federal law at the time such river is included in the national wild and scenic rivers system shall entitle the owner thereof to just compensation. Nothing in this Act shall constitute an express or implied claim or denial on the part of the Federal Government as to exemption from State water laws.

(c) Designation of any stream or portion thereof as a national wild, scenic or recreational river area shall not be construed as a reservation of the waters of such streams for purposes other than those specified in this Act, or in quantities greater than necessary to accomplish these purposes.

(d) The jurisdiction of the States over waters of any stream included in a national wild, scenic or recreational river area shall be unaffected by this Act to the extent that such jurisdiction may be exercised without impairing the purposes of this Act or its administration.

(e) Nothing contained in this Act shall be construed to alter, amend, repeal, interpret, modify, or be in conflict with any interstate compact made by any States which contain any portion of the national wild and scenic rivers system.

(f) Nothing in this Act shall affect existing rights of any State, including the right of access, with respect to the beds of navigable streams, tributaries, or rivers (or segments thereof) located in a national wild, scenic or recreational river area.

(g) The Secretary of the Interior or the Secretary of Agriculture, as the case may be, may grant easements and rights-of-way upon, over, under, across, or through any component of the national wild and scenic rivers system in accordance with the laws applicable to the national park system and the national forest system, respectively: *Provided,* That any conditions precedent to granting such easements and rights-of-way shall be related to the policy and purpose of this Act.

Sec. 14. The claim and allowance of the value of an easement as a charitable contribution under section 170 of title 26, United States Code, or as a gift under section 2522 of said title shall constitute an agreement by the donor on behalf of himself, his heirs, and assigns that, if the terms of the instrument creating the easement are violated, the donee or the United States may acquire the servient estate at its fair market value as of the time the easement was donated minus the value of the easement claimed and allowed as a charitable contribution or gift.

Sec. 15. As used in this Act, the term—

(a) "River" means a flowing body of water or estuary or a section, portion, or tributary thereof, including rivers, streams, creeks, runs, kills, rills, and small lakes.

(b) "Free-flowing", as applied to any river or section of a river means existing or flowing in natural condition without impoundment, diversion, straightening, rip-rapping, or other modification of the waterway. The existence, however, of low dams, diversion works, and other minor structures at the time any river is proposed for inclusion in the national wild and scenic rivers system shall not automatically bar its consideration for such inclusion: *Provided,* That this shall not be construed to authorize, intend, or encourage future construction of such structures within components of the national wild and scenic rivers system.

(c) "Scenic easement" means the right to control the use of land (including the air space above such land) for the purpose of protecting the scenic view from the river, but such control shall not affect, without the owner's consent, any regular use exercised prior to the acquisition of the easement.

Sec. 16. There are hereby authorized to be appropriated such sums as may be necessary, but not more than $17,000,000, for the acquisition of lands and interests in land under the provisions of this Act.

Legislative History

House Reports: No. 1623 accompanying H. R. 18620 (Comm. on Interior & Insular Affairs) and No. 1917 (Comm. of Conference).

Senate Report No. 491 (Comm. on Interior & Insular Affairs).

Congressional Record: Vol. 113 (1967): Aug. 8, considered and passed Senate. Vol. 114 (1968): July 15, Sept. 12, considered and passed House, amended, in lieu of H. R. 18260. Sept. 25, House agreed to conference report. Sept. 26, Senate agreed to conference report.

Public Law 93-622
93rd Congress, S. 3433
January 3, 1975

An Act

To further the purposes of the Wilderness Act by designating certain acquired lands for inclusion in the National Wilderness Preservation System, to provide for study of certain additional lands for such inclusion, and for other purposes.

Be it enacted by the Senate and House of Representatives of the United States of America in Congress assembled,

Statement of Finds and Policy

Sec. 2. (a) The Congress finds that—

(1) in the more populous eastern half of the United States there is an urgent need to identify, study, designate, and preserve areas for addition to the National Wilderness Preservation System;

(2) in recognition of this urgent need, certain areas in the national forest system in the eastern half of the United States were designated by the Congress as wilderness in the Wilderness Act (78 Stat. 890); certain areas in the national wildlife refuge system in the eastern half of the United States have been designated by the Congress as wilderness or recommended by the President for such designation, and certain areas in the national park system in the eastern half of the United States have been recommended by the President for designation as wilderness; and

(3) additional areas of wilderness in the more populous eastern half of the United States are increasingly threatened by the pressures of a growing and more mobile population, large-scale industrial and economic growth, and development and uses inconsistent with the protection, maintenance, and enhancement of the areas' wilderness character.

(b) Therefore, the Congress finds and declares that it is in the national interest that these and similar areas in the eastern half of the United States be promptly designated as wilderness within the National Wilderness Preservation System, in order to preserve such areas as an enduring resource of wilderness which shall be managed to promote and perpetuate the wilderness character of the land and its specific values of solitude, physical and mental challenge, scientific study, inspiration, and primitive recreation for the benefit of all of the American people of present and future generations.

Designation of Wilderness Areas

Sec. 8. (a) In furtherance of the purposes of the Wilderness Act, the following lands (hereinafter in this Act referred to as "wilderness areas"), as generally depicted on maps appropriately referenced, dated April 1974, are hereby designated as wilderness and, therefore, as components of the National Wilderness Preservation System—

(1) certain lands in the Bankhead National Forest, Alabama, which comprise about twelve thousand acres, are generally depicted on a map entitled "Sipsey Wilderness Area—Proposed", and shall be known as the Sipsey Wilderness:

(2) certain lands in the Ouachita National Forest, Arkansas, which comprise about fourteen thousand four hundred and thirty-three acres, are generally depicted on a map en-

titled "Caney Creek Wilderness Area—Proposed", and shall be known as the Caney Creek Wilderness;

(3) certain lands in the Ozark National Forest, Arkansas, which comprise about ten thousand five hundred and ninety acres, are generally depicted on a map entitled "Upper Buffalo Wilderness Area—Proposed", and shall be known as the Upper Buffalo Wilderness;

(4) certain lands in the Appalachicola National Forest, Florida, which comprise about twenty-two thousand acres, are generally depicted on a map entitled "Bradwell Bay Wilderness Area—Proposed", and shall be known as the Bradwell Bay Wilderness;

(5) certain lands in the Daniel Boone National Forest, Kentucky, which comprise about five thousand five hundred acres, are generally depicted on a map entitled "Beaver Creek Wilderness Area—Proposed", and shall be known as the Beaver Creek Wilderness;

(6) certain lands in the White Mountain National Forest, New Hampshire, which compromise about twenty thousand three hundred and eighty acres, are generally depicted on a map entitled "Presidential Range-Dry River Wilderness Area—Proposed", and shall be known as the Presidential Range-Dry River Wilderness;

(7) certain lands in the Nantahala and Cherokee National Forests, North Carolina and Tennessee, which comprise about fifteen thousand acres, are generally depicted on a map entitled "Joyce Kilmer-Slickrock Wilderness Area—Proposed", and shall be known as the Joyce Kilmer-Slickrock Wilderness;

(8) certain lands in the Sumter, Nantahala, and Chattahoochee National Forests in South Carolina, North Carolina, and Georgia, which comprise about three thousand six hundred acres, are generally depicted on a map entitled "Ellicott Rock Wilderness Area—Proposed", and shall be known as Ellicott Rock Wilderness;

(9) certain lands in the Cherokee National Forest, Tennessee, which comprise about two thousand five hundred and seventy acres, are generally depicted on a map entitled "Gee Creek Wilderness Area—Proposed", and shall be known as the Gee Creek Wilderness;

(10) certain lands in the Green Mountain National Forest, Vermont, which comprise about six thousand five hundred acres, are generally depicted on a map entitled "Bristol Cliffs Wilderness Area—Proposed", and shall be known as the Bristol Cliffs Wilderness;

(11) certain lands in the Green Mountain National Forest, Vermont, which comprise about fourteen thousand three hundred acres, are generally depicted on a map entitled "Lye Brook Wilderness Area—Proposed", and shall be known as the Lye Brook Wilderness;

(12) certain lands in the Jefferson National Forest, Virginia, which comprise about eight thousand eight hundred acres, are generally depicted on a map entitled "James River Face Wilderness Area—Proposed", and shall be known as the James River Face Wilderness;

(13) certain lands in the Monongahela National Forest, West Virginia, which comprise about ten thousand two hundred and fifteen acres, are generally depicted on a map entitled "Dolly Sods Wilderness Area—Proposed", and shall be known as the Dolly Sods Wilderness;

(14) certain lands in the Monongahela National Forest, West Virginia, which comprise about twenty thousand acres, are generally depicted on a map entitled "Otter Creek Wilderness Study Area", and shall be known as the Otter Creek Wilderness; and

(15) certain lands in the Chequamegon National Forest, Wisconsin, which comprise about six thousand six hundred acres, are generally depicted on a map entitled "Rainbow Lake Wilderness Area—Proposed", and shall be known as the Rainbow Lake Wilderness.

(b) In furtherance of the purposes of the Wilderness Act, the following lands (hereinafter referred to as "wilderness areas"), as generally depicted on maps appropriately referenced, dated April 1973, are hereby designated as wilderness and, therefore, as components of the National Wilderness Preservation System: certain lands in the Chattahoochee and Cherokee National Forests, Georgia and Tennessee, which comprise about thirty-four thousand five hundred acres, are generally depicted on a map dated April 1973, entitled "Cohutta Wilderness Area—Proposed", and shall be known as the Cohutta Wilderness.

Designation of Wilderness Study Area

Sec. 4. (a) In furtherance of the purposes of the Wilderness Act and in accordance with the provisions of subsection 3(d) of that Act, the Secretary of Agriculture (hereinafter referred to as the "Secretary") shall review, as to its suitability or nonsuitability for preservation as wilderness, each area designated by or pursuant to subsection (b) of this section and report his findings to the President. The President shall advise the United States Senate and House of Representatives of his recommendations with respect to the designation as wilderness of each such area on which the review has been completed.

(b) Areas to be reviewed pursuant to this section (hereinafter referred to as "wilderness study areas"), as generally depicted on maps appropriately referenced, dated April 1974, include—

(1) certain lands in the Ouachita National Forest, Arkansas, which comprise approximately five thousand seven hundred acres and are generally depicted on a map entitled "Belle Starr Cave Wilderness Study Area";

(2) certain lands in the Ouachita National Forest, Arkansas, which comprise approximately five thousand five hundred acres and are generally depicted on a map entitled "Dry Creek Wilderness Study Area";

(3) certain lands in the Ozark National Forest, Arkansas, which comprise approximately two thousand one hundred acres and are generally depicted on a map entitled "Richland Creek Wilderness Study Area";

(4) certain lands in the Appalachicola National Forest, Florida, which comprise approximately one thousand one hundred acres and are generally depicted as the "Sopchoppy River Wilderness Study Area" on a map entitled "Bradwell Bay Wilderness Area—Proposed";

(5) certain lands in the Hiawatha National Forest, Michigan, which comprise approximately five thousand four hundred acres and are generally depicted on a map entitled "Rock River Canyon Wilderness Study Area";

(6) certain lands in the Ottawa National Forest, Michigan, which comprise approximately thirteen thousand two hundred acres and are generally depicted on a map entitled "Sturgeon River Wilderness Study Area";

(7) certain lands in the Pisgah National Forest, North Carolina, which comprise approximately one thousand one hundred acres and are generally depicted on a map entitled "Craggy Mountain Wilderness Study Area";

(8) certain lands in the Francis Marion National Forest, South Carolina, which comprise approximately one thousand five hundred acres and are generally depicted on a map entitled "Wambaw Swamp Wilderness Study Area";

(9) certain lands in the Jefferson National Forest, Virginia, which comprise approximately four thousand acres and are generally depicted on a map entitled "Mill Creek Wilderness Study Area";

(10) certain lands in the Jefferson National Forest, Virginia, which comprise approximately eight thousand four hundred acres and are generally depicted on a map entitled "Mountain Lake Wilderness Study Area";

(11) certain lands in the Jefferson National Forest, Virginia, which comprise approximately five thousand acres and are generally depicted on a map entitled "Peters Mountain Wilderness Study Area";

(12) certain lands in the George Washington National Forest, Virginia, which comprise approximately six thousand seven hundred acres and are generally depicted on a map entitled "Ramsey's Draft Wilderness Study Area";

(13) certain lands in the Chequamegon National Forest, Wisconsin, which comprise approximately six thousand three hundred acres and are generally depicted on a map entitled "Flynn Lake Wilderness Study Area";

(14) certain lands in the Chequamegon National Forest, Wisconsin, which comprise approximately four thousand two hundred acres and are generally depicted on a map entitled "Round Lake Wilderness Study Area";

(15) certain lands in the Monongahela National Forest, West Virginia, which comprise approximately thirty-six thousand three hundred acres and are generally depicted on a map entitled "Cranberry Wilderness Study Area";

(16) certain lands in the Cherokee National Forest, Tennessee, which comprise ap-

proximately four thousand five hundred acres and are generally depicted on a map entitled "Big Frog Wilderness Study Area"; and

(17) certain lands in the Cherokee National Forest, Tennessee, which comprise approximately fourteen thousand acres and are generally depicted as the "Citico Creek Area" on a map entitled "Joyce Kilmer-Slickrock Wilderness Area—Proposed";

(c) Reviews shall be completed and the President shall make his recommendations to Congress within five years after enactment of this Act.

(d) Congress may, upon the recommendation of the Secretary of Agriculture or otherwise, designate as study areas, national forest system lands east of the 100th meridian other than those areas specified in subsection (b) of this section, for review as to suitability or nonsuitability for preservation as wilderness. Any such area subsequently designated as a wilderness study area after the enactment of this Act shall have its suitability or nonsuitability for preservation as wilderness submitted to Congress within ten years from the date of designation as a wilderness study area. Nothing in this Act shall be construed as limiting the authority of the Secretary of Agriculture to carry out management programs, development, and activities in accordance with the Multiple-Use, Sustained-Yield Act of 1960 (74 Stat. 215, 16 U.S.C. 528-531) within areas not designated for review in accordance with the provisions of this Act.

(e) Nothing herein contained shall limit the President in proposing, as part of his recommendations to Congress, the alteration of existing boundaries of any wilderness study area or recommending the addition to any such area of any contiguous area predominantly of wilderness value. Any recommendation of the President to the effect that such area or portion thereof should be designated as "wilderness" shall become effective only if so provided by an Act of Congress.

Filing of Maps and Descriptions

Sec. 5. As soon as practicable after enactment of this Act, a map of each wilderness study area and a map and a legal description of each wilderness area shall be filed with the Committees on Interior and Insular Affairs and on Agriculture of the United States Senate and House of Representatives, and each such map and description shall have the same force and effect as if included in this Act: *Provided, however,* That correction of clerical and typographical errors in each such legal description and map may be made. Each such map and legal description shall be on file and available for public inspection in the Office of the Chief of the Forest Service, Department of Agriculture.

Management of Areas

Sec. 6. (a) except as otherwise provided by this Act, the wilderness areas designated by or pursuant to this Act shall be managed by the Secretary of Agriculture in accordance with the provisions of the Wilderness Act. The wilderness study areas designated by a pursuant to this Act shall—be managed by the Secretary of Agriculture so as to maintain their presently existing wilderness character and potential for inclusion in the National Wilderness Preservation System until Congress has determined otherwise, except that such management requirement shall in no case extend beyond the expiration of the third succeeding Congress from the date of submission to the Congress of the President's recommendations concerning the particular study area.

(b) Within the sixteen wilderness areas designated by section 3 of this Act:

(1) the Secretary of Agriculture may acquire by purchase with donated or appropriated funds, by gift, exchange, condemnation, or otherwise, such lands, waters, or interests therein as he determines necessary or desirable for the purposes of this Act. All lands acquired under the provisions of this subsection shall become national forest lands and a part of the Wilderness System;

(2) in exercising the exchange authority granted by paragraph (1), the Secretary of Agriculture may accept title to non-Federal property for federally owned property of substantially equal value, or, if not of substantially equal value, the value shall be equalized by the payment of money to the grantor or to the Secretary as the circumstances require;

(3) the authority of the Secretary of Agriculture to condemn any private land or inter-

est therein within any wilderness area designated by or pursuant to this Act shall not be invoked so long as the owner or owners of such land or interest holds and uses it in the same manner and for those purposes for which such land or interest was held on the date of the designation of the wilderness area: *Provided, however,* That the Secretary of Agriculture may acquire such land or interest without consent of the owner or owners whenever he finds such use to be incompatible with the management of such area as wilderness and the owner or owners manifest unwillingness, and subsequently fail, to promptly discontinue such incompatible use;

(4) at least sixty days prior to any transfer by exchange, sale, or otherwise (except by bequest) of such lands, or interests therein described in paragraph (3) of this subsection, the owner or owners of such lands or interests therein shall provide notice of such transfer to the supervisor of the national forest concerned, in accordance with such rules and regulations as the Secretary of Agriculture may promulgate;

(5) at least sixty days prior to any change in the use of such lands or interests therein described in paragraph (8) of this subsection which will result in any significant new construction or disturbance of land surface or flora or will require the use of motor vehicles and other forms of mechanized transport or motorized equipment (except as otherwise authorized by law for ingress or egress or for existing agricultural activities begun before the date of the designation other than timber cutting), the owner or owners of such lands or interests therein shall provide notice of such change in use to the supervisor of the national forest within which such lands are located, in accordance with such rules and regulations as the Secretary of Agriculture may promulgate;

(6) for the purposes of paragraphs (7) and (8) of this subsection, the term "property" shall mean a detached, noncommercial residential dwelling, the construction of which was begun before the date of the designation of the wilderness area (hereinafter referred to as "dwelling"), or an existing agricultural activity begun before the date of the designation of the wilderness area, other than timber cutting (hereinafter referred to as "agricultural activity"), together with so much of the land on which the dwelling or agricultural activity is situated, such land being in the same ownership as the dwelling or agricultural activity, as the Secretary of Agriculture shall determine to be necessary for the enjoyment of the dwelling for the sole purpose of noncommercial residential use or for the agricultural activity, together with any structures accessory to the dwelling or agricultural activity which are situated on the land so designated;

(7) any owner or owners of property on the date of its acquisition by the Secretary of Agriculture may, as a condition of such acquisition, retain for themselves and their successors or assigns a right of use and occupancy of the property for such noncommercial residential purpose or agricultural activity for twenty-five years, or, in lieu thereof, for a term ending at the death of the owner or his spouse, whichever is later. The owner shall elect the term to be reserved. The Secretary of Agriculture shall pay to the owner the fair market value on such date of the right retained by the owner: *Provided,* That whenever an owner of property elects to retain a right of use and occupancy as provided for in this section, such owner shall be deemed to have waived any benefits or rights accruing under sections 203, 204, 205, and 206 of the Uniform Relocation Assistance and Real Property Acquisition Policies Act of 1970 (84 Stat. 1894), and for the purposes of those sections such owner shall not be considered a displaced person as defined in section 101 (6) of that Act; and

(8) a right of use and occupancy retained or enjoyed pursuant to paragraph (7) of this subsection may be terminated with respect to the entire property by the Secretary of Agriculture upon his determination that the property or any portion thereof has ceased to be used for such noncommercial residential purpose or agricultural activity and upon tender to the holder of a right an amount equal to the fair market value as of the date of tender of that portion of the right which remains unexpired on the date of termination.

Transfer of Federal Property

Sec. 7. The head of any Federal department or agency having jurisdiction over any lands or interests in lands within the boundaries of wilderness areas and wilderness study areas designated by or pursuant to this Act is authorized to transfer to the Secretary jurisdiction over such lands for administration in accordance with the provisions of this Act.

Applicability

Sec. 8. Unless otherwise provided by any other Act the provisions of this Act shall only apply to National Forest areas east of the 100th meridian.

Authorization of Appropriations

Sec. 9. There are hereby authorized to be appropriated an amount not to exceed $5,000,000 for the acquisition by purchase, condemnation, or otherwise of lands, waters, or interests therein located in areas designated as wilderness pursuant to section 3 of this Act and an amount not to exceed $1,700,000 for the purpose of conducting a review of wilderness study areas designated by section 4 of this Act.

Legislative History

House Report No. 93-1599 accompanying H. R. 13455 (Comm. on Interior and Insular Affairs).

Senate Report No. 93-803 (Comm. on Agriculture and Forestry).

Congressional Record, Vol. 120 (1974): May 31, considered and passed Senate. Dec. 18, considered and passed House, amended, in lieu of H. R. 13455. Dec. 19, Senate concurred in House amendment.

Public Law 94-579
Federal Land Policy and Management Act
Oct. 21, 1976

Bureau of Land Management Wilderness Study

Sec. 603. (a) Within fifteen years after the date of approval of this Act, the Secretary shall review those roadless areas of five thousand acres or more and roadless islands of the public lands, identified during the inventory required by section 201(a) of this Act as having wilderness characteristics described in the Wilderness Act of September 3, 1964 (78 Stat. 890; 16 U.S.C. 1131 et seq.) and shall from time to time report to the President his recommendation as to the suitability or nonsuitability of each such area or island for preservation as wilderness: *Provided,* That prior to any recommendations for the designation of an area as wilderness the Secretary shall cause mineral surveys to be conducted by the Geological Survey and the Bureau of Mines to determine the mineral values, if any, that may be present in such areas: *Provided further,* That the Secretary shall report to the President by July 1, 1980, his recommendations on those areas which the Secretary has prior to November 1, 1975, formally identified as natural or primitive areas. The review required by this subsection shall be conducted in accordance with the procedure specified in section 3(d) of the Wilderness Act.

(b) The President shall advise the President of the Senate and the Speaker of the House of Representatives of his recommendations with respect to designation as wilderness of each such area, together with a map thereof and a definition of its boundaries. Such advice by the President shall be given with two years of the receipt of each report from the Secretary. A recommendation of the President for designation as wilderness shall become effective only if so provided by an Act of Congress.

(c) During the period of review of such areas and until Congress has determined otherwise, the Secretary shall continue to manage such lands according to his authority under this Act and other applicable law in a manner so as not to impair the suitability of such areas for preservation as wilderness, subject, however, to the continuation of existing mining and grazing uses and mineral leasing in the manner and degree in which the same was being conducted on the date of approval of this Act: *Provided,* That, in managing the public lands the Secretary shall by regulation or otherwise take any action required to prevent unnecessary or undue degradation of the lands and their resources or to afford environmental protection. Unless previously withdrawn from appropriation under the mining laws, such lands shall continue to be subject to such appropriation during the period of review unless withdrawn by the Secretary under the procedures of section 204 of this Act for reasons other than preservation of their wilderness character. Once an area has been designated for preservation as wilderness, the provisions of the Wilderness Act which apply to national forest wilderness areas shall apply with respect to the administration and use of such designated area, including mineral surveys required by section 4(d) (2) of the Wilderness Act, and mineral development, access, exchange of lands, and ingress and egress for mining claimants and occupants.

Department of Agriculture
Office of the Secretary
Washington, D.C. 20250

Subject: Policy for Management of Wildernesses within the National Forests

To: Chief, Forest Service

The Department's wilderness management policy is not well understood. Some clarification is offered here, to gain broader awareness and acceptance of that policy. This is not an exhaustive list of practices or uses, but provides a statement of policy for the issues of most concern in managing National Forest wilderness.

The American people will be assured the benefits of an enduring resource of wilderness only if that wilderness resource is managed to protect its unique qualities. Wilderness management, to be effective, must have a basic set of objectives—applied uniformly, with latitude to adapt to the individual requirements of each area—which are understood and accepted both by Forest Service employees and the public.

The Department wilderness management objectives are:

To maintain an enduring system of high-quality wilderness representative of all National Forest ecotypes;

To perpetuate the wilderness resource for future generations;

To the extent that it is consistent with the first two, to provide opportunities for public use, enjoyment, and understanding of wilderness and the unique experiences dependent upon a wilderness setting;

To maintain plants and animals indigenous to the area by protecting the natural dynamic equilibrium associated with natural, complete ecosystems;

To accommodate and administer those "nonconforming but accepted" uses provided in the Wilderness Act and subsequent Acts in a way to minimize their impacts;

To maintain stable watersheds;

To consider the special protection needs of endangered plant and animal species and their habitats.

Forest Service wilderness management policy must be applied uniformly. Each wilderness, however, requires its own specific direction. This individual need shall be set forth in a management plan for each area. Such plans are to be developed locally with substanial local and regional public participation. The policies and plans shall be applied so that each area retains its wilderness quality; i.e., is managed on a "nondegradation" concept.

Efforts may be made, in modest ways, to improve wilderness quality by restoring natural conditions; practices which would result in the degradation of that quality will not be allowed. There is no place for vista clearing or any other form of "enhancing natural beauty" in wilderness.

Professional skill; knowledge of the Wilderness Act, subsequent related Acts of Congress, and USDA wilderness policies; good judgment; and public participation are essential components of wilderness management. The local manager should be given some latitude to apply common sense and practical interpretation to national management direction and policy.

General

Within wildernesses there shall be no timber harvesting, no manipulation of vegetation for watershed, wildlife, or forage purposes, and no use of motor vehicles, mechanical transport,

215

motorized equipment, installations, or structures other than as specifically provided for by the Wilderness Act or as stated hereinafter.

Visitor Use Facilities

Visitor use facilities are permissable only as needed to protect and manage the wilderness resources, and shall not be provided for the convenience of the visitor. Trails, built and maintained to the standard needed to protect the soil, water, and biological resources, may exist to properly distribute visitors throughout the wilderness. Bridges, made of native materials where possible, may be provided if their absence would subject the visitor to significant hazard or the riparian environment to unacceptable impact. Shelters will not be built, but those in place at the time of designation of the wilderness will be maintained until they need major rehabilitation or their use contributes to unacceptable impacts on soil, water, or biological resources, at which time they will be removed or destroyed. If necessary, to protect soil, water, biological, and wilderness resources, camping use may be restricted to designated sites; such sites may contain an identification marker and any facility specifically needed to protect the wilderness, such as a fire box in areas of extreme fire hazard. Existing, unsophisticated water sources such as hand pumps may be retained and maintained. Pit or vault toilets services by nonmotorized or nonmechanical transport may be emplaced where human waste disposal problems cannot be corrected by dispersal or reasonable limitation of visitor numbers. "Brow logs" may be used to reduce erosion at boat landings. Other facilities such as, but not limited to, boat docks will not be built in wilderness. Such existing facilities will be phased out and removed within ten years of designation of the area as wilderness.

Commercial Services

Commercial services needed for proper use and enjoyment of the wilderness are allowable under special use permits. Certain installations may be allowed for these services. Outfitter camp permits may provide for hitching racks and corrals made of native material. Such facilities should be designed to facilitate seasonal dismantling. The dismantling, however, can be waived provided use is intended during the next snowfree season and continued use of the location will not cause unacceptable impacts on soil, water, and biological resources. If a permittee was authorized to emplace or use tent frames with board flooring, wood siding, or built-in bunks—not generally of a temporary nature nor ordinarily permitted—in the season prior to wilderness designation, he may continue use until the facility needs replacement or major rehabilitation or their continued use would cause unacceptable impacts on soil, water, or biological resources. New installations of this nature will not be authorized in wilderness.

Emergencies and Administration

Emergency use of motorized vehicles and equipment and mechanical transport may be made by the Forest Service for search and rescue, fighting forest fires, or insect and disease epidemics. Nonemergency use should occur only in unquestionable instances of wilderness management need by the Forest Service or cooperating agency. Proposed uses of chemicals for control of outbreaks of insects and diseases must be approved by the Assistant Secretary.

Hydrometeorological devices existing when the area is designated may remain so long as the operating agency agrees to convert to miniaturized equipment, adequately camouflaged, each time a device needs replacement. State game and fish agencies may conduct fish-stocking programs approved by the Forest Service, using aerial drops on those waters where such aerial stocking was in practice prior to wilderness designation. State agencies, reintroducing animals in a project approved by the Forest Service, may use mechanical transport, including helicopter, only upon a determination by the Assistant Secretary that the reintroduction is desirable and that no practical alternative mode of transportation exists.

Nonconforming but Accepted Uses

The Wilderness Act provides that certain uses, generally considered as "nonconforming" to wilderness environments, may continue in wildernesses. Where grazing had been established before designation and is continuing, installations and improvements for grazing are permissible only as needed to protect wilderness resources—including soil, water, and biological resources. Where the use of aircraft and motorboats had become established prior to designation as wilderness, their continued use may be permitted at locations, times, and in such manner as is provided in the management plan for that wilderness, so long as that plan concludes that such continued use is necessary and proper for use of the wilderness. Hunting and fishing shall be in accordance with applicable State and Federal laws and regulations. There may be wilderness locations so popular with nonhunters during the hunting season that hunting closures by the State agency should be negotiated for limited areas less popular with hunters in order to provide autumn wilderness experiences for both hunters and nonhunters.

The establishment of new water projects or parts of projects may be permitted only upon specific authorization of the President. Existing water developments will either be made as esthetically compatible as possible with the wilderness environment or removed. Maintenance of such existing developments will be by primitive tools unless case-by-case authorization is granted by the Regional Office for motorized maintenance methods.

Philosophical Basis of Wilderness Policy

As writer Michael Frome notes in *Whose Woods These Are: The Story of the National Forest,* "the modern concept of wilderness was born and reached fruition in the Forest Service." Aldo Leopold, who won creation of the Gila Wilderness in 1924, the Nation's first, stated that "the administration of the National Forests of America has for its real purpose the perpetuation of life—human, plant, and animal life."

Leopold is credited with considering the predicted timber famine "a matter of quality rather than quantity," and suggested that "the emphasis on logging under intensive forestry be limited to richer, accessible forest regions, capable of producing high-quality timber, while dedicating remaining regions to various forms of recreation, game management, and wilderness."

While Leopold introduced the wilderness idea and was responsible for establishing the first area in New Mexico, Robert Marshall brought the concept to maturity during his career as Director of Recreation in the Forest Service. Marshall developed the administrative regulations under which the Forest Service proceeded, on its own, to protect over 14 million acres of National Forest land as "wilderness," "wild," or "primitive" areas, prior to congressional passage of the Wilderness Act of 1964.

The Forest Service should be proud of its leading role in wilderness administration. Forest officers engaged in wilderness administration today should be guided by their predecessors' wise counsel:

Leopold: "Recreation is valuable in proportion to the intensity of its experiences, and to the degree to which it *differs from* and *contrasts with* workaday life. By these criteria, mechanized outings are at best a milk-and-water affair. Recreation is not their only, or even their principal, utility. Ability to see the cultural value of wilderness boils down, in the last analysis, to a question of intellectual humility. Raw wilderness gives definition and meaning to the human enterprise."

Marshall: "The National Forest System is uniquely fit to provide two distinct vacation environments: One, the comfortable and modern; two, the peaceful timelessness where vast forests germinate and flourish and die and rot and grow again without relationship to the ambitions and interferences of man."

These observations are as valid today as when they were made, and the value of wilderness will increase as our society becomes more dependent upon complex technology.

Let's continue our record of excellence in wilderness administration through uniform application of these policy guidelines.

M. Rupert Cutler
Assistant Secretary for Conservation,
Research, and Education

Index

About the Author

Lloyd C. Irland was born in Chicago. Summer experiences in the woods of Wisconsin led him to study forestry, receiving a B.S. at Michigan State University in 1967, and an M.S. from the University of Arizona a year later. Following military service, he served briefly as an economist at the Chicago Board of Trade, and then completed a Ph.D at Yale University. He has worked for the U.S. Forest Service in Louisiana and on short assignments in Oregon and Washington. From 1973 to 1976, he taught forest economics at the Yale School of Forestry and Environmental Studies. In 1976 he took his present position with the Maine Forest Service.